INTRODUCTION TO
EMILY DICKINSON

INTRODUCTION TO

EMILY DICKINSON

by

HENRY W. WELLS

HENDRICKS HOUSE, INC., NEW YORK

To

Eunice de Chazeau

PREFACE

This book is at the same time a study of Emily Dickinson and an experiment in critical method. The introductory pages contain much of the author's apologia which might, under slightly different circumstances, have been relegated to a preface. The character of the experiment is sufficiently indicated even by the titles of the major sections into which the book is divided. All that is required, then, by way of preface may easily be contained within the pleasant task of somewhat informal and expanded statements of acknowledgements. In this case the acknowledgements are, even beyond the custom in such matters, of very real moment.

First, I must acknowledge more debts than can briefly be stated to Mrs. Millicent Todd Bingham, editor of *Bolts of Melody,* author of *Ancestors' Brocades,* daughter of Emily Dickinson's friend and first editor, and herself, to say the least, an outstanding workman in the field. Although prior to 1945 I had published some criticism of the poet and written still more for the clarification of my own mind, it was not until Mrs. Bingham's books appeared, both materially enlarging and clarifying the subject, that I thought of expressing my own views in book form. Not only has she read my manuscript, informed or convinced me in certain matters, and generously argued with me in others, but, together with her publisher, has been of invaluable aid in permitting a liberal use of quotation, a privilege not always enjoyed by Emily's critics. Of comparable value has been the help and advice of the poet and critic, Genevieve Taggard. In her poetry she brilliantly develops many values derived from Emily; in her criticism, both written and vocal, she shows a sensitivity and sprightliness which literary appreciation always demands and seldom receives. I am deeply grateful to her. All students of Emily are, of course, indebted to George Whicher, but not all in quite so intimate or comprehensive a manner as myself. I can truly sympathize with Professor Whicher since I, who am both teacher and writer, remember how heroically he attempted to teach me to write when, a long time ago, I was an obstinate undergraduate at Amherst. Although I have approached Emily from a number of angles not, I think, found in his critical biography, I enthusiastically express my debt to him in his capacity as exponent both of the English language and of the Amherst poet. Finally, I am indebted for useful hints to Lionel Trilling and the poet, Eunice de Chazeau.

I take pleasure in acknowledging the great generosity of Little, Brown, and Company in permitting me to quote from *The Poems of Emily Dickinson* (1937), edited by Martha Dickinson Bianchi and Alfred Leete Hampson, and of Harper and Brothers for similar generosity in allowing me to quote from *Bolts of Melody* (1945), edited by Mabel Loomis Todd and Millicent Todd Bingham.

Henry W. Wells

March, 1947

CONTENTS

INTRODUCTION TO EMILY DICKINSON

INTRODUCTION

The first words of *Leaves of Grass,* showing how well Whitman understood one of the major problems of his age and ours, offer the briefest explanation of the plan of this book on Whitman's chief contemporary in American poetry. Life Whitman saw as divided between the personal and the public, between the flowering of the individual and that of society. As he expresses it, he sings of himself, "a simple, separate person" and yet also utters "the word democratic, the word *en-masse.*" As the nineteenth century advanced, it became increasingly evident that personal and social interests were commonly opposed or even at swords' points. Capitalism, Protestantism, and Romanticism alike stressed the rights and privileges of the individual, while a growing awareness that some social organization alone could conquer the moral anarchy of *laisse faire* renewed a stress on men's public responsibilities. Typical complementary tendencies of thought manifested themselves in the rise of new psychological and sociological theories, as developed by philosophers of the soul, such as Freud, and philosophers of the state, such as Marx. Ever since the dawn of thought in China or in Greece, two such departments of thought have been discernible; yet not until the tragic acceleration of human living in the Western World of the last century and a half, have the horns of this basic human dilemma spread so widely apart.

Throughout the nineteenth century writers whose interests lay largely in the regions of mysticism, metaphysics, or art commonly depicted life as a personal problem; to such men the soul was infinite and within itself might rise to the highest perfection. According to this belief, directly inherited from the Renaissance, education became primarily a problem of developing the individual. Thinkers whose interests, on the contrary, lay largely in regions of politics or economics, naturally envisaged life as a public problem. According to the progressive thinking of the age, men were to seek an equality of opportunity; their basic desires were all much the same; and there was little need to worry about the happiness of the individual provided he live in a healthy and well-organized state. Without such a state, the majority would inevitably continue to bear the burdens of privation, war, and misery. Which, then, was the chief factor, the individual or society? The times pressed this ubiquitous problem more urgently than ever before, and more tragically than hitherto failed to provide adequate answers.

In the following introduction to Emily Dickinson the two paths will be followed in succession, though not without a continued awareness of both or even without their occasional conjunction. The first section, a biography of the spirit, views Emily in terms of her extraordinary personality and genius. It relates the unique story of her writings in prose and verse, how they have only gradually been recovered and printed, and how they have been received by readers and critics. It glances at her personal peculiarities, placing her within the limited group of men and women distinguished by genius, and even by a genius in certain respects highly abnormal. It examines how successfully she utilized and transcended both her genius and her sex, her provincial world and her personal relationships, until her poetry, though still personal, became highly expressive of our common human experience; how, in other words, she rose from the personal to the universal. It further considers how she perfects what lies imperfect within us all—or, in other words, how she sharpens and refines what in others remains inchoate and crude. All persons cherish in some degree their legacy of childhood, cultivate mature powers of thought and introspection, live emotionally, have moments of pleasing fancy, and are taught by the sternest of teachers, death. Integrity of soul, personal courage, and faith are to some extent known to the millions; or at least so well known that, when superlatively exhibited in an Emily Dickinson, they are viewed with understanding, admiration, and delight. All these aspects of her work prove, broadly speaking, to be personal, and are most readily described in such terms. Together, they are the subject matter of the first part of this study.

With the second section the point of view undergoes a material shift. Here Emily is viewed in her relation to the periods of literature before and after her own lifetime, and likewise in relation to her own environment. This section considers her in her more limited aspects, as a woman, a New Englander, a recluse in the provincial town of Amherst, a Protestant, and a perplexed victim of outstanding problems of her own day—and ours—as friction between science and religion, reason and non-reason. It reviews her relation to certain traditions, literary, philosophical, and mystical; it considers her poetry in the light of romantic standards of sensitivity; and, finally, it examines her work in relation to the social, economic, and political organism of her age. Even in the case of so marked an individualist as Emily, both her own writing in itself and its reception throughout succeeding generations reflect far more of these social forces than a superficial and specious view leads one to suppose. All art, no less than all theology, remains in vital contact with these peculiarly terrestrial movements.

But it will not suffice to view Emily's art both personally and impersonally, in relation to herself and to her cultural and social environment. A rounded consideration of any art work must always include or even be crowned by a view of its peculiar medium and technique. If the works of a poet are studied without reference to biography and "influences," without reference to facts and ideas, the study, if prolonged, is almost certain to become thin. Nevertheless, the more intimately we approach the very words of the poet, the lines and brush strokes of the painter, the harmonies and sounds of the musician, and the movements or costume of the dancer, the nearer we come to the intoxicating wine of the art itself. In moments of aesthetic enthusiasm the rest may even appear merely the container, the glass holding the precious juices. Art has both its content or meaning and its form. Under analysis we necessarily lean upon its obvious biographical and intellectual values as well as upon whatever we discern of its inevitably more elusive technical nuances. The study of form both is and is not the totality of art study. In any case, it may be thought of as the cream; and, by a natural inversion in literary criticism, as customarily in all the time-consuming arts, the cream is left to the last. It is, therefore, in the third or final part of this book that attention falls on the poetry considered more severely as an entity in itself.

The peculiarly confusing manner by which Emily's works have thus far been brought to the light of publication almost justifies her own aspersion on publication as the auction of the mind of man. Readers and critics have, consequently, overlooked the breadth and variety of her work, representative of the very highest type of genius. Her own conscious aesthetics have been too little considered. In the extravagant adulation, even the imperfections of her indiscriminately published works have as a rule been disregarded, to her own loss. Her contributions to the diverse types of art in which she excels, such as poetic aphorism, light verse, and ecstatic lyricism, remain to be carefully distinguished and described. Her use of imagery and abstraction and her imaginative transmutation of nature are also outstanding mysteries in her achievement. The enveloping forms and patterns of her poems, her singular and original mastery of rhythm and rhyme, and, finally, her explorative and highly imaginative use of words repay the most careful investigation from all who would enhance their appreciation and enjoyment of her poetry.

In an overall view of Emily Dickinson it must appear how myopic much of the study of her work has thus far been. Bewildered or thrown off their familiar guard by so rare a personality and such unusual work, her critics have too often followed routes of least resistance. A narrowness amounting to barrenness or flat irrelevance has been the result. Several books dealing with her life or even with her works from the most exclusively personal point of view have debated the riddle of her love affairs.

As yet the material has been lacking for a full historical documentation, and so carefully were these personal secrets originally guarded, that it seems doubtful if such evidence will ever be found. A few writers, as Mrs. Millicent Todd Bingham, rather darkly hint that there is no dark secret at all, though Professor George Whicher's book, *This Was a Poet,* goes far toward establishing a reasonable outline for her emotional life. It might be better to describe Professor Whicher's most admirable and dignified volume as a cool frame for the fiery colors of Emily's impersonally-personal lyrics. Whereas a number of women—including Martha Graham in her notable dance, *Letter to the World*—have stressed Emily's love affairs, scholarship in masculine hands has begun where it too frequently ends, with the timid effort to place Emily against her Puritan and provincial background. It is difficult to say whether the result has been more to labor the obvious or to conceal the truth. Her poems have been likened to those of Emerson, her ideas to those of Thoreau or Theodore Parker. Her verses have been ingeniously compared with those of the early Puritan, Anne Bradstreet. All this is helpful in its way, but also misleading.

The significance of Emily Dickinson lies in the fact that her kinship is closer to all great poets than it is to any of her contemporary New Englanders. As an individual, an amazingly alive person and a genius, she should be seen first of all against the background of the greatest individuals, persons, and men of genius, and not against a background of the men and women of the town of Amherst. In short, the helpful critic comes not to bury Emily but to praise her. She stands in company with the chief poets, seers, mystics, and visionaries, far more nearly than with those men and women to whom she wrote actual letters. Her poems, are, as she well termed them, letters to posterity, inspired by ideas, feelings, and an awareness of form and beauty reaching back to the worlds of Sappho, Plato, Simonides, Meleager and Martial, Tu Fu and Li Po. With more recent poets she also has much revealingly in common, as with Omar, Shakespeare, Herrick, Blake, Burns, Heine, or the German mystic, Angelus Silesius. This book aims to deliver Emily from the claws of personal interpretation and to place her personality upon a more distinguished height, not of Amherst Hill, but of Parnassus; it aims for the first time to examine her work closely against the perspective of the world's major poetry. And, finally, it aims to justify this station not only by reference to the subject matter of her verse—its personal emotions and general ideas—but by an investigation of her poetic techniques from an aesthetic point of view.

PART I

REPRESENTATION OF MAN

1 *TREASURES OF VERSE AND PROSE*

The equally vivid and elusive personality revealed in the works of Emily Dickinson no more clearly invites a commentary than the extraordinary history of the manner in which these works have attained publicity. A sound foundation for an interpretation of her writings calls for some preliminary statement of what these writings are, how they have reached us, and in what manner they have thus far been received. The canon of Emily's works is very far from being as yet established. It is well to know first of what one speaks, even though this requires a brief factual summary of publications to date. The outlines of Emily's life may also be helpfully traced by way of introduction.

These contours are classically simple. She was born in 1830 in a stately brick house on Main Street, in the small town of Amherst, located very nearly in the center of Massachusetts. Here, in 1886, she died. She remained unmarried. Her immediate family consisted of a brother, a sister, a singularly colorful father, who was a successful business man and politician, and a singularly colorless mother. Her parents died in 1874 and 1882 respectively. Except for a year at Mount Holyoke Seminary, located some ten miles from Amherst, she was never for any considerable length of time removed from her emotionally exacting family life. As a young woman she enjoyed a reasonable amount of travel, visiting Washington, Philadelphia, and Boston, everywhere she lived seeing what might pass for a fair portion of the world. But Emily was not warmly pleased with the society which she saw, and gradually even the local society of Amherst, in which she had once fully participated, grew irksome to her. She became excessively shy, avoided crowds, had small liking for church, and wilfully shut herself up within her own house and grounds. Here Miss Dickinson received visitors on occasions, although with an odd habit of ensconcing them in the drawing room while she herself sat in the hall. She preferred to dress in white. This physically restricted existence she professed to enjoy greatly, for she was a very high-spirited person, much given to dramatizing her own life.

The outline of her uneventful days is easily reconstructed. She did housework, labored long and lovingly in her garden, read widely, and above all studiously labored over her poems. She could be extremely bitter concerning men and women whom she disliked, but with men whom she admired — and apparently loved — she naturally assumed a subordinate role. According to the best of the none too good evidence now available, the Heloise of Amherst was in love with three men, two being her instructors in her early years, the third and more seriously beloved man, a preacher. This trinity taken together added up to Abelard. All were considerably older than herself. One suspects that her affection also involved an ardent desire for her own intellectual and spiritual growth even in the field of her poetic art. The preacher, the Reverend Charles Wadsworth of Philadelphia, was married before Emily first met him, and not long thereafter moved to the Pacific Coast. Their meetings were few and at long intervals. All three of these men died during Emily's lifetime, the first two while she was herself young. Whether her affections went out with her accustomed violence to still other men, cannot be known, though it remains, of course, quite plausible that they did. In any event, the Amherst gossip concerning her was doubly vague, being largely posthumous, after her reputation as a poet had been established. Of some importance to her and of even more to posterity was her purely literary friendship with the distinguished Bostonian man of letters, destined to be a coeditor of her poetry, the somewhat pompous but by no means insensitive Colonel Thomas Wentworth Higginson. Their relationship remained for the most part on epistolary terms.

From childhood this amazingly sensitive and imaginative New Englander devoted much time to writing. She loved to write and to receive letters. As a young girl she composed light sketches in prose. And throughout her life she wrote poems. Certain of these, which their author may be presumed to have thought the better of, she bound in small manuscript booklets, described by her biographers as fascicles. Others remained on the highly miscellaneous scraps of paper frugally used for composition. Some are in clean drafts, some in an amazingly confused condition. During her lifetime she failed to make the contacts with publishers which might have led to the publication of a book of poems, although there is a reasonable suspicion that she would have welcomed such publicity had circumstances permitted and her moods of paradoxical pride and humility been moderated. In any case, she sent copies of a few of her poems to friends active in the literary world. A small handful of lyrics received publication, whether at her own desire or against it cannot be definitely ascertained. Colonel Higginson, who had read at least fifty of her pieces during her lifetime, and other of her friends advised against publication on the ground that the pieces were too much opposed to current conventions of verse-making. She died, vaguely aware that she had left a precious legacy to posterity, but reconciled with a gamble on posthumous publication as preferable to the embarrassment of publication during her own lifetime either at her own expense or at the risk of others. A very large number of manuscripts she carefully preserved, leaving them in the possession of her younger sister, Lavinia. Over fifteen hundred of her pieces—many of them, however, extremely brief or even fragmentary—have thus far been published. So secretive has this New England family been regarding its treasures, that it cannot be said how many still remain unknown, but the probability is that only a relatively small number are now unprinted and that these will scarcely alter her position in literature or our picture of the character of her work.

The story of the publication thus far, though fairly familiar and recounted in part, yet at somewhat confusing length, in Mrs. Bingham's volume, *Ancestors' Brocades,* is so extraordinary, and so vaguely grasped by most readers of American literature, that recapitulation seems warranted. Numerous misconceptions have also arisen concerning the poet's reputation, which should be avoided or corrected.

Lavinia Dickinson, the first owner of the manuscripts bequeathed by Emily, was as undistinguished in intellectual attainments as her sister had been eminent. Even letters she wrote with difficulty, and she read virtually no literature; she had no understanding of her sister's verses. Her sole distinction, not to be ignored, consisted of proficiency in irate and imaginative vituperation. Moved partly by affection for her sister's memory, and partly, I suspect, by a yearning for pin money, she sought to have the poems published. Lavinia in 1886 found herself living in a large house with a personal income far smaller than that available to her brother and sister-in-law next door. There was no member of her family to whom she could reasonably turn for assistance, or who had any interest in publicity. Fortunately, across the fields lived a young professor of astronomy and his talented and attractive wife, Mabel Loomis Todd, who had been one of Emily's close friends in the closing years of her life. To Mrs. Todd, then, Lavinia naturally turned for the needed aid in preparing the manuscripts and conveying them to a publisher.

Realizing the peculiar difficulties of this problem, Mrs. Todd herself turned for advice to Emily's most trusted literary friend, Colonel Higginson. The Colonel in time found a publisher willing to undertake the task, with the result that three small volumes were slowly prepared and produced successively in 1890, 1891, and 1896. Observing that Emily's letters had at least something of the brilliance of the poems and were far more readily digested by readers fifty years ago than the verses, the same editor produced in 1894 a collection of letters, containing also nearly a hundred short poems. In the editing Mrs. Todd at all times performed the greater part of the work, and as the labor advanced increasingly lifted the burden borne by Colonel Higginson. In 1896 this chapter of the editorial record abruptly concluded. By that time five hundred poems had been published while an equally large number had already been copied by Mrs. Todd. Indeed, she her-

self retained till her own death in 1932 and then handed
on to her daughter over six hundred unpublished poems
and poetical fragments. A large number of highly valuable manuscripts were also in the possession of Emily's
sister-in-law, Susan Dickinson. Legally there was a grave
question as to the ownership of the manuscripts. Had
Lavinia given all her collection outright to Mrs. Todd,
or did the ownership of all Emily's poems revert to the
Dickinson family? The copyright of all the publications,
in any case, indisputably belonged to the Dickinsons.

The cessation of publication in 1896 was occasioned by
a dispute concerning a small piece of land, resulting in
a lawsuit between Lavinia Dickinson and Mrs. Todd.
Again money was the chief agent, for Lavinia in this
instance found that her dependence upon her lawyer
forced her to bring suit. The trial became a notorious
case, involving the town of Amherst in a flood of unsavory gossip regarding the alleged conduct of the late
William Austin Dickinson, Emily's brother, and Mrs.
Todd. This suit precluded for the time being any further
coöperation between Mrs. Todd and the Dickinsons and
made it difficult or impossible for Mrs. Todd to continue
her editorial tasks. Emily's niece, Martha Dickinson, best
known as Madame Bianchi, became for the time the literary representative of her aunt to posterity. She produced
a collection of hitherto unpublished work, *The Single
Hound,* in 1914, and supplemented this later with other
material. The current collected edition, edited by Madame
Bianchi and Alfred Leete Hampson, appeared in 1937.
This is still the most important book by Emily Dickinson. It contains all the poems originally published by
Mrs. Todd and Colonel Higginson, grouped in the earlier

part of the book, as well as all the pieces subsequently uncovered by Madame Bianchi and her friend. The sum of this magnificent collection amounts to slightly more than nine hundred items.

In 1932 Mrs. Todd died; in 1943 Madame Bianchi died. But Mrs. Todd had copied many pieces thus far unpublished, and her editorial labors were now resumed by her daughter, Mrs. Millicent Todd Bingham. Thus in 1945 a new volume of Emily's poems, bearing the dramatic title *Bolts of Melody,* appeared, whose title page announced the joint editorship of Mrs. Todd and Mrs. Bingham. This contains more than six hundred poems or fragments, and is the second and, to date, the last standard collection of Emily's work. Here, then, are in all over fifteen hundred pieces for consideration.

The record even today remains incomplete, though presumably not gravely so. More serious, however, is the objection advanced by certain zealous scholars that the existing texts are so imperfectly edited as to be an insecure basis for literary criticism. In the opinion of the present writer, however, this objection is invalid and pedantic for the following reasons.

In the first place, no perfect edition, and, in this sense of the word, no definitive edition, of Emily's poems, is possible short of a transcendental heaven. A number of her manuscripts are so heavily rewritten as to make it wholly impossible to discover her intentions. Frequently she writes out several versions of the same stanza, leaving it uncertain which she prefers. More often she displays the vexing habit of listing as many as eight or ten words, any one of which may be used in a certain phrase and no one of which she marks as preferred. Almost unprecedented problems confront the editor, who must choose as his own taste determines, and this taste obviously cannot be subjected to an absolute.

Doubtless a few faults may legitimately be found with Emily's most recent and by all odds her most scholarly and conscientious editor. Mrs. Bingham has not given us the perfect book, nor is it, of course, to be expected that she could do so. Since no group of trained scholars has ever examined any considerable number of Emily's poems, the work of none of the editors thus far can in the fullest sense of the word be judicially appraised. Judgment must be partial. Errors or misjudgments seem neither numerous nor important. The general inference is that Mrs. Bingham, aided by the earlier efforts of her mother, produced a careful, faithful, and judicious version of the uniquely difficult random material at her disposal. Herself a scientist, daughter of an astronomer, the wife of a distinguished scientist, trained in accuracy and in the best standards of modern research, and dedicated to an inherited responsibility, she inspires her reader with considerable confidence. With her mother's personal intimacy with the poet to guide her, her versions of the poems in *Bolts of Melody* can hardly be regarded without sincere respect. Moreover the quality of these poems by no means differs so widely from that of the earlier pieces as to induce any deep suspicion of them either. The ground, then, is not so treacherous as certain persons zealously interested in the strictest standards of literary scholarship might lead us to infer. Academic prejudice to the contrary, in literary criticism courage is an even more valuable virtue than scrupulosity. And Mrs. Bingham as editor unquestionably possesses both virtues in marked degree.

Mrs. Todd made very careful copies of by far the larger number of poems first published under the editorship of Madame Bianchi. Professor Whicher, Emily's most competent biographer, and others have happily been able to check on a number of pieces. As a result we have a considerable list of corrections or variant readings for poems edited by Mrs. Todd in the nineteenth century and by Madame Bianchi in the twentieth. Furthermore Mrs. Bingham in her *Ancestors' Brocades* publishes many letters exchanged between Mrs. Todd and Colonel Higginson which throw much light on their editorial policy. With this evidence on hand, certain reassuring conclusions may be drawn. There seem to have been no deliberate frauds. In the light of their own literary standards, which were by no means despicable, Mrs. Todd and Colonel Higginson were fundamentally honest, and Madame Bianchi was no more than on occasion amateurishly inept and singularly obstinate. The nineteenth-century editors undeniably did a certain amount of rewriting. That they went quite as far as Bishop Percy in editing the popular ballads, which is suggested by Professor Whicher, seems to me a distinct exaggeration; but their liberties were undeniably considerable. Their motives, thoroughly clear and aboveboard, were to regularize Emily's imperfect rhymes, eccentric grammar, and harsh phraseology. Mrs. Todd was far from being obtuse, and perhaps once in a score of times her versions may please even the modern reader more than Emily's own words. No poem is ruined by such editing; few, it seems, are gravely hurt. The presumption is that Mrs. Bingham and others have already revealed Madame Bianchi's most serious offenses, and that Mrs. Bingham herself as well as others have been frank in treating the early work of Mrs. Todd. Quarrels between families have at least the value of providing reciprocal corrections. On the whole Mrs. Todd appears to have made more changes, for nineteenth-century taste demanded such alterations, and not till some thirty years after her death did Emily appear a truly great poet whose works forbade change. Presumably Madame Bianchi committed more errors but partly from a lack of imagination, partly from family piety, made fewer deliberate alterations. All the editing thus far will unquestionably be reviewed in the course of years, and both the scholars and the public are highly justified in demanding a new and improxed text. Pocket editions of selections of various lengths are also highly desirable. Nevertheless, all their imperfections and personal bickerings notwithstanding, Emily's editors thus far have done her creditable service; their most questionable action has been to secrete the manuscripts instead of opening them to the public under the jurisdiction of a great library. Unfortunately, separate interests as to copyright threaten long to delay a complete and scholarly edition. But this affords no reason for the neglect by the critics of American literature of one who is very possibly our foremost poet. Aesthetic criticism of any work, entirely regardless of its authenticity, is legitimate. And not only this. With much confidence it may be held that the best edition of Emily's poems which will ever reach the public will afford a picture of her work only in very minor respects different from that available in the two volumes now at hand, under the editorship respectively of Madame Bianchi and of Mrs. Bingham aided by her mother. The scholar will already have marked in Madame Bianchi's volume the variant readings afforded by more conscientious hands. He will be wary of the well known and thoroughly innocent practices of Mrs. Todd and Colonel Higginson. Circumstances encourage neither timidity nor delay. An improved text, perhaps unavailable for a generation to come, may in slight measure increase the clarity of our judgment. But in a cloudless sky the sun is at all times presumably bright, no matter what is the progress of its course; it is clearly discernible for what it is; all its cardinal properties of shape, color, energy, and warmth appear unmistakably. So is it with Emily Dickinson today. No one need in a pedantic folly regret that he lives too early in the day to appreciate adequately and even to the full limit of his potentiality the remarkable legacy with which in so strange a manner she has endowed us.

This legacy does not consist exclusively of her poetry. There are the letters, which have at times been even so extravagantly admired as to raise the question of their proportionate value and their true place in Emily's literary bequest. The letters will profit far more than the verse from final editing. True, many are known to have been lost, and others to have been mutilated by sensitive friends who valued personal feelings more highly than the pleasure of an inquisitive public. The next inclusive edition of her correspondence will fill in many minor gaps left by the first editor, Mrs. Todd, and may well include as many hitherto wholly new letters as those already in print. The letters, being written by Emily, are, of course, generally fascinating, often sprightly, and sometimes of great intensity and power. In addition to her own are some revealing letters written to or about her. In the latter category stands the account hurriedly jotted down by Colonel

Higginson to his wife late on the evening when he had his first and most memorable interview with the poet. This letter was published by Mrs. Todd in her revised collection. Emily had studiously prepared for the interview with all the arts of a great actress. Already one of the foremost living masters of aphorism and epigram, she knew precisely what she wished to say. Weakened, stunned, and thoroughly exhausted from his meeting, the Colonel retired to his inn to relate to his wife his fresh and uncomfortably burning impression. With a mind and heart tingling with excitement, and a need to unburden himself of so harrowing an experience, he recorded Emily's appearance and words in the most spontaneous and convincing manner. Colonel Higginson was the Boswell of women. His malleable mind perfectly caught the imprint of Emily's diamond. Perhaps no letter which she herself wrote contains so much of herself as this record of an eventful interview. As the more masculine mind of the two, she fairly impregnated this veteran of the Union Army with her poetry, which, aided by the midwifery of Mrs. Todd, was to be born many years later, thus giving birth to all Emily's posthumous fame. His account must be regarded as one of the most notable items in American letter writing.

The wisest manner of envisaging her own letters, attractive as they are, is to regard them as the background to her poems. Only a small minority of persons, for some reason or another prejudiced against verse as a whole, will today actually prefer the prose. Their ratio of value in this regard has been declining. When first published, the letters sold well, though never as widely as the poems. The highly feminine and hyper-emotional quality of the correspondence, so largely addressed to Emily's feminine friends, was much in the Victorian manner, whereas the bolder and starker idiom of her verses sacrificed contemporary interest for immortality. As Emily, by nature a letter writer, lucidly discerned, her poems constituted her personal-impersonal "letter to the world." The republication by Madame Bianchi of the letters in 1924—without acknowledgment to Mrs. Todd—won a sudden burst of appreciation for Emily's prose. A few discerning men of letters at that time were so far impressed by the correspondence as to prefer it to the verse. Time, as might be expected, has sifted their value, so that today the letters are recognized as for the most part charming occasional writing, the poems alone as truly eminent literature. However well Colonel Higginson might play Boswell, his friend was no Doctor Johnson. Her poetry far surpassed her prose and her epistolary skill. This is no doubt partly owing to the circumstance that a valuable correspondence is commonly the product of a relationship between two gifted people. Emily addressed many undistinguished men and women on whom the full force of her mind would have been lost.

Even if much real aid in the interpretation of her greater art may be had from Emily's letters, it is well, then, to realize that they differ widely and most instructively from her verse, affording no ultimate clue to the latter. The prose letters to friends are in relatively grey, everyday tones, against which the lyrical letters to posterity stand out in flaming contrast. One art is an art of paste, the other of pearl. With her letter writing Emily cajoled her friends, soothed them in their distresses, encouraged them in their pleasures. An element of condescension exists in her familiar correspondence. The letters show her as a character actress, a player on the wide stage of society. Of all her correspondents recorded by Mrs. Todd, only Colonel Higginson consistently called forth her more serious thoughts on life and art. In her letters she discloses her social charm, but only in her poems does she unlock her own heart. Her genius belonging chiefly to the more subjective forms of expression, only the poems show the full force of her mind and personality. It is true that if we possessed frank letters to any man with whom she was in love, we might well have at least a more intimate expression of her heart in prose. Yet it is neither certain that she actually unburdened her heart in this fashion or that she would have been especially felicitous in so doing. Fundamentally shy, she shunned the revelation of herself to others or even the more literal or prosaic expression of herself to herself. Her own personal interests and those of her future readers were happily identified. In the use of verse, rhyme, and the formalities of poetic expression she found both an escape from an unbearably naked confrontation of her own soul and a generalization of her emotions enabling her to write great verse, necessarily of universal meaning. The almost invariable rule is that a writer's love-poetry will be more successful as literature than his amorous correspondence. Thus even in this section of letter writing so commonly prolific, the advantage remains on *a priori* grounds strongly with verse. To conclude, it becomes both a delicate and an important matter to hold her correspondence—published and unpublished—at its proper evaluation, neither neglecting it as commonplace or trivial nor allowing its more speciously personal character to win for it an exaggerated esteem. Moreover, the contrasts between the verse and prose become even more valuable than the similarities. It is notable that both poems and letters are by the same hand, but still more noteworthy that Emily perfectly distinguishes between a letter to a contemporary and one to posterity, between familiar colloquy and pure art. The poems inevitably attract the keener interest.

2 *READERS AND CRITICS*

Preliminary skirmishing is not quite finished with a review of the general contents of the writings on which Emily's literary character rests. When we meet someone whom we wish to know, we are not satisfied to know him only through direct communication; we wish to know what impression he has made on others. To record what thousands of readers have experienced becomes realistic and significant, while to insist too narrowly upon one's own interpretation appears less original and creative than arrogant and egotistical. The creative critic interprets the reception of his author quite as much as he elaborates a personal analysis. During the fifty years in which Emily Dickinson has been known as a poet, the reception of her works has been as unusual as their actual character or the strange story of their publication. Many of the gravest errors popularly encountered on the subject as a whole arise not from individualistic or subjective views but from popular errors as to how her work has been received. To build a new interpretation, one first reviews the old, both the erroneous and the discerning.

The very boldness of Emily's poetry has discouraged the critics, whereas the public, which sometimes trusts its instincts, has accorded her wide appreciation. Her poetry has received the tribute of no volume of general appreciation or aesthetic criticism, and even the occasional essays on her work have as a rule wanted sharpness and originality of viewpoint. Highly general and flattering statements commonly serve to express the enthusiasm of the critic without closely defining Emily's unique contribution to literature. There is the growing awareness of a great poet without an ample statement of the qualities of her greatness. Many of the most warming tributes and penetrating discriminations have been incidental comments or asides by non-professional as well as professional reviewers. Thus one among the finest and least known short statements of her gifts may be found in a chapter in *Adventures in the Arts,* a book of miscellaneous essays on several arts by the well-known American painter, Marsden Hartley. One of the more stimulating if also one of the more perverse articles is the study by R. P. Blackmur in *The Southern Review* (1937), where with an elaborate parade of detail and a peculiar obtuseness to the essential aspects of her art, the writer describes Emily as a second-rate poet, author by chance of half a dozen perfect poems, and bungler in hundreds. Emily has had her enemies, the learned English critic, Andrew Lang, being among the most savage. The vicissitudes of her fame are peculiarly instructive. The reviewers of her earlier volumes were much less enthusiastic than the public, while for the last score of years her eminence has been secure and her reputation steadily on the ascent.

Not the leading essays, but the leading points of view in the miscellaneous appreciations best repay attention. It is less rewarding to note what in detail has been said of her than to note who have cared to read her, to praise, or to imitate. Answers to such questions aid the further problem why she has been read and what her readers have sought and found. The answers prove somewhat surprising, for they reveal her as possessing that extraordinary breadth of appeal to the most diverse classes of readers which is the surest token of a true master. Her collections of little poems have proven Shakespearean in the scope of the audiences they have received. Yet the peculiar history of her life together with that of her reputation have ideally lent themselves to intellectual snobbishness. Because so few persons—if, indeed any—appreciated her adequately in her lifetime, it has been assumed that to enjoy her at all constitutes a badge of superior merit, witnessing how much more enlightened are the twentieth-century intellectuals than those of the preceding century. Every deprecatory or condescending word by a Colonel Higginson can too readily be cherished as a stepping-stone to self-congratulation on the part of the more recent reader. It may well be argued that the honest appreciation by Colonel Higginson of Emily's essential qualities evinces more genuine literary insight than the communion of self-congratulation exchanged by current fashionable opinion.

From Emily's exceptional life it was easy for opinion a generation or two afterwards to construct an ideal legend of the unappreciated artist come ironically into posthumous fame. Emily's contemporaries did not scorn her. In no proper sense had they the opportunity to judge her, well or ill. She certainly did not pine from harsh criticism, for she had little formal criticism, and from her local friends the verbal comments were presumably cordial enough. She died from Bright's disease, not from a broken heart or the injured pride of unappreciated genius. When her books were published, they received a few cordial notices from clearly discerning critics, as William Dean Howells, and, what is more significant, a warm reception from the common reader. Contrary to Colonel Higginson's fears, the books sold remarkably well. By

1904 seventeen editions of the first collection had appeared, and reprints of the seventeenth are known to have been issued in 1910, 1915, 1916, and 1920. Ten editions of the Second Series had been printed by 1894, and copies thereafter were dated 1901, 1904, 1913, 1916, and 1923. Two thousand copies of the Third Series were printed in 1896 and the book was many times reissued thereafter. There were also combined printings of the First and Second Series. Merely from these bibliographical facts it becomes clear that Mrs. Todd's early efforts as editor were well appreciated.

The many letters which reached the editors directly or through the publishers afford fascinating evidence of the diversity of tastes which Emily's poetry was daily satisfying. Several of these are quoted or described in *Ancestors' Brocades,* and for such helpful material we are truly in debt to Mrs. Bingham. The testimony is democratic. A certain southern woman, of Huntsville, Alabama, chiefly valued the therapeutic property of the poetry. "Why not publish the remaining poems of Emily Dickinson", she wrote, "for a Christmas present to the sorrowing? Her fingers touch the chords that soothe the aching heart, then why withhold anything of hers from suffering souls?" The English reviewers were uncommonly hostile or supercilious. Yet from England came ample evidence that not the reviewers, professional politicians in the world of letters, but the broader consensus of the people spoke with wisdom and discernment. Colonel Higginson, for example, received a note from two otherwise unknown English women. This letter, which considerately contained a self-addressed envelope, naively bearing a British stamp, is a model of courtesy and understanding. The ladies, "although perfect strangers, venture to write" to Colonel Higginson asking that more of Emily's poems be published. As this obscure but most enlightened and civilized pair of Emily's admirers express the situation: "The exquisite originality of her style seems to us to open a new world of poetry, and we cannot help grudging the idea that there may be other verses as beautiful, which we may not be privileged to read."

Mrs. Todd and Colonel Higginson naturally turned first to her simplest lyrics and those of the most popular emotional appeal. Yet neither their own taste nor the materials at their disposal permitted the publication of the cheaply popular. However much their volume may have offended reactionary critics, it contained nothing to pamper and evidently little to offend the general public. Emily's reputation has been in every respect precisely the reverse of the usual. Instead of being popular in her lifetime and forgotten by posterity, she has been as popular with posterity as she was unknown during her life. Instead of being discovered by the intelligensia and slowly appreciated by the public, she was discovered promptly by the public and later all but abducted by the cult of spiritual snobbery. A wide audience quietly enjoyed her long before she became the fashion of a literary advanced guard. First popular among readers, she was later imitated by writers. The history of her fame offers more support to a democratic than to an aristocratic regimen within the world of books.

Although for a score of years after the publication of their first installment Emily's poems were widely read and had a few prompt and distinguished champions, they gained no substantial critical recognition for twenty-two years, and became actually famous only thirty-two years thereafter. One readily envisages the story as a tragi-comedy in five decades. In the first two acts the tension is latent and thoroughly submerged. Only the most acute observer can see anything inevitably dramatic. The turn-ing point occurs in the year which witnesses the outbreak of the First World War, when Madame Bianchi pub-lished her collection, *The Single Hound* (1914). This was a memorable year in American literature. Carl Sand-burg in *Poetry* published his first group of poems, in-cluding his best known lyric, *Chicago*. Vachel Lindsay produced his first really important volume, *The Congo and Other Poems*. Robert Frost achieved his first and per-haps his greatest success with *North of Boston*. Edgar Lee Masters published his historically important work and his sole masterpiece, *Spoon River Anthology*. Edwin Arlington Robinson, though publishing little in this year, was preparing his first thoroughly mature work, very shortly to appear in *The Man Against the Sky*. Elinor Wylie was in a similarly critical moment of her career. Conrad Aiken produced his first volume. It can safely be said that no more eventful year occurs in the entire his-tory of American poetry. In short, Emily was reborn precisely when American verse was reborn. There may be something accidental in these events, but there is also much more of profound significance. American critical opinion could only appreciate its finest lyrical poet when the country as a whole began to be productive of good verse in considerable quantity. Emily's own style had been in advance of American taste by over half a century.

The fourth act came in the twenties, with its own climax just ten years after Madame Bianchi's first offering. In

1924 Emily's triumph actually began. In other words, she became a major figure in the eyes of literary opinion only during the decade after the first world holocaust. A new subjectivity and subtlety, with an element of futility that need not be considered at the moment, entered the consciousness of English poetry approximately with the appearance of T. S. Eliot's *Waste Land* in 1922. In 1924 Madame Bianchi produced *The Life and Letters of Emily Dickinson* (the earlier collection of letters had for some time been out of print), together with a volume most mistakenly called *Complete Poems*, while in England Conrad Aiken edited a more aptly entitled *Selected Poems*, with a discerning introduction. The triple blow deeply penetrated into the critical mind of the English-speaking world, and as result a fashion of lavish praise promptly emerged. Finally, the thirties deepened the triumph and demonstrated beyond question that Emily's high reputation was to be lasting rather than a mere fad. This decade, commencing with the centennial of the poet's birth, also began, in 1930, with the publication of three appreciative but rather too romantic biographies. The decade ended with an academic accolade, the final evidence that Emily had at length entered the marble halls of fame. She received what was in essence a posthumous honorary degree from Amherst. In 1939 appeared the admirable study, primarily biographical and historical, by a distinguished scholar at Amherst College, Professor George Frisbie Whicher. Professor Whicher's aim was to state the facts of Emily's life and all known facts concerning her writings, with whatever historical commentary might be brought to bear to show Emily as no less a miracle than hitherto supposed but yet also the direct heir and product of New England society for more than two centuries. The thoroughness and accuracy of his work is incontestable, while it goes without saying that much keen appreciation of the poetry is shown, although the book is primarily a background study and is literary criticism chiefly by indirection. It ranks among the foremost works of academic commentary yet published in America.

Even the best publications on Emily have never proved as valuable or revealing as the imitations. Poets in America and England, and even in South America and Europe, commenced in the nineteen-thirties to turn to her as a major source of literary inspiration. She became probably the most vital single force in the development of the English lyric. The most creative among the new generation of poets studied her and acknowledged her strong influence upon them. Hart Crane, poet of unequivocal genius, celebrated her in lyrics, and in his masterpiece *The Bridge.* Conrad Aiken put successfully into practice what he had preached as a singularly discriminating critic. W. H. Auden declared that his love for her verse first determined him to be a poet. That unsurpassed master of the craft of the modern lyric, Wallace Stevens, clearly studied her art, as did Marianne Moore, Leonie Adams, Mark Van Doren, and, in England, Stephen Spender, Sylvia Warner, W. J. Turner and many of the ablest British practitioners of modern lyricism. Such revivals as the recovery of Gerard Manley Hopkins or even the belated cult of John Donne appear almost ephemeral beside the steady pressure exercised by her sure skill upon the artistic ideals of the best of the younger writers. The strong influence of her style becomes all the more remarkable when it is observed that her subject matter in itself offered such small attraction to writers naturally most deeply moved by the vast menace of twentieth-century war, capitalism, economic collapse and profound social unrest. The abiding purity and profundity of her art and artistic insight quietly made for her a solid foundation in the world's literary consciousness at a time when the whole world itself wavered and trembled in the throes of a collective agony.

To be praised is relatively unimportant, to be imitated is of serious consequence, but to be read and enjoyed is of still greater moment. A survey of reading habits unmistakably shows that she is one of the most widely read and truly appreciated poets in America today. Her reputation becomes all the more remarkable when it is recalled that the destiny of her poems no less than that of her life has been an austere triumph. Her family undeniably placed certain obstacles in the path of her writing both when she was alive and after her death. Without in the least entering into unpleasant or unsavory details, it should be noted that quotation from her poems, their use in anthologies, and the somewhat bulky and unsatisfactorily edited edition in which for the last twenty years they have been read must have done much to discourage popularity; yet all this has failed to check the tide of her fame. Her conspicuous place in innumerable anthologies and on the shelves of even the smallest public libraries attests her hold upon the public mind. The people demand her at all costs.

Her poetry wins attention from a wide range of readers. She belongs almost equally to the people and to the cults. Experiments have shown that many of her simplest lyrics strongly attract children. Even groups of negro children, for example, in a large New York City primary school located near the Harlem slums have been found to respond enthusiastically to certain of the poems. At the other extreme her concision, her boldly imaginative use of language, her strict sense of form, her emotional and moral intensity, and her profound subjectivity have ingratiated her work to the most warmly acclaimed radical leaders in current literature. Her imperfect rhymes and irregular rhythms attract persons with ears attuned to the nuances of modern music. In her aggressiveness she seems masculine, in her deep spiritual gift for absorbing suffering she appears feminine. Realists and scientifically trained readers are drawn to her unprecedentedly sharp and specific imagery and statement, mystics and the religiously inclined to her contemplative poems. Conformists find that she accepted her environment, rebels hold that she rebelled against it. Optimists discover in her work faith, hope, and ideal beauty; pessimists find in it a withering scorn of human life and a frank look at nature, accompanied by stoical fortitude. One reader notes her piety, another her atheism. Professor Whicher finds her the heir of Jonathan Edwards, whereas Sister Mary James Power, in her recent volume, *In the Name of the Bee,* discovers her to be a Catholic in all but name. Few readers may admire all her verses, but almost all admire some. In turn she addresses the intellectual, the passionate, and the fanciful. In the eyes of her readers she may be witty, wise, or ardent, a lover of man or a lover of nature, a rebellious child or an adoring angel, an unabashed emotionalist or an austere sage. Her vision being both for this world, and otherworldly, she attracts the most diverse groups. No reader can be too young or too old, too simple-hearted or too sophisticated, to find what must be in his eyes an all but perfect expression of experience. Seemingly narrow, a provincial woman, unmarried, and, during the years in which she composed her greatest poems, much of a recluse, a writer of tiny poems, a perfector of miniatures and a professed believer in the microscope, she achieved a breadth that draws the multitude to her as to a common focus. Being supremely human, she appeals to humanity. Moreover her magnetism and personality as an imaginative genius arrest the attention. Everyone may have a unique conception of her, but all recognize the personal element in her work. Like a lover or a religious leader, she has the gift to appeal to the individual as well as to evoke from him the strongest sense of her own identity. Although ideally speaking she addresses all persons, she speaks to each one separately and in turn becomes heard through the strength of her own individuality. To a review of this personality, considered in its most personal aspects, the pages immediately following are devoted.

3 *GENIUS AND ABNORMALITY*

Although the personal element in Emily Dickinson's verse must always be of more moment to the world at large than this element in her life, the two are inextricably bound together, and the normal pattern of our thinking confronts us first with the woman and second with her life's work. It may well be more important to us that she was a writer than a person, but she could hardly have been the one without being the other, and it proves most striking of all that she became a genius. Biography in the American field or in any other seldom presents so unmistakable an example, for she conforms to all the many connotations which the word genius has come to bear. Even after scholars have placed her in her environment and shown the ways in which she supposedly conformed to the norm of her nineteenth-century New England culture, it remains apparent that she did become both abnormal and strange. No explanations can keep us from feeling in the end that there was something a bit weird about her after all. Our grasp of psychology, whether acquired in the schools or in life, at once brings to attention her abnormal tensions and her many marks of eccentric behavior. Her fellow townspeople recognized her as a freakish and an alarmingly original character; posterity prefers to regard her as belonging to the foremost order of genius.

The word has many shades of meaning, almost all not only relevant to Emily but highly applicable. She resembles the biological "sport", the type unaccountably unique, and perhaps even indicative of a new turn in the evolution of the species. Deeply as her roots undoubtedly go into her environment and tradition, she stands markedly aside from that tradition, having her tryst, if not with infinity or immortality, as she herself pleasantly declared, at least with the succeeding century. Genius to some writers virtually means inspiration, and of this Emily undeniably had a lion's share. The concept implies a phenomenally fruitful creative imagination, and this, too, was hers. Beyond her strong powers of reason, she was guided primarily by her intuition, by her daemon, or her star. That, too, is genius.

In each creative field genius obviously takes on slightly different aspects. Whoever possesses it in religion is a seer, or a saint; above all, he is a seer of visions, and such Emily emphatically not only saw but realized and expressed. She possessed much of the fervor and dedication of the saint, much of the insight and penetration of the religious or metaphysical sage. In her we find that almost unbelievable concentration upon a single species of creative task, so useful to the race, so characteristic of genius, and so painful to the pregnant minds which bear its burden. The strong bias and personal distortion common in genius, often leading to ascetic severity, one notes in Emily. Genius is neither acquired nor inherited, but a personal birthright; it is the most common fatality of greatness; and this quality also appears in the poet, for she was dedicated to poetical expression from childhood, however much the hard school of life and her own intelligence ripened and matured her art. That her only authentic portraits represent her as a young child or girl, somehow helps us to realize this phase of her character.

Pictorially the young Emily takes her place beside the young Mozart. The genius we think of as living outside the norm in mind, in conduct and possibly in morals. Emily certainly soared beyond normality in mind and manners, and potentially if not actually in morals. (There is the well-known legend that one day Lavinia rushed into her brother's house with the appalling news that Emily intended to run off with a married man! What could be done to stop such madness?)

In the popular mind genius is closely connected with the notion of "the artistic temperament". Not all persons with such temperament are believed to be geniuses, but in popular thinking all geniuses are supposed to possess such a quality. Largely because of this spirit in Emily, Colonel Higginson arrived at the melancholy conclusion that she was his "half-cracked poetess". In his correspondence with her he was primarily aware merely of an eccentric. She rarely addressed her own envelopes, rarely signed her own name to letters addressed to him, wrote in a wildly imaginative style, uttered the most extravagant statements, and disregarded the most sanctified laws of literary composition. He distrusted her mind, but probably thought no worse of her than of other women who wilfully refused to be conventional. When he actually saw her, his impression changed. He confessed the terrific tension of her personality, the electrical shock of her mere presence; he found himself positively terrified when with her, and thoroughly exhausted when he had left the room. This was to be in the presence of something more than either eccentricity or madness. It was unmistakably genius, whether for better or for worse. And Emily had the gifts not only of a great poet but of a great actress.

Her social appearances were few but all the more calculated and devastating. With full energy of soul and body, she mastered an effect, at the same time that her position was fundamentally sincere to the degree of stark tragedy. Here, again, was personal and aesthetic genius.

As the most fruitful form of a consuming enthusiasm, genius burns itself to make a torch for mankind. The genius of the true artist is always enthusiastic, extravagant, and Dionysian. Such attributes become wholly obvious in Emily. Her fiery temperament glows all the more fiercely beneath her cover of Puritanical reserve. In a curious but valuable little poem, "I cannot dance upon my toes", by her usual figurative indirection she vividly describes her own state of mind. Outwardly she remains humorist, inwardly a soul dedicated to life's most devastating forces. With a pen artful as Degas's brush, she paints a troupe of awkward toe dancers at least striving to appear ecstatic. Within her own soul, she declares, are wilder dances fit to "lay a Prima mad!" With a delightful New Englandism she declares that in her heart, "it's full as opera!" Genius, then, in this classical, platonic, and Dionysian sense Emily shared to a superlative degree.

The querulous science of a more aging civilization than that of Euripides acquaints us today with speculations on the relation of genius to madness. Thus genius comes to be defined by certain schools of psychology, notably those closest to Jung and Freud, as a fruitful madness, like a pearl within an ailing oyster, or ambergris in a sick whale. Shakespeare's intuition that all greatness is to madness near allied has been subtilized and refined into a labyrinth of obscurity. It stands far removed from our present purpose to psychoanalyze Emily, nor, I presume, do most students of American thought look forward to a possible treatise on the subject. The broad outlines of the case readily suffice for the present. To fail to recognize grave abnormality in Emily's life or at least the reflections of this condition in her poetry, constitutes a serious omission. Equally serious an error would it be to focus so acutely on the background of the abnormality as to overlook the serene perfection of the art in the foreground. In a preliminary study, and for what may be called a background awareness, the distraught conditions of Emily's life possess considerable value, comparable in importance to the background of her New England culture. Without her abnormality she could not have produced the type of art which she achieved, nor without those normal tendencies toward abnormality in every human breast could the public enjoy this art as it does. To draw a picture of Emily as a typical New Englander would be palpably contrary to fact. In the first place, the normal New Englanders were far from normal, at least if we judge by Emily's father, brother, and sister. But the general principles involved require no special scrutiny.

Neither is it fruitful to elaborate the evidence for the painful experiences which Emily suffered in actual life. Enough in other connections has already been indicated, even in the rapid summary of these preliminary pages, to demonstrate her tragic frustrations, the grave and almost fatal struggles within her own psyche, and her intense neuroticism. Of vastly greater concern is the relationship between her obvious tensions and her perfect art, her distorted and crucified life on the one hand and her most comely and proportioned poems on the other. In her case even more clearly than in most instances of genius, it becomes plausible to believe that her literary efforts supplied an insurance of her ultimate sanity. Not only by the strenuous labor of composition did she occupy herself and sustain a hold in existence. A preventive was unquestionably attained by the discovery of ideal aesthetic forms wherein the heady wines of madness might once and for all be poured and sealed. The Aristotelian psychology of tragedy was once more vindicated. Emily's life was built about this formula. Was she mad or sane? Neither of the direct answers proves satisfactory. Her own imagery indicates better solutions. She was mad in this world but sane in eternity. Her fondness for such concepts as eternity, immortality, heaven, and infinity, her thirst to live in the absolute, all reflect her successful transformation through art from perplexity to serenity, and her ability to come out upon the safe side of her distresses. Her firm art kept her upon the lee shore, providing the breakwater which saved her from being blown out to sea. Although her outward conduct in her last years seemed strangest to her friends, she almost certainly passed through the most strained periods of her emotional life considerably earlier. Emily overcame her emotional difficulties partly with the aid of time but also with the help of her activity as creative artist.

Only a small percentage of her poems unmistakably reflects her struggles in that phase of genius akin to madness, although these are often the poems most widely and legitimately admired. Among her verses may be found many instances of coolly stated aphorism, clear and calm description, and poised, humane and natural gaiety such as might conceivably have come from the hand of a writer unwrung by life's more melancholy pressures. Much of

her ethical, religious, philosophical, and mystical poetry
has at least no obvious ties with her inner struggles. Her
technical quest for the exact word or phrase, the emotionally fitting rhyme or the precise statement need, ideally
speaking, have no immediate bearing upon her abnormali-
ties. Yet it must be noted that in actuality her quest for
perfection in art seems partly motivated on therapeutic
grounds, and her intellectual search for truth to have been
in no small degree a strategy to outwit her emotional
confusion: the mental clarity behind the emotional storm.
In all such cases the relation to abnormality, even if
established, remains, however, indirect or oblique. Many
poems of a more frankly emotional context directly por-
tray the spiritual mastery of a nervous or psychical dis-
order.

Emily's finest poetry may be viewed as the autobiography of a victorious struggle against acute pain that was
in a sense madness and threatened total prostration of
her personality. Unforgettably she describes her moods
of extreme depression. She subtilizes between the various
shades of fear, anguish, crisis, numbness, and despair. Her
heightened capacity for ecstacy or joy proved, of course,
no less an evidence of abnormality than did her extreme
sensitivity to human ills. Especially in the love poems
and in those numerous pieces neither classified by her editors as love poetry nor obviously such but covertly and
fundamentally of this description, one detects signs of her
tragic dislocations. This may be seen in such magnificent
lyrics as, "After great pain a formal feeling comes", or
"There's a certain slant of light On winter afternoons".
Emily discloses the history of the lover's madness even
more objectively than Robert Burton, author of *The*

Anatomy of Melancholy. Even many of the physiological symptoms of such madness she vividly describes, as attacks of fever, frigidity, trembling, numbness, and dizziness. Her poems themselves afford a relentlessly faithful record of a soul which has passed through experiences as pathological in the life of the individual as prison camps infested with torture are pathological in the life of a state.

Had her nervous afflictions been less sharp, she would probably have composed less powerful verses, or in any case verses of a very different kind; had they been greater, she would have succumbed and produced no poetry whatsoever. Her life, as woman and as poet, hung at times in an agonizing balance. Her position further suggests that other poets have been less fortunate in this relation between life and art. William Blake, for example, may well have been more pathologically involved than Emily; it is certain that his prophetic books bear blemishes from his abnormality such as nowhere deface her work. On the other hand Emily's timid bid for fame during her own lifetime was eclipsed by a group of Cambridge poets— Longfellow, Lowell, and Holmes—who were either too sane or two feebly mad to achieve the fine fury virtually requisite in the lyrical or the poetic imagination. The contemporary public in making their art its standard lost those psychological benefits of art immemorially helpful to mankind. It remained wholly ignorant of art as a purgative ritual. The Cambridge poets rivalled neither an Aeschylean tragedy nor an Aristophanic comedy, whereas if Emily never duplicates a tragic chorus by the one nor an abandoned comic chorus by the other, she at least sounds depths of tragedy and heights of mirth unknown to the strikingly bourgeois favorites. She is far the better poet, and why? Though so terse an answer may appear to beg the question, this chapter points the way with the mere observation that, unlike them, in a superlative degree she was in the possession of genius.

Emily Dickinson outlived and outfought her madness much as she outdistanced her provinciality. After the manner of the true genius, she turned both her highly emotional disturbances and her notably provincial environment, forces which equally threatened her poetical success, to her own good account. Both battles she won in the name of genius. With the more subjective and intimate of the two struggles the reader is the less concerned, partly because the details necessary for a full discussion have been lost with the minor personalia of the past century. With the more epic struggle between the local and the universal, the temporal and the eternal, the merely personal and the completely human, the reader is vastly more concerned, since the evidence is here both fuller and more potent, and her successful transmutation through genius is accordingly the main subject of the first part of this book.

4 *ON SEEING MICROSCOPICALLY*

Emily Dickinson's life and works show a mind uniquely capable of perceiving the particular and achieving the universal. Not only is this constructive process the supreme exercise of her imagination; its parts themselves become instinct with imagination, since this faculty alone discovers what details are worthy of recording, what language or symbol makes them vivid, and where the core of universality lies within the enveloping sphere of the individual's experience. Intuition and inspiration enabled Emily, by employing the right image and right word for it, to discover in the heart of her own being the common heart of Man.

With peculiar insight she realized that a microscopic vision most readily leads to infinity. As she so pointedly observed, "microscopes are prudent in an emergency". Her understanding of the problem not only agreed with the traditional views of the mystics; it curiously paralleled the efforts of distinguished scientists, her contemporaries, who were more and more successfully investigating the universe through exploration of the atom. Whether we look inward into the human body or outward to the heavens on a night of stars, we recognize reality as composed of similar particles. Life is simplified, explained, and reduced to its essence by interpreting the vast whole in relation to the minute particle.

Emily needed the infinite because she found herself in a personal predicament; in the modern world she needed infinity much as in the ancient one Saint Augustine required a knowledge of God. She was compelled to find some way to forget not only her pain but herself, to discover some manner of rising through and above herself to the impersonal. She could not merely forget herself in a view of human society or of the much vaster entity, nature. Salvation lay only through interpreting, translating, and transcending the immediate till it became some form of absolute, till her own personal love, joy, and sorrow grew comprehensively human and even of cosmic significance. Her poetry grew to be that chemistry or rather alchemy of the soul whereby this magical transmutation was achieved. This was accomplished not by objective reference to history, sociology, or natural science, but by the discovery of a universal form within the self.

From the shallow grandiosity prevailing in the taste of the bourgeois nineteenth-century—as in Longfellow or in Tennyson—Emily Dickinson was wholly free because of her complete sincerity and command of reality. The popular poets were grandiose; she was truly grand. Her self-disciplined insistence in poetry upon the actual, personal experience, or observation, her complete disregard for the specious generalities and idealisms of the age, insured her unique success. The better conscience of the times failed to endorse the main effort of the age, the ruthless imperialism of the industrial and capitalistic nations, as of the United States in the direction of Mexico and of Great Britain in that of India. As a result, the laureates of imperialism, from Tennyson to Kipling, were invariably shallow and tumorous. The poet who lived quietly in the dignified brick house in Amherst, and loved her father at the same time that she despised his political and capitalistic schemes, was free from the vicious, highly masculine, and Anglo-Saxon hypocrisy. Others might find their reality in colonial empire; she won a more legitimate conquest in the wars of her own imperial soul.

The notion that one must retire in order to advance is not, of course, peculiar to Emily Dickinson. With a purely materialistic view of life, Voltaire counselled men to cultivate their gardens. While Emily was commencing her career as poet, Thoreau sought retirement at Walden and in the woods of Maine in order to set his own heart in harmony not with an artificial, eighteenth-century garden but with the wild and sublime heart of nature. Emily, like Voltaire, cultivated her garden; for she was the daughter of a well-established country squire and far removed from the pioneering spirit of the woodsman. In her singularly intimate garden, however, she grew not the practicable flowers and vegetables which Voltaire would have men cultivate but the mystical flower of flowers, the rose of the universal heart. As highly cultivated as the neo-classical Voltaire, as thoroughly idealistic as the romantic Thoreau, she combined the better genius of two centuries.

Drastically and systemmatically she rejected the broader and more specious ideals of her times to concentrate on her microscopic eye. She discountenanced many social allegiances. No Union short of the universal union of mankind held charms for her, since anything less became diversive in her profounder vision. In her eyes to be catholic it was necessary for her to be more than Catholic, or, in other words, to be universal. Thus she belonged to no church or congregation. Although she lived through two periods in which her country was at war, patriotism as a life-motive signified relatively little to her. It may have been in part from this tendency that she declared that to her war seems an oblique place. Moreover, a want of conventional patriotism and not a lack of awareness of war characterized her thinking, for, as we shall shortly note, the imagery of her poems shows her keenly aware of wars in progress. It is true that she accepted America and in one poem boasted of the stars in the American flag as symbols of an indomitable idealism essentially distasteful to materialistic Britishers. But this poem remains a marked exception, and the stars clearly signify to her rather states of the mind than states of the Union.

Particularity with a Lowell, a Whittier, or a Frost not uncommonly takes the form of regionalism. Emily's more drastic position in this respect should be closely observed. Since relatively little is known of her uneventful personal life, her biographers have dwelt at length upon her environment, almost always described as of New England rather than of America. Her poems have, very properly, been likened to Emerson's; they might even better be likened to those of the more aesthetically minded Thoreau. It has been noted that she followed countless patterns of New England living; that she was a typically idealistic New England spinster; and that her tendency to metaphysics and religious speculation and experience recalls that the greatest of Puritan divines, Jonathan Edwards, had lived only seven miles from her own home. The present writer has previously written on Emily exclusively from this point of view in a chapter dealing with her mind in *The American Way of Poetry*. Professor Whicher has much more amply expounded the same point of view. Its validity is, I suppose, incontrovertable. Yet how relatively trivial it seems in the general picture of her poetical achievement!

The essence of the case is clearly that while she was of New England she was only incidentally of New England, and in the end completely transcended her heritage, which she only partially accepted, and from which in some respects she violently revolted. She herself, to be sure, declared that she saw "New Englandly". Whether or not she saw that way, she certainly did not invariably write that way, for no one else in New England thought of the simple device of using that adverb. She scrupulously avoids in her poetry almost all words which might be termed local allusions. There are, with the exception of half a dozen references to the town of Amherst, almost no allusions by name to places or people in New England. In this respect it is significant that she refers somewhat freely to more exotic points in geography; and while she has perhaps only one geographical allusion to a hundred in Whitman, she does refer more than once to China, India, the Himalayas, Cashmere, Africa, Russia, Norway, the Alps, Vesuvius, and Mexico. Knowing and confessing that she was inevitably regional to a certain degree, she made deliberate and successful effort to free herself from fetters of regionalism. The sentimental variety of regionalism, shortly to become so popular, she would have thoroughly abhorred.

The town of Amherst has since taken some measures to claim the poet who as a poet in no way claimed the town as hers. Whatever realism she possessed by no means encouraged her to envisage Amherst as Dante viewed Florence. Her verses never mention Amherst College, and we know that as a mature woman she took no active part in the religious, political, or corporate life of the community. In Amherst she undeniably had a few close friends, but her deep, spiritual type of democracy discouraged her from making friends familiarly with all the town. Her business was to write in such a fashion that a century later all the town would be reading her verses.

Neither church, country, region, nor village claimed Emily's soul. As one of the most fastidious of minds, she had an extraordinary genius for detail. Besides, she was a woman, and there are even a very few poems in which her sex temporarily gets the better of her universality. This is naturally the rule in her ample personal correspondence. Perhaps more clearly than anyone, Emily understood the difference between the social letter and the letter to posterity. Each demanded particularity, but of a different species. One required the personal reference, the other, the symbolic image. Most of her published letters are delightfully informal, chatty writing, full of allusions to local persons and places, with personalia of all sorts, and a plentiful use of concrete references which the modern reader either fails to understand or grasps much less fully and in a very different sense than originally intended. Her personal letters are the gossip and chatter of time; her poems, the gossip of eternity. Even where the same subject matter occurs, as in an account of a death, a wedding, a garden, or a blackbird, the viewpoints will be leagues apart. How the poet universalizes her theme will be the subject of the next chapter. It remains to observe in this how important her realism and concreteness became, and how, more specifically, she practices her vision with the microscopic eye.

The only messages she got each day, she declared, were bulletins from eternity. As she frequently repeated, eternity was not another time but an absence of time, a living in a sufficient and more vital present. It was merely the present life resting on a firm foundation, that foundation being a manner of experiencing and not a species of religious faith. Eternity—or art—and imagination provided a very modest manner of viewing a very commonplace present. Her most sublime poems are jottings in the diary of an enlightened soul.

Her microscopic eye amounts merely to her keenness in observing both her physical and social surroundings and her own psychological experiences, in other words, both inner and outer reality. As the basic manifestation of the outer world, nature strongly attracted her. That she was to some extent driven to nature after unsatisfactory encounters with human beings, need not detain the present argument. The immediate point is the freshness and acuteness of her observations. The relation of her thought to the rise of American science in the great age of naturalists, from Audubon to Burroughs, is likewise an important topic for later discussion. For the moment it must suffice that the details which she saw she saw with the eye of the artist, employing her marvellous mastery of the precise word to translate this experience into verse. Indeed, the precision of her observations of nature resembled that which in part made their expression possible—her precise and exhaustive study of the dictionary. With her verbal art at her disposal, it became relatively easy for her to draw her frank and uncanny pictures of a bird eating a worm, a snake dividing the grass, a bat, a mushroom, or any other of nature's lesser creatures, pleasant or unpleasant. The coloring of each season, the variable tones evoked by distance and light, reflections in moving water or impalpable tints in clouds she detected and expressed much as the impressionist painters, unknown to herself, were doing at the same time in France. In accuracy of color she rivals Claude Monet, in accuracy of line, Toulouse Lautrec. She unhesitatingly examines surrounding nature, with an emotional and imaginative mind amply sufficient to transform her realism into the loftiest idealistic art.

Her happiest hours seem to have been passed out-of-doors, but her poetry also memorializes with similar specificity her life indoors. Coventry Patmore might write sentimentally of the angel in the house; Emily Dickinson writes simply and directly of the woman in the house. She is as much the laureate of housekeepers as Homer was the laureate of warriors. Without perhaps fully grasping its significance, many of her critics note her tireless liking for domestic imagery. Like Shakespeare, she is fond of depicting costume, especially feminine costume. Her allusions carry us to every part of the house—even the most remote. Her poetry explores attic and cellar, parlor, dining-room, kitchen, bedroom, closet, and hall. To her sensitive and sympathetic eye the view out her second-story window assumes almost infinite importance. She sees the tree, green in summer, naked in autumn, white in winter, the edge of a wall, and a distant steeple, while all the lights of the sky play a clairvelux for her minute contemplation. The various household activities receive her attention. To her the unending war of the housewife against the spider takes on a higher meaning than the war between the States or the political chaos in

Europe. Candles and lamps glow softly in her pages. She surrounds her readers familiarly with chairs and sofas. Even on the tomb she serves a "marble tea". Emily Dickinson is in fact the only person in America who really made transcendentalism practical.

The world of her poetry has no place for the mob and unfolds no broad communal stage. There are only a few characters, intimately known. These persons are in no case, of course, presented in the manner of fictional or dramatic figures, since such full-length portraits cannot be given in the lyric or the aphorism. Interested as Emily primarily was in Man rather than in the varieties of men, characterization in the usual sense remains, like war, oblique to her world. It is her satirical sense which chiefly evokes it, as may be seen in her brief account of the hard, successful business man whose face would wound a stone hurled at it, in her harsh drawing of the specious and conceited preacher, or in her pictures of the soft but venomous sentimentality of her sister-in-law, Susan Dickinson. Her characters are otherwise not described, but felt emotionally. They are, of course, never named. But we know that she is moved to write of persons for the most part only when they are most intimately known to her, as her father, mother, sister, her closest friends, and her lover. Such is the narrow circle which in her own fashion she knows minutely.

Above all, she knows herself. Her most searching and relentless microscope is turned inwards, and after the manner of the finer Puritans she searches out and reports not only her moments of greatest pleasure but her hours of almost unbearable pain and her own spiritual blemishes. Nature becomes largely an organ for the expression of her own moods through her art. She records not so much her friends and lovers as their effect upon her. How she receives a letter or a piece of bad news, or how she endures either a joy or a bereavement, become her favorite themes. In this spiritual reporting she is not only personal; she is mercilessly exact. Minute shades of spiritual difference she records in far greater poems than those relative trifles where the eye dwells more on shadings among the clouds than on their spiritual import. She becomes an artist in the field of the psychologist Freud no less than in the field of the naturalist Audubon. Even the philosophy of the soul she turns into austere gnomic verse, as rich in aphoristic ore as Omar's *Rubaiyat*. Totally without knowledge of scientific system or method, a precision highly agreeable to the scientist she emphatically possesses, thus indicating one more phase of her love of microscopes.

5 *CIRCUMFERENCE*

To grasp the character of Emily's mind it is helpful to consider the meaning which she attaches to the words "circumference" and "microscope". The circumference is the limit of a thing. Thus the circumference of the world is infinity, immortality, eternity, and the absolute. An individual is an atom. To see him it is necessary to see microscopically, and hence all vision confined to the problems of a personality is microscopic vision. Such vision may be fruitless or fruitful. To arrive at the core of any individual or of the self, it becomes necessary to pare away the soft exterior. Emily's self-appointed task as poet and as thinker was to examine personality with microscopic vision, to digest whatever the mind affords in knowledge of the external or the internal world, but ultimately to fix attention only on the eternally human qualities. The incidental purged away, the eternal Man must emerge. To perceive this humanity is to rise from pettiness to full human stature; to express it is to be the pure artist, the true lyric poet.

In the privacy of her thoughts and in the quiet of her upstairs room Emily labored to dissolve whatever was ephemeral or trivial in her experience and to achieve the universal. With unsurpassed frankness and a truly zealous gaze she faced herself, her family, and most intimate friends, her immediate neighbors and the house, the garden, and the landscape wherein she found herself. By seeing not only minutely enough but clearly enough, she succeeded in dismissing the transient nature of whatever she saw and in affirming its lasting value. She found the circumference of Amherst in the world and of herself in the universe. This mental action as stated in general terms necessarily assumes a philosophical complexion. But Emily was a woman, and not only feminine but pragmatic. Both her sex and her New Englandism taught her pragmatism. Well aware as she certainly was of the ideas on which her habits of life were founded, to her the highest importance rested in the way of life and not in any doctrine, however truthful. Her vexed and frustrated soul called for spiritual release, but not for flight. She aimed frugally to utilize whatever was her fate, either good or ill. Her duty was by no means to lose her identity, but to enlarge it to the limit defined by its circumference. The limit was the world in human terms. If she could write poems about love and death, nature and housekeeping, joy and pain, in such a fashion that, potentially at least, all persons could be her sympathetic readers, she would necessarily achieve the goal that her spirit demanded. Writing a letter to posterity became for her the best way of making life meaningful, enjoyable, and bearable. For the greater part of her life she remained physically in Amherst. Through her poetry she most nearly succeeded at the same time in dwelling in Amherst and in subduing the world.

To write a poetry serving this function required a specific type of discipline. She found herself forced to discover a subject and an idiom as far as possible free from narrowly temporal or geographical limitations. She acknowledged that she must see New Englandly, and unquestionably she knew herself to be a daughter of the nineteenth century, even though of its radical elements.

Without morbid fear of the contemporaneous, or, for that matter, of the antiquarian or the prophetical, she aspired to reach the impersonal through the personal. That she succeeded, the evidence of time attests. The question is merely how she solved her difficulties. In her success she does, of course, what every true artist does, and does it superlatively well.

A surprisingly large number of her poems are merely philosophical aphorisms in verse. These seldom prove to be her best pieces, but no one at least in English excels her in this type of writing; and the presence of so large a proportion of work in her collection which remains indisputably generalization gives a suggestive clue to the character of the rest. Her more figurative, lyrical, and imaginative poems retain the feature of generalization present in the more frankly intellectual pieces at the same time that they gain in poetic power through their freer, more symbolical, and less didactic manner.

Most of the poems are in a quite literal sense out of time and place. They bear few references to any country, town, local custom, or literary or social tradition. Although Emily Dickinson has often been associated by her critics with the metaphysical poets of a school of Donne, it is noteworthy that she almost wholly avoids the spate of learned allusion found in Donne's poetry. Her own life was her chief mythology. History, which is the science of time, practically does not exist for her poetry, which is the art of eternity. In this connection her treatment of the American Civil War proves of considerable interest. One touching poem with this war as a background expresses the affection of a mother and her son. The mother has died many years before the son falls in battle. Emily imagines their meeting in heaven. Not even the heavenly country, however, is of the essence of the poem, for it deals far more with sheer affection, the agonies of delay, and the joys of surprise, than with conventional ideas of immortality. Unlike Whitman, Emily Dickinson never contemplates the social or political aspects of the particular conflict.

The stage of her poems is bare of all but essentials. Not only does she never name her lover; never does she relate anything of him which surely leads her biographers to his identity. The entire purpose of her lyricism spells the nemesis of the biographer's somewhat irrelevant curiosity. It becomes pleasant to employ, like Emily, the fiction of immortality and to imagine her smile at learned frustration and her spiritual victory. Avidly she describes how her lover turns about in a room or how his shoes creak behind an opening door, because these are incidents of grave emotional value, however trivial they may seem to all but the microscopic eye initiated in the deeper values of life. Of merely prosaic fact or decorative ornament she gives nothing. The baroque eloquence of seventeenth-century learning stands as removed from her as possible.

She writes of men's deepest emotional experiences as those which they most obviously share in common. Again and again it is clear that some specific event occasions a poem, but all matter superficially belonging to the occasion has been omitted. This enables the reader to make the emotion his own. Life has for him, as for Emily, supplied the pertinent occasion. Like Emily, by recognizing the experience objectively, he is enabled to throw off a confining and an uncomfortable emotional burden.

Her imagery remains at the same time vivid and, as far as possible under the circumstances, universal. In using physical nature she prefers to study the nuances of what is basically familiar, exactly as when she analyzes human nature. Sun and moon, trees and waters, cloud and lightning, the passage of the seasons and the hours of the day, are imagery in the most powerful and serious of her so-called nature poems. Although in this field she observes minutely, she is the opposite of pedantic, for she cares as a poet no more for scientific learning than for historical learning. Her observations seem almost always fresh yet almost never recherché. No personal vanity dictated lines of hers marred with far-fetched snatches of semi-scientific naturalism typical of Victorian poets infatuated by fashions in the literature of the Darwinian period. She never elaborates genre pictures of nature, in the manner of Robert Frost enjoying the activities of New England blueberry pickers, lumbermen, or small farmers. With far too austere a mind to linger over the regional, the trivial, or the merely external, she seeks in nature only the forms and impressions applicable to her language of the universal.

Her reluctance to use the proper names of persons or of local places as dictated by her thirst for the universal is duplicated in her reluctance to employ names of classes or species in nature. It pleases her to write a minutely accurate and vivid description of a hummingbird without naming it. In a similarly imaginative and unpedantic fashion she writes on snakes, bees, robins, woodpeckers, and other creatures. She prefers not to name the stars. The purity of her style even extends to writing a memorable poem on the snow without calling it by name.

Something of her art for nature imagery she unquestionably learnt from the book she knew best, the Bible.
This applies here, of course, rather to the poetical than
to the historical parts of the Scriptures. Notably in the
King James version the Hebrew poetry is so translated
that the reader rarely becomes conscious of the least exoti-
cism in the scene. The accounts in Job and Psalms, for
example, of the grander aspects of nature, the allusions
to sun, moon, and stars, day and night, clouds and snow,
wind and rain, mountains and the sea, bear for the most
part no specific reference to Palestine. The references
are not to one country but to the religious interpretation
of the whole world as created by one God. Milton's
paraphrase in *Paradise Lost* of the creation myth in Genesis gives a similar instance of the universalizing effect
of the Hebrew upon modern poetry. Obviously, the religious element in each case greatly aids in the broadest
possible applicability of the imagery.

After nature, religion supplies the chief source for symbolism in Emily's most serious poems. She chose nature
first as the body of experience which men have most in
common and religion second as their next most binding
tie. Indeed her special use of religious imagery, as in her
fondness for the resurrection theme, most clearly shows
that she intuitively understands the religious imagery
itself as a reflection of nature myths. Her treatment of
Christianity becomes, at least from an intellectual point
of view, one of the most remarkable features of her work.
From Christian literature she culls whatever attracts her
almost as would a complete outsider, a poet, let us say,
of Islam or of Japan. Recalling her well-known tendencies
to skepticism and heresy, not to mention blasphemy, it be-

comes virtually impossible to say how many of her allusions to Christianity represent belief and how many mere metaphor. One point, however, is clear. She touches the major tenets of each sectarian creed without affirming her allegiance to any one but instead leaving the reader all the more skeptical as to her belief in any sect whatsoever. So it has come about that her heart, at least, has been claimed by disputing commentators for both Catholic and Puritan thought. Even the inconsistencies within that delicately poised sect, the Church of England, are less remarkable than those in Emily, for Anglicans infrequently think or write with zeal on any side, whereas Emily's writing carries imaginative persuasion and passionate energy even where its total effect discourages belief.

She possesses an excellent command over the terminology chiefly favored by the Calvinists. Her poems abound in references to election, predestination, and grace. They show her thoroughly familiar with the austere and rigid practices of puritan believers. All this in a poet of Amherst is by no means extraordinary. But that she should write of the more typical beliefs and attitudes of Catholicism in a manner that would hardly seem strange to a Florentine of the fourteenth century, does indeed evoke wonder. The whole subject of her relation to religious belief will be carefully considered later. At present, emphasis need fall only on an eclecticism too glaring to be for a moment denied. The consequence of this eclecticism is by no means shallowness of thought but depth and breadth of poetical content. Although glancing at all sects, she never for a moment becomes a sectarian, any more than she becomes a nationalist, a regionalist, a typical Victorian, or, in any strict sense of the word, a provincial. To religious imagery and religious experience she commonly turns her most zealous attention as to one of the deepest and most nearly universal reservoirs of human experience. But of the type of religion that has also on so many occasions been divisive, promoting bigotry, intolerance and parochialism, she has nothing. She never creeps into the narrow house of a cult and closes the door. In her religious imagery no less than in her nature imagery, she stands in the open, upon a mountain top, under nothing more confining or oppressive than the stars.

When Emily writes that the poet deals with familiar matters of daily life, known superficially to everyone, but known profoundly only through imaginative vision, she by no means advocates a vulgar familiarity or a trivial realism. Her concern is clearly not with the affectations or gadgets of an hour, the whims or fashions of a moment, but with basic emotional urges of mankind. In seeking the familiar, she seeks and achieves the profoundly human. This point of view explains much of her own conception of individuality, genius, and self-expression, in all of which she believes, but not entirely in the commonly received manner. It is true that her poetry is deeply subjective, that she seeks to express herself, and that in a measure her work reflects the romantic ego. Like Whitman, she sings herself. But Whitman, no more the pragmatist but much more the opportunist than Emily, sought to identify himself with contemporary America. The poet of Amherst, on the contrary, much more successfully than Whitman actually sang the song of the universal. He had the theory of this, too; but he mastered less of the practice. Moreover the romantic doctrine of self-expression as formulated by Rousseau opened wide the flood gates for a popular debauch of eccentricity, to which in all her serious thinking the poet of Amherst was unalterably opposed.

This was her last and greatest trial. In her struggle against the transient and the ephemeral Emily easily resisted the seductions of nationalism, sectarianism, and all other organized divisive movements among mankind. Her bitterest struggle and most signal triumph lay in her battle with the romantic ego, in the innermost wars of self. She believed that in any individual lay the core of the universal which, if isolated, would end isolation. Here lay the dangerous pass, the crucial testing ground in her adventure. How could she as artist and as woman cultivate so advanced a self-consciousness and avoid egoism? How could she in her rebellion against society and with her obviously unconventional habits of life, write poetry and live a life ordered by the higher conventions of the universal? In last analysis the criticism of her work on this score presents difficulties almost as grave as those which she faced in her own spiritual and creative quest. Yet with confidence it can be said that, a few bizarre passages or unfinished stanzas to the contrary, her verses are individual without eccentricity, and strongly distinguished by their very lack of egoism. The universal manhood which she so sorely needed and bravely sought she attained.

Her achievement may, however, be examined further and its various parts broken down for analysis. In the following passages of this study a few of her most notable means for realizing a universal humanity will be successively considered. Such an approach becomes the more desirable because in the two volumes wherein today her poems are collected the arrangement fails to give a clear picture of any one of her principal qualities or interests. The volume compiled by Madame Bianchi is, to be sure, more bewildering, with the dazzling profusion and confusion of its nine hundred poems, than is that judicially edited by Mrs. Bingham, with its six hundred. But in any case, some critical effort is required to segregate the poet's main insights and her remarkable understanding of the nature of man considered as an individual. One basic experience which all men have in common is that of having been children. A large number of Emily's poems either deal with childhood or have a fancy attractive to the child at the same time that they delight adults. Emily appeals to the eternally childlike within the heart. With her vigorous intellect she dwells philosophically upon the ageless problems of the mind. By virtue of her sensitive heart she appreciates the eternally recurrent states of the impassioned soul. Her imagination freely indulges in those flights of fancy reminding us that all men are dreamers and all should be laughers. With unsurpassed insight and power she discerns what vital meanings the common experience of death holds for life. Her poetry shows her dual devotion to intellectual truth and emotional sincerity, for at the same time that she accepts the emotions, she stands for reality as opposed to sentimentality. Finally, despite her deep suffering, or rather because she has faced and outfaced suffering, she voices that courage, faith, and joy in life without which the individual and the race can achieve no flourishing existence. She herself simply defined the function of her art: "I winnowed what would fade." Or as she wrote elsewhere: "The Absolute removed the relative away."

6 *SYMBOL OF CHILDHOOD*

With a true instinct for the universal, Emily Dickinson turned to childhood as a basic experience shared by all persons. Her treatment of the subject shows her awareness that the theme is not quite so sure to be intelligible as might appear on superficial consideration. It is true that all men have been children, but Emily well knows how readily many forget their childhood or how far they stray from it. Although a legacy which all possess, it is one which some squander or neglect till it becomes almost wholly dissipated, but which others cherish till it yields a constantly increasing income. Childhood resembles the penny in the biblical parable: it may be buried in the earth where it may rust away from disuse or be set to profitable loan and in the end returned tenfold to its giver. To Emily, childhood is a mysterious pearl of great price. Rightly used, it buys the way to heaven; lost, it signifies also the loss of the soul. There is no gift which Emily mentions so often with praise, and none whose opposite wins from her such utter condemnation. The antithesis of childhood is that least excusable of all human vices, pomposity. Emily's emphatic hatred of pomposity is second only to her reverence for childhood as clue to her sense of values both in life and art.

Her verses abound in references to childhood, allusions all the more significant since they emerge in unexpected places. So revealing is her habit in this respect, that all her art may be thought of as a superstructure upon the basis of her regard for childhood. Scratch the surface of her verses, and the childlike will be found below. Dig beneath the imagery which resembles the shrubs and grass covering the surface, and childhood will be discovered as the basic soil. A few critics have even cast aspersions upon her mind on this account, as though beneath all her surface brilliance lay nothing better than childishness, skittishness, or girlishness; as though here were a serious flaw in the character of the woman and in the substance of her poetry. This viewpoint proceeds from a misunderstanding, an inability to perceive that the conception of childhood in her poetry is much more than merely literal, possessing instead a strong symbolic value. What is it that she really means by introducing the theme so persistently?

Although her view is doubtless connected with attitudes commonly found among poets of the Romantic Movement, it differs considerably from theirs, which are as a rule more literal and more sentimental. When Emily speaks of herself as a little girl, she does not as a rule mean this in a literal sense, nor is she actually writing poetry for children whenever an unmistakably childlike quality enters her verses. She is putting her childhood to loan. While her Romantic associates generally admired childhood as a thing in itself, dwelling upon its spontaneity, its credulity, or its innocence of the world, she interprets it symbolically as the shorter end of a wide ratio, that between the individual mind and the vast forces surrounding and penetrating it. She realizes how like a child is the discerning adult, who knows how little he knows, how much remains unknown. Her feeling for life in this respect much resembles the picture drawn by psychology describing our consciousness as only a minute part of the contents of the human soul. Emily does not wish romantically to be a child again, as Whittier yearns sentimentally in his *Barefoot Boy*. Her usual attitude toward childhood is one of mature retrospect. She has perceived the individual as both vast and little. In one of her most revealing phrases she refers to children as "Little groups of continents just going home from school." How much, how little we can achieve in life, she exclaims in one of her aphorisms. True, even the most limited soul is unthinkably vast. Infinity, she asserts is the very law of our being. But while experience is immeasurably great, understanding is immeasurably small. Look inward, and the soul becomes unspeakably minute. It resembles the tiny men and women as seen in the Taoist landscape paintings against a background of limitless nature. The individual is tiny, like the merest insect, or as he actually appears when seen from distances secured from a mountain or an airplane.

Where such reflections are concerned, mythological images are always the most potent. The truth which Emily seeks to convey through symbols is not that the child is mighty—a sentiment rather crudely embraced by Wordsworth—but that men are as little children in contrast to the divine. She takes very literally at least one familiar saying, namely, that men are children of the gods. This thought has itself been abundantly symbolized in both Christian and non-Christian mythologies. The creatures of the gods remain always far beneath them in magnitude. This holds equally true whoever the god may be. Emily's poetry is very largely concerned with love, either of an unspecified divinity, or of an almost equally unspecified human lover. In Christian theology

there is no higher love of God than that of the cherubim
and seraphim, represented in art as infants about the
celestial throne. Greek religion provided not only the
image of the adult Venus, but that of Eros, or Cupid,
the infant adorer of his mother. Emily instinctively understood the sagacity in these mythologies, for she herself
contained the seraphic flame and the spark of Eros. Since
triteness and mere imitation may be suspected in the more
familiar Christian imagery, a passage in which she approximates the classical thinking serves as the better confirmation. One of her love poems, "We learned the whole
of love," begins with the statement that lovers have step
by step gone through the alphabet of love, its words,
chapters, and book, till the revelation has closed. They
have discerned what has by another poet been called "the
intelligence of love." The greatest depths remained still
to be surmised. Divine forces immeasurably greater than
any individual could either define or conceive passed
through them, of which their consciousness became only
dimly aware. Their highest spiritual wisdom was attained
as they realized themselves children before an Infinity
infinitely greater than they:

> But in each other's eyes
> An ignorance beheld
> Diviner than the childhood's
> And each to each a child
>
> Attempted to expound
> What neither understood.
> Alas, that wisdom is so large
> And truth so manifold!

This passage helps to define what Emily does and does

not mean by her copious allusions to childhood. At least
in her more serious moments she has far more than the
merely childlike in mind; by this reference she violently
casts away all the pomposities and empty posturings of
adult mentality. The very human childhood is on her
tongue, but the seraphic childhood in her heart. The
image, like almost all her images, remains strikingly
realistic, while the meaning, like almost all her meanings,
embraces the scope proper to metaphysical poetry. With
the false humility that ironically conceals both cowardice
and pride, she has no commerce. Her lofty spirit never
grovels, simpers, or crawls. But a true and profound
humility she possesses. Its antithesis, as already observed,
is pomposity. Emily by her own acknowledgment had
listened to sermons of proud and loud-mouthed men who
achieved the maximum of littleness by shamelessly revealing their arrogance in the face of God. Such men
knew all, believed all, and told all. Emily thought differently. Of the little which she knew, she had only a little
to tell. Today that little in the intrinsic power of its
spiritual insight wholly eclipses their pompous posturings.
They were fires of straw, while her light gently proved
itself a star. The "gentlemen who see," like her father,
flaunted their faith, although her microscopic partical was
destined in the end to outlast their most pompous edifices.
Emily's life with an arrogant father at home was the precise analogue of her life with the arrogantly conceived
Father of Calvinistic theology. Both taught her through
the irresistible power of antithesis the lesson of seraphic
wisdom. It was a lesson which few have read so well.
One is reminded, however, of the somewhat over-facile
story of Saint Augustine, who found in the child playing

on the sand an object to check his own overweening pride.

Emily discloses her outlook in a number of passages where she likens not herself but the acknowledged sages of the world to children. "I can't tell you but you feel it," is a lyric affording an instance. Here she declares that neither she nor anyone else really knows the mysterious beauty and meaning in an April day. She imagines God in heaven as a schoolmaster attempting to explain the mystery to the saints and sages of the Church. "Saints with vanished slate and pencil Solve our April day."

> Modest let us walk among it,
> With our "faces veiled,"
> As they say polite Archangels
> Do, in meeting God.

The "they say" is extremely typical of Emily. She makes no dogmatic assertions about God, either here or elsewhere. It merely pleases her and serves her purpose to use the orthodox image in this context. Another poem employs a symbol of childhood to expose man's universal ignorance of nature. All nature the poet likens to a small-town New England circus with tents free to children during their half-holidays from school on Wednesday afternoons. We have seen only the outside of the tents. If nature could only let in the sages on some such a Wednesday! Unfortunately "the taciturnity of nature" remains as Shakespeare also has described it. For the quality which Emily regards as the basis of all spiritual insight, the language has no name. "Humility" will not strictly serve; it has embarrassing connotations and proves in no regard quite satisfactory. Once or twice, as we have seen, Emily uses "modesty." But she is a poet, not a reasoner in quest of terms. She finds sufficient her own almost infinite variations on the theme of childhood. The world which her father imagined as a battleground of contesting capitalists she imagines as a nursery of souls. In her poem, "What is paradise? Who live there?" she even imagines heaven in the same terms. So great is her reverence for the universe, with its infinite stores of truth and beauty, that she can fancy no individual in its presence, either in this world or hereafter, as other than a child.

The strangely pervasive character of the child image in her poetry discourages exhaustive illustration. Anyone surveying her work from this point of view readily amasses notes far too numerous to itemize or even to tabulate. An extremely large number of her poems mention childhood; she is thoroughly accustomed to refer to herself while an adult as a "little girl." A vast number of pieces are subtly modulated to contain intimations of the child psychology. These express what has just been called her seraphic vision. Finally, a very fair number of poems are so obviously naive as to be admirably adapted for reading to the young. Although her fundamental view of childhood is symbolical, philosophical, and mystical, she digresses and relaxes sufficiently often, and has a sufficiently warm and human heart, to write scores of little lyrics which have actually been collected and compiled into an anthology for children.

Most indicative of the persistence of the child theme in Emily's poetry is its emergence in places for which only some penetrating or philosophical explanation can account. There seems at first no obvious reason why it should appear. An example occurs in her well-known poem on the solemn departure of summer, "These are the days when birds come back." Four stanzas depict the idyllic days of Indian Summer, suspended in a haze of deceptive calm, with tinted leaf and floating seed. The poem concludes:

> Oh, sacrament of summer days,
> Oh, last communion in the haze,
> Permit a child to join,
>
> Thy sacred emblems to partake,
> Thy consecrated bread to break,
> Taste thine immortal wine!

One must sympathize with certain basic elements in Emily's understanding of life to perceive why there is any allusion to childhood here, and what the allusion signifies. Another of her best known lyrics gives its reference to childhood the distinction of a place in the concluding stanza. "I dreaded that first robin so," depicts the deadly irony of a delightful spring day at a time when the beholder is laden with sorrow. Robin, daffodil, and bee greet her with their accustomed cheerfulness. Courtesy compels her to acknowledge their salutations, but their greetings by contrast only deepen her own pain:

> Each one salutes me as he goes,
> And I my childish plumes
> Lift, in bereaved acknowledgment
> Of their unthinking drums.

In another instance Emily writes a strangely beautiful and whimsical poem on death. She imagines that Death is a friend—perhaps a lover—who takes her for a ride in his carriage. Three or four scenes are specified as the most

notable sights beheld on the way. It is wholly typical of
Emily's mind that the first of these should be a school
with its playground: "We passed the school where children played At wrestling in a ring." Properly understood,
such images have great importance.

How unromantic and un-Wordsworthian is Emily's
view of childhood generally may be inferred from a tart
little poem, "Who is it seeks my pillow nights?" This
is a slap in the face of Sunday School morality. The
nightly visitant is Conscience, but her prim behavior is so
wryly described as to render the grim Nurse thoroughly
ridiculous. The poem marks one of Emily's heterodox
impudences. Its sly and witty mockery of stupidity and
superstition bring it nearer to Voltaire than to the British
pietists. Blake in *Songs of Experience* similarly ridiculed
that dull nursemaid, Conventional Morality. Emily was
far too sophisticated to discover any prerogative to virtue
either in nurse or priest.

She was far from deifying childhood. One of the few
persons living today who recalls her remembers hearing
her speak only once. When this person was extremely
young, Emily tartly addressed her from her garden: "Go
away, you nasty child!"

Although the symbolical meanings of childhood are
greatly preferred by Emily, it is clear that she had a
genuine interest in childhood, both in herself and in her
neighbors. In illustration of the importance which she
attached to her own girlhood, the poem "A loss of something ever felt I," possesses special value. This lyric states
that her very first recollection is that she felt something
missing in her life and silently mourned the loss, as
though an exiled monarch. Long afterwards in adult life

she finds herself in the same position, and, incidentally, suspects her lost palaces to be other than the City of God. She finds her most characteristic state of mind rooted in her earliest years. The woman has merely enlarged what the child began. As illustration of the importance which she attached to childhood in general, may be mentioned her poem, "Heart not so heavy as mine." This recounts the joy experienced by a saddened woman hearing a boy passing under her window whistling a tune. Emily had a keen interest in juvenile books and books strongly appealing to the young. So, for instance, her own poetry mentions Cinderella, Bluebeard, and Little John; and she has a very lively poem, "I never told the buried gold," based on the romantic tale of Captain Kidd. Most of her pieces on animals, especially those in *Bolts of Melody,* are clearly written within the range of the child's mind. In a few of her less successful compositions she even came perilously near to the sentimental insipidities of the usual children's verse of the Victorian era. It will be recalled that at least four of the extremely small number of her poems to receive periodical publication during the last century appeared in *The Youth's Companion.* In short, Emily occasionally wrote simply and directly of children and for children. Her more naive passages strangely contrast with much of the eminently intellectual material in her poetry. As a rule, however, when alluding to childhood she deals in motives much too profound to appear upon the surface, belonging to what may properly be termed the symbolical and veiled features of her art.

7 POWER OF THOUGHT

Although Emily Dickinson knew and loved childhood and utilized its meanings symbolically for particular purposes of her life and art, in the course of years she developed as a writer of considerable intellectual force. The relation of her thought to her art has as yet been only lightly touched by her critics. Intellect hardens her poetry. Without her powers of thought both the woman and the artist might have been plunged into a crater of consuming emotions and rendered wholly ineffectual. Although she is neither a systematic nor a great thinker, she challenges attention intellectually far more than do most poets or novelists. In various parts of this study, phases of her thinking receive attention, as her understanding of theological concepts, her almost instinctive grasp of ideas in aesthetics, her trenchant ethical criticism, and at least her personal reaction to current advances in the natural sciences. None of these fields, however, shows her at her best as a thinker. Her keenest observations belong to the category of the psychological, nor is she negligible in more liberal fields of philosophy.

As a thinker she is not only pragmatic, but feminine. One of the most self-critical of her aphorisms notes that the mind lives like a parasite upon the heart. The observation proves in her case only too true. Emily thought for a purpose. She sorely needed to think, since from her earliest years life presented her with hard problems in an eminently personal form. Whatever limitations her thinking possesses, they certainly are not academic. Defiant in her attitude toward much of her brief training in Mount

Holyoke Seminary, as far as can be seen she gained little or no positive benefits from it. As she herself told Colonel Higginson, she had virtually no formal education. Nevertheless, the desperate situations into which, as a rebel and a genius, she was forced by her intransigent heart threw problems rudely in her face. A person of sharp natural intelligence, she met their challenge. In thought she found aids to save her ship from many a perilous crash; even where her thinking achieved no other palpable utility, it occupied her spirits, disciplined her emotions, and proved a salutary exercise. Restless as her mind was, and fertile as her imagination became in conjuring up new and disconcerting difficulties, she found thought more a blessing than an embarrassment. Her limitations in scope appear, to be sure, more clearly in the strictly intellectual field than in any other, for this domain was the most severely restricted for her by her sex and social position. Nevertheless, even here she attained a certain width, for she brought to poetry a mind far more alert than most popular poets of the nineteenth century. Her thinking is sharper though possibly less significant than Whitman's; inferior rather quantitatively than qualitatively to Emerson's or Thoreau's; and considerably more vigorous than any intellectual elements which Longfellow, Whittier, Lowell, or Poe succeeded in injecting into their verses.

Emily was both priest and sinner, interrogating her own soul and reporting her own confessions. Like a devout Calvinist, she summoned her heart and mind before the private bar of reason and conscience. Pointedly as she employed general terms and much as she contributed to the refinement of their meaning, her function as poet made her ablest in describing the psychological states which she experienced and for which thought in her own day had no names. Her extraordinary powers of introspection mark a mind stimulated and empowered to stimulate others. That she grasped the essential meaning of psychological theories of the divided personality appears in such a lyric as, "I felt a cleavage in my mind." "A doubt if it be us," affords still more penetrating insight into the same problem. Emily observes that when a disaster threatening prostration falls upon the soul, collapse may be averted if the individual for a time mercifully exchanges his own identity for a new. Dwelling by no means far from the borders of madness, to which genius is proverbially allied, her microscopic eye recognized with an almost scientific precision on how fine a thread sanity hangs. Her poem, "The brain within its groove Runs evenly and true," relates how the swerving of the least splinter may turn repose into chaos.

Many of her poems are little essays in psychology. Such a masterpiece in miniature as, "After great pain a formal feeling comes," might be cited in this regard. It gives a searching and realistic description of a state of mind. "There is an arid pleasure," shows the same type of subtle delineation. Her curiosity explored outstanding problems of the psychologists. Thus she has a number of fascinating lyrics dealing frankly with questions of memory and forgetfulness. "A thought went up my mind today," gives an interesting statement on a theme later included under the subconscious. The poem is a mere psychological jotting. Emily observes that a thought has come and gone which she vaguely realizes she has had at some earlier time, although she can neither locate its origin nor account for its latest emergence and disappearance. The deeper student of human nature, she realizes, must look beneath the surface of things. Patience, for example, is viewed as a singularly deceptive quality. Beneath its calm smile lies a hidden turmoil. Emily understands, also, that a crisis marks the end of a long and often well-concealed development. As she expresses it in a terse aphorism, "Slipping is crash's law." She is fond of making distinctions within the psychological realm, as in a poem which begins, "The difference between despair And fear . . .". Even her poems lacking theoretical conclusions often show a disciplined and highly intelligent way of thinking. "I found a phrase to every thought I ever had, but one" is a singularly interesting excursion into semantics. "I measure every grief I meet With analytic eyes," gives a valuable picture of her customarily critical attitude. The whole world to her tended to become a vast psychological laboratory. She watches life with the coolness and objectivity of a physician. "I've seen a dying eye," shows how sharply she kept watch by the couch of a hopeless invalid. Her mind found itself thoroughly at home along this border line between science and philosophy.

Passing from her more psychological to her more distinctly philosophical observations, one moves on the whole from her fresher, more original, and inspired poetry to the less brilliant and more didactic pieces. Even here, however, her general ideas emphatically have substance and pith. In one respect in particular her method indicates to what an unusual degree for a poet she pursues a purely intellectual course. Approximately a hundred and sixty of her poems, or in other words over a tenth of the total number published to date, take the form of a brief poetical definition of some abstract idea named in the first line. Among the ideas so defined are pleasure, thought, peril, perception, time, possibility, experience, delight, renunciation, skepticism, wonder and suspense. The inference is that her thinking was guided to a surprising degree by the fascination that words possessed for her. She evidently pondered numerous words whose meaning concerned her deeply. They were the key terms in her own writing and thinking. She may well have responded sharply to them in conversation; more likely still, her mind may have underscored them in her daily reading. In many cases her poem begins very simply with the verb to be: "Faith is," "Fame is," "Death is," "Doom is," "Denial is," "Exhilaration is," "Expectation is," "Experience is," "Glory is," "Grief is," "Heaven is," "Hope is," "Life is," "Love is," "Prayer is," "Remorse is," "Revolution is," "Risk is," "Surprise is."

This habit in her writing was connected with the devoted study of Webster's Dictionary, which virtually from childhood was one of her favorite books, studied, read, and digested almost as she treated her Bible. She disciplined her mind with frequent attention to this dictionary. Her vocabulary is both large and definitely that of an intellectual. Thus in a poem on romantic people who mistake the climax of a love for its entire course, she declares that such lovers mistake a perihelion for the total orbit of a planet. Regarding her devoted study of abstract terms in the language of the soul, it is safe to hold that she frequently consulted her dictionary, profited by her reading, but proceeded with a more profound definition or explanation than the mere lexicon afforded. Among her little poems may be found a comprehensive lexicon of the heart. Emily's exacting mental processes are almost as

far removed as possible from the thinking of the average
woman writer of sentimental verse. The strongly intellectual flavor of many of her poems may be fairly judged, for
instance, by the first three lines of one of her brief lyrics:

> Delight is as the flight,
> Or in the ratio of it
> As the schools would say.

A large number of distinctly intellectual passages in
her work fall under two categories, those revealing her
intellectual mysticism, distinguished by subtle discriminations in metaphysical idealism, and those disclosing her
strong conviction in the zestfully dynamic character of life
and of the universe. The first category will be analyzed
in a later chapter on her mystical and idealistic ideas, the
second, in another chapter on the optimistic faith behind
her thinking as a whole. Her indomitable trust in the
unexpected, her insatiable curiosity, her firm will to live,
receive at her hands a certain amount of philosophical
explanation and defense. In these two fields she is a distinctly vigorous thinker, indeed almost an original one.

By some literary critics thought is regarded almost as
alien matter in poetry. The poetry must in any case
transcend the thought, or the poem remains not poetry but
philosophy. Hence the question arises of Emily's position
in respect to the two elusively related fields. It must be
admitted that the thinker and the poet in her work are not
always perfectly integrated—in what artist are they? A
few of her poems suffer from an excess of emotion and
dearth of thought; a considerable number from a ratio
more favorable to thought than to feeling. Although a
few of the little poems defining her favorite ideas have

great beauty and really extraordinary power, others undeniably remain somewhat dry and didactic. These pieces
taken together place her less surely among great poets
than among famous writers of prose aphorisms or among
those pre-Socratic Greek thinkers who committed their
maxims to somewhat prosaic verse. Certain of her more
intellectual pieces have quite as strong a biographical as
an aesthetic value. Not masterpieces in themselves, when
read consecutively or in a general review of her verse
writings, they help to build, block by block, the structure
of her thought, the edifice of her mind. They take their
place beside the aphorisms of Pascal or the epigrams of
Emerson. Even if they fail materially to enhance her
stature as a poet, they are indicative of that stature. They
resemble trial flights. Such pieces may be said to tune
the engine of her robust mind. They are exercises with
one hand; efforts in which she gives attention to only
one phase of her personality. They become eloquent with
indications. If a traveler on the approaches to a city sees
stately buildings in its outer ring of suburbs, he infers
true magnificence for the major buildings lying before
him in the city's heart. So Emily's lesser and more distinctly dialectical pieces serve to introduce those major
poems and nobler lyrics in which, whether within ten,
twenty, or thirty lines, her united powers are stretched to
their height. She knew well enough how to create in art
a marriage of thought and emotion, as well as of substance and form. Her poetry could hardly be the virile
art that it is, had she not understood thought as an essential constituent part in the full dignity of the human
personality. Thought she conceived as prime minister,
the highest servant to the kingly heart.

8 *LIVING BY THE HEART*

That life is primarily a matter of warm feelings and ardently cherished values is attested by the use of the word heart, literally the central organ of the body, to stand for the emotions, the core of human existence. Feeling, like thinking, is an ubiquitous element, as air; our feelings may subside till they become almost imperceptible; but they sleep lightly and are easily aroused. The unfeeling is ultimately the dead. Emotions are, in fact, far more extended through life than thinking. It is they which give life its tone and meaning, constituting its motive force, its impulse, and its end. So close are our feelings to us, that we take them largely for granted; they are so intimate that the intellect finds peculiar difficulty in examining them; searching for them the key is lost to objectivity or perspective. We know that art is the emanation and transfiguration of our emotional life, yet the emotions in art commonly escape analysis. One somewhat fantastic school in modern criticism even denies their existence in art, though experience emphatically proves the contrary. It is so much easier to discuss an artist's ideas or technique than his feelings, and the entire realm of the heart is so far invisible and interior, that we often neglect to comment upon it. Yet reflection shows it to be actually the basis of all arts: the heart remains the heart of the subject. In the case of the lyric poet, the vision of man becomes overwhelmingly that of the emotions. The phenomenal richness of the emotional life in Emily Dickinson's poetry witnesses her supremacy in this realm of expression.

While no comprehensive analysis of her emotions is proposed here, at least so vital a part in the general estimate of her literary character cannot well be taken for granted. What shall be thought of that marvellous heart which came to rest some sixty years ago in the New England village where it first embarked on its extraordinary adventure? The first comment is undoubtedly the commonplace observation that, marvellous as this heart was, it was remarkable above all for being a part of the great heart which beats through mankind in common. Though she was a marked woman, a genius, highly abnormal and super-sensitive, her feelings are basically ours; we follow her through the wide scale of her emotions, recognizing her as spokesman for one general humanity. She is conspicuous because she is both like ourselves in quality yet ampler in the proportions of her own emotional life. Emily sought for the universal in the development of her intellect, in her meditations upon childhood, on death, on personality, and on human courage, and in her strong and often exuberant exercise of the imagination. In no respect did she so brilliantly succeed in being human as in her expression of the heart's profound music.

As the preëminently emotional art, music gives the most direct and searching expression of the feelings, thus affording the most satisfactory clues for the unravelling of all phases of the subject. The most revealing terms for the psychology of the emotions are not the scientific terms at all, but the Italian substantives commonly used to indicate the emotional tones in music. Each poem, stanza, or line in Emily's lyric poetry might be glossed with an appropriate term from musical scores. Her lyrics, like music, sing within the heart. The poems fall into perfect

allegros, andantes, largos, or prestos; they have their forte
and pianissimo, their brio and diminuendo. Tones are
low or high, heavy or light, austere or sprightly. The
richness of emotional texture is perhaps their most remarkable single feature. The poems provide an advanced
course in the emotions; most popular verse is a kinder-
garten beside them.

The simple terms for describing the soul, used before
psychology became a science, throw strong light upon the
character of her work. The poems in turn express exalta-
tion, joy, hope, suspense, depression, fear, pain, pathos,
pity, and despair. There is scarcely an emotion to be
named for which Emily has not an expression at least
equal to any in English poetry. Mention of a few representative poems helps to give force to a statement not
likely to be challenged. She is a poet of ecstasy; "Title
divine is mine," one of her love poems, indicates her
ardor. Repeatedly she describes herself as a drunkard
and a debauchee. She writes worthily of rapture:

> And creatures clad in miracle
> Go up by two and two.

Among her many poems on the ecstasy of dawning
might be mentioned, "Musicians wrestle everywhere."
Her poem, "Exhilaration," is thoroughly typical of her
seraphic heart. Her lyrics on hope are almost too numerous to mention; they commonly include the symbol of
immortality. More typical of her acute dramatic feeling
are the poems depicting suspense, where the heart hovers
in a refined agony between hope and despair. Emily discovers amazingly expressive language for this condition
of doubt, a state far less pleasant than unpleasant. Suspense leaves us

> Staking our entire possession
> On a hair's result,
> Then seesawing coolly in it
> Trying if it split.

This passage, coming unconventionally at the end of a poem ("Robbed by death, but that was easy") has vastly more power when read in its context than when examined outside it.

Emily is absolute mistress of pathos, rarely if ever descending to popular sentimentalities of her age and achieving instead a most genuine tenderness. She ensures the sincerity of her expression by her distinctive nuances in words:

> Now when I read I read not,
> For interrupting tears
> Obliterate the etchings
> Too costly for repairs.

One of her little elegies begins with lines unsurpassed in grave tenderness:

> We cover thee, sweet face,
>   Not that we tire of thee,
> But that thyself fatigue of us . . . .

In short, there is something wonderfully moving in Emily's language, on the one hand simple and direct, on the other, imaginative and distinguished.

The central emotion of tragedy is agony, well known to this lyric poet. "I like a look of agony," commences one of her most penetrating little poems, showing how steadily, honestly, and discerningly she faced and outfaced extreme grief. But she did even more than this. Of

the highest importance to her as a poet was her ability
to perceive at the same time two landscapes of the soul—
joy and pain, bliss and horror. As few other writers,
she understood the drama of the emotions, the aesthetic
values of suspense, climax, and ultimate devastation. In
this instinct for the dramatic element in the lyric she most
resembles the Elizabethans in general and John Donne
in particular. But she becomes even more remorseless
and emphatic than they. Among her typical pieces are
her expressions of depression and despair. "After great
pain a formal feeling comes," has the classical finality
of a Greek ode. This poem was apparently one in a group
which was happily produced in some kind of sequence
when first published in the volume, *Further Poems by
Emily Dickinson,* edited by Madame Bianchi. They describe a woman prostrated by a shock. Even to record the
first lines of such pieces often indicates their quality fairly
well. They include such lyrics as, "There is a languor of
the life," "There is a pain so utter," "It ceased to hurt
me, though so slow," and the short lyric beginning:

> From blank to blank
> A threadless way
> I pushed mechanic feet . . .

Pathos and despair meet in the moving and highly feminine poem of which the first stanza reads as follows:

> I tie my hat, I crease my shawl,
> Life's little duties do
> Precisely as the very least
> Were infinite to me.

This is the very anatomy of misery. Emily becomes match-
less in her descriptions of a state of paralysis following

disaster, for most writers probably too much a blank to admit description. She found clues to the expression of the hitherto unexpressible. Her lines, "I've dropped my brain, my soul is numb," might be cited among the numerous powerful instances in question. In her psychical biography she also tells how new life stirs over these frozen seas. Recuperation no less than degeneration becomes her theme. To use her own words, she writes "Anecdotes of air in dungeons."

From her own experience Emily deduced something of the Aristotelian doctrine of purgation, although she was far too tender-hearted to follow the ancients in disparaging pity. Her view, many times repeated, is that the greatest joy follows the greatest suffering and is made possible by it. "A wounded deer leaps highest," the opening sentence in one of her most inspired creations, may be taken as a statement of this favorite thought. Since she desired the highest pleasure, it was according to her own doctrine necessary to pass through the greatest pain. As she more than once declared, personal crucifixions are essential in the complete life; Christ did the wisest in suffering most. Thus her philosophy of life was largely based on her view of the emotions, and doubtless developed as the fruit of her own deeply moving experiences.

As previously noted, her powers of expression are made possible through experiences far too shocking to be entirely normal. Although she addresses the average world, she herself is in a sense not of it. This is, at least, the distinction between her abnormal life and—if the phrase is admissible—her normal art. In a review of her emotions it becomes necessary at least to glance at outstanding evidences of emotionalism heightened to the pathological.

A few of her poems make this condition especially clear. Thus the lyric, "I years had been from home," gives a singularly vivid picture of a neurotic condition. This unfortunate adventurer of the heart has lived for years in exile. He returns to his home, looks fearfully at door and window, touches the latch, and flies forever in the utmost terror, wholly overcome by the agony and chaos of his own heart.

An emotion must have its cause or source; many have also their object or direction. But when the spirit enters into a particular emotional state, there may be no definite object to the feeling, nor even a conscious cause. The heart is glad or sad, without the mind's knowledge why. Such states of the soul Emily often describes. To impersonal nature, for example, she often responds emotionally. Without love or hate she nevertheless feels herself overcome as it were by a sea of emotions, bright or dark. Poetry recounting these experiences is peculiarly subjective. It is a type of lyricism in which Emily excels.

She further excels in the exposition of those emotions which have a more specified object, as her relation to family, friends, and lovers, to God, to animate or inanimate objects, usually long familiar to her, which she loves, toward flowers, birds, and insects. In these instances the emotions become, to use a helpful but somewhat old-fashioned word, the affections. If we use the word in this sense, her affections bear scrutiny.

One of the chief of Emily's frustrations, and one of the ironies chiefly intensifying her whole emotional life, was her inability really to love God. The personal God, beloved by Heloise, Dante, or Patrarch, was unavailable to the thankless heir of John Calvin, who found the Calvinistic God so thoroughly unlovable. Emily was too inbred a puritan to feel no loss in this estrangement from an approachable divinity. The cavity left in her emotional life by her failure to find satisfaction in any communal God, she attempted in part to fill by the intensification of her personal devotions. With an almost shocking boldness, she applied to her lover the terms and sentiments commonly ascribed to Jesus. Her father, who held so powerful a position in her life, became an analogue for God, the Father of Heaven. And for Emily, as for Blake, the Holy Spirit commonly became art. Her poetry is on the whole serious because of the serious life forced upon her, especially through the complete dislocation of her religious affections. Under other circumstances it would have been possible for her to have found emotional release in at least an imaginative familiarity with exotic gods. So Matthew Arnold looked longingly to the gods of Greece, and Emerson to some extent to the still more ancient and remote gods of India and the East. But no genial or imaginative mythology came between Emily and the bitter-sweet experience of real life. For her the veil of the Temple was wholly rent. She faced nakedly the stark reality of an actual world and a metaphysical idealism emanating from it. This austere condition heightened all her emotional experience.

The love of God denied her, she turned all the more fervently toward nature and toward man. To what extent her love of nature was genuinely contained and to what extent it merely symbolized or sublimated her more personal affections, so far as concerns this analysis is material for a later chapter on her symbolism and imagery. At least according to the appearance of the case, she emphati-

cally did love nature, both in its inanimate and its animate
forms. Her affection for nature was probably as simple
and direct as any other of her loves. Moreover it was a
love of deep understanding, an understanding not so
much of any physical law or phenomenon, as of the precise emotional response induced by a precise examination
of the objects. Nature became the vast organ upon which
Emily as poet played the throbbingly emotional music of
her life. Just as the absence of any satisfactory religious
outlet for an emotion channeled her feelings elsewhere,
so the absence of any adequate love for the fine arts further intensified her existence. One of the most pathetic
incidents in her biography is the story of the joy with
which, shortly before her death, she greeted for the first
time the great classical composers, as Bach and Mozart,
when played on her own piano by her friend and future
editor, Mrs. Mabel Todd. Besides literature and her own
writing, Nature became her closest, most constant, and
most beloved friend. Once she declared that the death
of a flower occurring in her childhood marked her for
life with irredeemable grief. Nature also supplied her
with inexhaustible delights. It alone responded to all
her moods and encouraged them, offered her no real
embarrassments, and remained faithful. Their moods
might not always agree in time, but they appeared to
proceed from fundamentally the same deep wells of
feeling. From a sociological point of view the reader
may question the fervor and constancy of her devotion
lavished upon flowers, birds, and animals or even stones.
For all of them she felt more warmly than the average
human being for his family and closest friends.

Nevertheless, the most intimate of personal relationships comprise the background of most of her poems, especially of her strongest. As a whole these poems, transcending all mere accidents of personality, constitute, in her own words, a letter to posterity. They are also letters dealing with or addressed to her closest personal acquaintances. A number, as the slight little poems dispatched with gifts, were literally epistles to neighbors. Most of them concern incidents in her life with her intimates. Her joys and griefs are commonly shared. Thus many of the lyrics dealing with death were occasioned either by her loss of her friends or by their losses of their friends. Some such elegies were originally included in letters of condolence. Her heart flowed outward, to her lovers, her father, mother, sister, brother, and at least a select company of neighbors, relatives, and friends. All the circumstances in her life and culture aided her regard for these individuals and enhanced the warmth and intensity of her affection. Artificial social conditions made her days and years a veritable hothouse for breeding emotions. The Romantic Movement of which she was in a sense the heir, in a sense herself a member, extolled emotional living. Family sentiment and pride, especially in provincial New England, enhanced it. Her position among American poets became almost unique. Whitman and Poe lived largely in their dreams. Mere conventional sentiments sufficed for Longfellow and Lowell. Only Emily Dickinson lived primarily by the inexhaustible fires of an eager heart. So of the human heart itself she became, through the discipline of her art, a supreme spokesman.

9 *RELEASE OF FANCY*

Among the mental functions needed for the fulfillment of the personality, Emily Dickinson would unquestionably have included fancy. In the selective process followed in these pages, aiming to catch the profile of her literary character, this quality may receive attention, serving here, as it served in her life, as relief between the pressure of the warmer emotions and the cold reality of death. A streak of humorous fancy cut a bold diagonal across her tragic mind, like a light and colorful vein across the surface of a New England ledge. Without this lightening and exhilarating feature, her personality could not be the fascinating paradox which it is. Fancy became an essential ingredient in her economy of existence.

Concerned primarily with the thing rather than with the word, we must confess that no term in this regard provides a wholly clear or satisfying impression. "Fancy" has suffered from contradictory overtones and implications. To Shakespeare and the Elizabethans it signified love, with all the traditional whimsicality of passion. The more sober writers of the romantic school of Wordsworth and Coleridge employed it frequently but with a degree of condescension. Although they wrote from time to time in a manner which they termed fanciful, they held such writing as tainted with triviality, a mere dilution beside the work of the robust imagination. Wearied with the excessive vogue of the term in romantic authors, recent criticism has allowed it to fall into relative disuse. Yet it may be revived to good purpose, especially where nineteenth-century writers are the subject, for it has now thrown off old pedantries without as yet acquiring new.

As used here, fancy is a flight of imagination for its own sake, with considerable ingenuity and at least a dash of the comic or whimsical. It is, to be specific, the quality distinguishing the imagination of Aristophanes, most fanciful of all European poets, from that of Aeschylus, certainly one of the most deeply imaginative. In its surface quality, fancy is spontaneous or even naïve. The child-mind is rich in fancy; dreams are compounded of it. The exuberant and the macabre are two of the moods in which it operates most freely. As one of the modes of imaginative release, allied to imaginative humor, it served much the purpose among the creatively minded romantic poets which wit served among the socially minded Augustans. Fancy has its roots in the primitive; and it is therefore natural that in the art of the present century the surrealists have frequently shown a retrospective concern with arts of primitive peoples.

But it is as a normal function of the human spirit, not as a feature of literary movements, that fancy is considered here. Emily lived in a world of fancy; it was a domain which she inhabited, much as in the political sphere she was a citizen of Massachusetts. In her social life her fancy was more conspicuous than in her writing. The explanation lies in such a poem as "A wounded deer leaps highest", already cited in other connections. In this lyric Emily declares that the deeply hurt spirit resorts to jests and playfulness to conceal its wounds from public inspection. Such was her own practice through life. A wild and somewhat hectic fantasy characterizes many of her earliest writings, both in verse and prose.

Her familiar letters and school compositions abound in such a quality, and, according to reliable reports, her conversation flashed with it. To staid puritan citizens of Amherst she appeared somewhat as Hamlet to the Court of Denmark: an eccentric known for wild and whirling words. This mood serving as her most familiar defense in society served also as a happy relief in a minor, though a considerable number of her poems.

The vein flows most freely in her gayer verse and in those colorful lyrics wherein her imagination is most exuberant, relatively uninhibited and, as it were, on a holiday. A fairly large and by no means unimportant section of her poetry may be described as light verse. Some of this is frankly humorous, most of it patently fanciful. The imagination of her graver emotional poems, though related to her fancy, has a far different quality. Nor should her serious poems using the quaint imagery associated in English poetry with the Metaphysical School of John Donne be regarded as part of her free exercise of fancy. Such a lyric as, "My life had stood a loaded gun", wielding the image of the gun through twenty-four lines, much as Donne protracts the image of the compass in one of his most celebrated songs, possesses a far different flavor from her poems of fancy. The metaphysical poems are serious, dry, witty, intellectual; the truly fanciful lyrics exuberant, warm, humorous, and spontaneous. Even the most macabre of Emily's pieces have a lightness of touch missing in the forced sobriety of metaphysical wit.

Some of the most popularly known and admired of Emily's works belong to this category. Conspicuous in the group are such pieces as, "I like to see it lap the miles", her whimsical account of a railroad train as a

new species of horse and wagon, and "By my window
have I for scenery Just a sea with a stem", her charming
lyric likening a tree to an ocean. In each instance her
imagination toys pleasantly with a far-fetched metaphor.
Any such figure may with a legitimate extension of the
term be regarded as a flight of fancy. The fanciful poem
is merely a universe enlarged on the plan established in
the atom of the phrase. With the dexterity of a circus
rider successfully guiding two swift horses, Emily combines the apparently incongruous figures of horse and
train, ocean and tree. Although neither poem is intended
to be imaginatively profound, each becomes stimulating,
fascinating, and suggestive.

Her fancy often proves the most striking as, in its more
macabre forms, it impinges upon the serious without quite
aspiring to high seriousness. Three representative pieces
serve sufficiently for illustration. "Because I could not
stop for Death", is a brilliant lyric imagining death as a
caller at the poet's house. He takes her for a ride in his
carriage, a thoroughly bizarre and entrancing journey. "I
felt a funeral in my brain", is a weird little poem wherein
Emily imagines herself in a stunned condition attending
her own funeral, or perhaps it would better be said that
the funeral visits her. A fancy similar to that in Goethe's
account of the stormy orgies of Walpurgisnacht lends a
wild splendor to Emily's picture of a storm: "An awful
tempest mashed the air." Imaginary beings rush across
the sky,

> The creatures chuckled on the roofs
> And whistled in the air,
> And shook their fists and gnashed their teeth,
> And swung their frenzied hair.

Sharp incongruity between the commonplace and the sublime supplies the formula for a number of Emily's more fantastic flights. She combines the indoors with the outdoors, the ephemeral with the long-abiding. A poem on a storm and its passing begins with the bold image, "It sounded as if the streets were running", and concludes with the observation that, "Nature was in her beryl apron, Mixing fresher air." Another piece oddly combining Emily's twin passions for housekeeping and nature commences:

> She sweeps with many-colored brooms,
> And leaves the shreds behind,
> Oh, housewife in the evening, west,
> Come back, and dust the pond!

The little lyric continues with comparisons of the clouds and their reflections to ravellings of dust and thread, and the breeze to spotted brooms. The ending is purely magical:

> Till brooms fade softly into stars—
> And then I come away.

Another piece still more boldly reduces the solemnity of the grave to a New England parlor. In the tomb Emily will await her lover, making her parlor orderly and setting "the marble tea".

Throughout her nature poems her fancy takes its bravest and farthest flights. This seems due to two causes: first, to the figurative character of all her nature poems —actually about her own moods and not objectively descriptive of the outer world—which therefore places the poems initially on a symbolic footing, a springboard for further fancies; and second, to the detachment from an objective treatment of personal life, tending to place such pieces in the category of light verse. While nature often expressed Emily's saddest or gravest moods, it was also her playground, and at all times a relief from the stress of living, if not an ampler release. In the presence of nature her fancy becomes exuberant, especially in her reflection of the more expansive aspects of sky or sea. Thus in her brief poem, "The red blaze is the morning", she fancies the stars as sparks left from the wide burning of day. This lyric is obviously more fanciful and less serious than the noble little poem, "The largest fire ever known", likening the sunset to a cosmic but disregarded conflagration. Traditionally among poets, the sun is god of the powerful and earnest imagination, the moon the goddess of irresponsible fancy. Emily has a comparatively long poem, "I watched the moon around the house", abounding in the most far-fetched conceits. The poet lifts her eyeglass upon her as a lady might inspect a stranger in the town; she speculates on the moon as a stemless flower, a head fallen from the guillotine, a thoroughly supercilious observer of human affairs. Such incongruous images are somehow rendered harmonious by the poet's art.

A still longer and more carefully worked out poem studiously preserves a whimsical style. "I know some lonely houses off the road", is a rather girlish effusion written, however, with consummate skill. Based upon Emily's irrational fear of robbery and violence by night, it remains, nevertheless, largely comic, in the purely entertaining manner of a ghost or murder story. Two thieves break into a lonely house inhabited by an aged couple. Emily confers an eerie excitement on all the images. Al-

though much more self-conscious than her more typical
and serious art, this lyric, by virtue of its discreet fantasy,
holds a significant place in the general picture of her
verse.

Whereas this poem remains girlish and virginal, a
number of Emily's still more attractive lyrics are frankly
and artfully attuned to the childlike mind. More than
once for the enlivening of her verses she ingeniously introduces the image of the circus. An instance especially apt
for reference here is her curious fantasy, "I've known a
Heaven like a tent", in which she compares the breaking
clouds in a glorious display of light to the disappearing
of the American travelling circus. Her genuine and homebred fancy contrasts with Longfellow's more famous,
exotic and facile image on the tents of the Arabs. Another pleasant poem with at least a juvenile flavor, "I
never told of buried gold," likens the sunset light upon
the hill to the inaccessible treasures of Captain Kidd.
Once when describing bright reflections in water, she is
reminded of a colorful band of vanishing pirates.

In a few extreme instances Emily carries her fancy to
heights of the fantastic suggestive of the advanced
achievements of modern surrealists, those artists who,
while gaining a reputation for innovation, have learnedly
leaned upon passed schools of the macabre, the grotesque,
and the bizarre. She combined her conscious with her
subconscious, her imagination with her dreams, to create
striking and emotionally convincing effects. One piece,
"In winter, in my room", describes her terrified flight
before a snake. The poem concludes with words that may
be regarded as literally true: "This was a dream". Modern
commentators have added the observation, a Freudian

dream. Less readily subject to Freudian interpretation, but
in the same general category, is the more successful and
fantastic lyric, "I started early, took my dog, And visited
the sea." The piece continues with an account of mer-
maids rising from "the basement", of frigates extending
to her their hempen tackle mistaking her for a mouse on
the strand, and of a tide rising to cover her till she flees
in terror before the monster of the deep, in the end breath-
lessly effecting her escape, though to the last a silver
water laps her heel.

Emily's life and poetry would have been much the
poorer had they lacked this breezy and exhilarating element. Fancy was a major ingredient in her humor, an evidence of her vitality, and her triumph over graver weights
continually tending, like the monster of the sea, to drag
this Ariadne beneath the waves. Her fantasies have made
a definite contribution to modern art and poetry, quite
apart from the major achievements of her highly serious
poems. They are the sparkle and exuberance of her
normal and beneficent imagination. For the present argument, the importance of the faculty which created them
weighs more than the literary contribution. In a sober,
literal-minded, puritan world, Emily rightly envisaged
the vital place of the fantastic in the fully developed personality of the eternal Man.

10 *ANGEL OF DEATH*

Emily sharpened her taste for the sweetness of life by turning repeatedly to partake the bitter sacrament of death. That a large proportion of her poems deal with death has inevitably been remarked, but it may be regretted that her unique treatment of the subject has received little scrutiny, especially from her ablest biographers. It presents a major issue; many of her finest poems are involved; and so extraordinary is the breadth of her vision that on the whole there is remarkably little morbidity to discourage reader or critic. Death became for Emily the supreme touchstone for life. As a subject it holds an equally dominating position in the field of her verse. Herein lies one of her most striking and original contributions to poetry and to thought.

Some day a discerning publisher may cull from her bewilderingly numerous productions an anthology of poems dealing with death. Such a book would be vital and exhilarating, and neither eccentric nor depressing. It would also be one of the world's great collections of lyrics. In fact, her editors have already made valuable steps in this direction, for with discernment for which they have too seldom been credited, they have gone far to segregate her poems on death into practicable compartments. Perfection in choice and arrangement could hardly be expected in initial efforts; nevertheless the reader is much facilitated by what has thus far been done. Criticism need only call attention to this achievement to place at the reader's easy disposal substantial materials for the hypothetical anthol-

ogy as indicated above. Although by no means all her
poems dealing primarily with death have been segregated,
sufficient have been so treated as to make an impressive
and thoroughly representative garner. At least a quarter
of all her works deals chiefly with this theme. Nearly a
fifth of them or, to be more explicit, two hundred and
ninety pieces, are included within the separate garners.
Though obviously dealing with death, the first sequence
bears in Madame Bianchi's volume the interpretative title,
"Time and Eternity". This group consists entirely of poems
previously edited by Mrs. Todd. It is Part Four of the
Poems, containing over a hundred and forty items. Part
Five, "The Single Hound", includes a sequence of twenty-
one poems of the same character, proceeding from number seventy-one to number ninety-one. In Part Six,
entitled "Further Poems", the sixth section consists of
twenty-three such pieces. Finally, in *Bolts of Melody* the
section called "The White Exploit", pp. 181-224, contributes ninety-four poems. These four groups taken together adequately reveal Emily Dickinson's interpretation
of her favorite theme.

By every lover of her poetry these hundred and thirty
pages should be read consecutively. Within them lies a
large part of her most serious writing, for they contain
little of that light or humorous verse, little of those casual
or reflective jottings, constituting so considerable a part
of her remaining work. Here are her most carefully
wrought lyrics, her most uncannily compressed aphorisms.
The aesthetic and emotional power of her verses on her
preferred theme, when all are read consecutively without
dilution of her lighter materials, becomes overpowering.
There is a unity here resulting not from a philosophical

system but from a sensitive and subtle personality. The total effect is of great symphonic music constructed with the recurrence of certain solemn themes always in variations and entirely without prosaic repetition. Among nearly three hundred poems, no two are closely alike. The lyrics reveal the working of an astonishing mind, which attains a maximum of variety and scope through concentration upon a single point. Behind this vast expansion and rigorous limitation lies still another and even more amazing paradox. Death becomes a gateway to vitality, lifelessness to life. The ultimate of the positive hinges upon the ultimate of the negative. From a simple formula comes a bewildering riddle, and from a riddle proceeds an emotional solution. A problem is resolved more by an act of defiance than by philosophy. Emily outstares death; she looks so intently and piercingly upon it that its terrors vanish, as fog before sun. Intellectually she leaves death exactly where she found it, namely, a mystery. Emotionally it has lost its venom, but not its awe.

What threatened her life as a poison she transubstantiates both for her life and art into the most nourishing of foods. To Emily death ceases to be a mere theme or problem and becomes the key to art, to beauty, and to life. The mortal foe that kills the feeling, stops the heart, ends all emotion, becomes the savior that arouses the feelings, stirs the heart, and is the true begetter of emotion. Life gains its values through destruction of itself. By narrowing itself to the frugal inches of the grave, it expands to the limitless and the infinite. Such are the riddles which her poems themselves divulge, turn over gently in the hand, examine from all angles, till they almost cease to be riddles and become the most homely and familiar thoughts, entering spontaneously into the subconscious stream of thought, and, one might almost add, into the blood stream.

—Few labors could be more superfluous than the paraphrase in dull prose of what Emily has herself stated in forceful, clear, and ringing verse. The difficulty is not to comprehend any one of her lyrics, but to piece hundreds of them together until they make in our minds the satisfying pattern which they assuredly constituted for her. The poems, therefore, present far less a challenge to the conventional literary interpreter, concerned with exposition and clarification of alleged difficulties in the text, than to the imaginative philosopher seeking for a synthesis from materials of bewildering richness.

Death becomes for Emily the mountain of vision. Like the highest summit in a range, it commands the panorama of the whole. From this elevation of the thought of death Emily looks down for the first time with enlarged understanding upon love, hate, nature, art, religion, humanity, and all those concerns of mind and soul that severally engross her attention elsewhere. Through the clarifying experience of death she reaches a pragmatic solution of life's other problems. Emotions hitherto consuming or destructive lose their devastating power. The violent feelings evoked by death at the same time resolve themselves by their own fury and level off lesser spiritual disturbances, as a gale may level the coruscations of petty waves.

Death is the revealer. Emily sees and experiences much that lies far beyond the vision and understanding of the average of mankind. Her attitude toward the orthodox or conventional views of death immediately provokes attention. And here, as always, her own position proves to be neither logical nor simple. In general, she neither denies nor affirms the popular orthodox and naïve Christian conceptions of death and immortality. At one moment, to be sure, she may seem to accept the naïve belief in a pseudo-physical resurrection and reunion with one's friends, family and lover; but in the next moment she denies assurance of this, and pronounces herself in favor of infinity in preference to such a literal-minded immortality. With her views on death her views on all the other major problems of her life are intimately concerned, especially those on reality. When leaning the most heavily upon her mysticism, she found time unreal, and the real wholly within the human mind and adhering to "the now". In short, reality was a property of the present tense. Hence immortality, when more seriously understood, possessed no objective reality but only an inner reality. This is the conventional mystic doctrine, to be considered more fully in later sections of this book dealing specifically with her mysticism and with her analogues to earlier mystical poets, such as the German, Angelus Silesius. Ordinary sorrow or separation would not, she assumes, have been powerful enough to open her eyes to this supreme and mysterious truth. The only effectual angel of spiritual truth is death. In his presence the mysterious reality becomes clear, and the true or esoteric meanings of immortality, eternity, heaven, and infinity are disclosed. Thus death becomes the supreme teacher of esoteric truth.

Death is also the supreme incident in life. We slip into life unconsciously. Whereas no one can meditate on his coming birth, both our own death and the death of friends become subjects on which the soul is disciplined in wisdom. As the goal is more significant than the nondescript starting point, so to the thoughtful death becomes more meaningful than birth. Since for Emily, at least, death is symbol of reality, it becomes not the bitter dead-end of the grave—though on one level it remains that—but the gateway to reality and hence to life, joy, and ecstacy. Emily had a passionate devotion, if not a normal urge, for three men who died during her lifetime. Death, which is a spiritual crisis, set them for her within a new and superior realm of being. Sealed by death, they became doubly real. If she found herself still short of complete happiness, this was less because she had not as yet been reunited in a future heavenly existence, than because her mind was still to some extent earthly and dull, as yet incapable of complete self-sufficiency and imaginative mastery. The ultimate ideal lay beyond her, as, in her opinion, beyond all human beings. This ideal was perfection, an hypothesis of the human mind, and one of her nearest approximations to a vital concept of God. Death still remained in a metaphysical sense the fulfillment of love.

In a homelier and more natural sense it was also the progenitor of love, since it begot our tenderest and most readily participated feelings and actions. As she repeats through many poems, our precarious existence, the fact that we may at any time die, gives life its greatest warmth and poignancy. This rule obtains at all times. It reaches the intensity of dramatic truth, however, when a friend falls into some mortal danger. Then we show our greatest solicitude; our heart and actions become most truly loving. His physical crisis may prove our spiritual crisis. Immediately after death, the beloved enters into a new reality within our own minds. In the purely mental world which he then inhabits, free from all material accident, we see him most clearly, love him most, and recognize best our own relations to him. We learn for the first time both how much we have loved him and how much more we ought to have loved him. The human being faced with the imminence of death also discovers that he lives more acutely. Each hour becomes the more precious to him as he realizes that it carries him nearer to his last. Death is the austere mother from whose breast humanity drains the richest nutriment for the human heart.

Death was Emily Dickinson's closest and dearest friend; like her other lovers and close friends, he was her teacher, differing from them chiefly in that he was her best and most constant instructor. In strange and wonderful fashion she lived continually in his presence. He was infinite, the one lover who could never leave her. She did not believe in the God of her Calvinistic fathers. A god whom she did believe in was this Death who was also the Lord of Life, the God whom she came to know much less from books than from experience. Her own book was dedicated largely to him. Although there were no idle or vulgar familiarities possible between such a god and a mortal woman, her intimate knowledge of him made him her special favorite. In several poems she uses the familiar image—as already noted, probably suggested to her by experiences with her flesh and blood admirers—of death taking her for a pleasurable ride in his horse and carriage. Long after she confined herself within her house, ceasing to travel in any actual coach, she took these imaginary rides with her mysterious friend. In one poem she terms him Death, in another uses his other name of Lord.

He was all the truer friend and the less jealous in that
his chief pleasure was to take her calling on other friends
otherwise beyond reach of eye or voice. Death was her
chariot of triumph. It was also her chariot of genius; the
horses were Pegasean; Death was Apollo; and this was
the chariot of her song.

But Death was not altogether so simple for her as he
has been thus far described. Her fascinating friend was
capable not only of infinite mercies but of infinite dup-
licities and betrayals. He was neither wholly good nor
evil. Indeed he was virtually a pantheistic conception,
from whom all human and non-human reality proceeded;
god of man and of nature, of good and of ill, of the divine
and of the physical. If he was the gateway to the eternally
true, he was also the gateway to the eternally false. He
was both God and the devil. In his esoteric aspect he
proved beautiful as Apollo; in his material and vulgar
aspect a grim, agonized and horrifying corpse. If he was
source of infinite joy, he was also source of a finite pain
so vast as to be, practically considered, also infinite. Both
idealist and realist, Emily not only dreamed of the mystical
meaning of death, discovering in him a benign divinity;
she scrutinized a corporeal death, finding it terrifying and
infernal. Her philosophy combined an idealism as pure as
that of a Renaissance Platonist, for example, Pico della
Mirandola, with that of the popularly conceived terrors
of Albrecht Dürer's dance of death. Unlike many New
Englanders of the transcendental period, Emily was no
sentimentalist. In a remarkable manner she combines an
almost oriental spirituality, suggesting Hindu mythology,
which frequently represents death as an angel, with oc-
cidental realism, firmly behind even the exterior fan-

tasticality of the dance of death. This contradiction or
paradox in her nature vastly enriches her poems on death,
increases their dramatic poignancy and tension, and begets
at times a fantasy allied to macabre humor. Hence, too,
the pathos with which she dwells upon death-scenes and
scenes of bereavement, as well as the almost clinical
realism with which she gruesomely paints actual scenes of
the dying. Death is the more fascinating to her as she
finds in it the quality which Marc Antony discovered most
alluring in his lover—infinite variety. Brief as her lyrics
are, in many of them this multi-dimensional character of
death proves stated or implied. Who would not be wholly
fascinated by a creature so richly compounded of good
and ill, pleasures and pains? Remorselessly she notes the
pity of death as it afflicts children, and as bit by bit it saps
the strength and glory of aging man. Virtually no phase
of the problem, pleasant or unpleasant, ecstatic or revolting, has she left unexplored.

Her taste for the infinite is still further whetted by
death, for to her death is a supreme challenge to a dynamic imagination. No one really knows what lies beyond the grave. Is there a blank, or precisely what? That
common folk should die, is plausible enough to her; but
how a genius, stored with intensified vitality, can be imagined as dead, passes her understanding. She could with
difficulty conceive her own extinction, and when beneath
the spell of her inexhaustibly powerful and fascinating
poetry, the thought of the extinction of Emily's soul
actually delivers a formidable shock to our own credulity.
But, again, what lies beyond death? She no more knows
the answer than did the notorious villain in Christopher
Marlowe's *Edward the Second,* who in death went as a

traveller, "to discover countries yet unknown." In the
last analysis death fascinated her most in being for her
the ultimate mystery, as the Elizabethans describe it, the
undiscovered Northwest Passage of the soul. She did not
believe the Christian explanation, nor did she hold for
long to any other. A supreme gambler of the soul, she
actually preferred to doubt. The restless, creative power
of her verses springs largely from this healthy skepticism.
Had she been a doctrinaire mystic believer, she would
probably have lost her keen sense for the drama of life
and declined into mystic silence.

With such a theme, the almost measureless scope of
emotion, musical phrase, linguistic nuance, and psychological or speculative subtlety found in Emily's poems on
death becomes intelligible. In these poems we seem to
hear all instruments and all voices, a potent and romantic
symphony, firm in texture, fantastic in variation, with the
mastery of complete understanding and achievement. It is
positively misleading to specify individual masterpieces,
where such exist by the score. However deep a mystery
death might be, it conferred assurance on Emily's art.
Although not uniformly magnificent, almost all her poems
upon the theme are highly distinguished. The condition
to be kept most in mind is that the quality and character
of her work demand here that for the fullest enjoyment
all the poems be read consecutively and experienced as
one supreme expression of her life, her vision, and her
art. Here Emily Dickinson's genius comes to its ultimate
flowering. Individual lyrics are sparks of light, brilliant
stars, but above all creating a cosmic pattern upon the
sky. The fires of imagination burn in death's darkness,
creating the maximum of splendor, the consummation of

awe. The splendor of the individual star is as nothing within the splendor of the firmament. Emily's philosophy is electic, her poetry organic. Massive and difficult to conceive aesthetically as the whole is, we perceive it as forming one entity. From such knowledge we recognize the true manner of envisaging and enjoying the greatest of her art.

11 *INTEGRITY OF SOUL*

When Polonius advises his son to be true to himself and so of necessity false to no man, his statement is equally individualistic and optimistic. The assertion means that to be true to one's self safely establishes one's entire ethical relation to the world. The key to life's problem is so far, at least, declared to be found, in that self-perfection is confidently held the summation of man's duty. Parenthetically one notes that Shakespeare's intention is not quite so clear as Polonius's words. Did the dramatist chiefly mean to ridicule the sententiousness of his times by placing these words in the mouth of the egotistical minister? Did he cast a shrewd aspersion upon the egocentric doctrine beloved by his times? Or does he thoroughly approve the maxim? The first and third assumptions are not altogether inconsistent; it is for the third that the strongest case can probably be made. In a neo-Senecan play such as *Hamlet,* there is good reason to suppose that in company with the great majority of advanced thinkers of his age Shakespeare approved that neo-Senecan individualism and moral optimism which Renaissance thought bequeathed by direct descent to Emily Dickinson.

It would be ill-advised to separate two ideals which she so commonly finds united, that of personal integrity and personal courage. Her belief in the individual man amounts to a faith in his ability to resolve the major problems of life. The emphasis upon individuality accounts for one of the chief formal distinctions in this book, that between her expression of the individual and her reflection of the racial experience, heritage, and hope. Although she never in any complete sense stood alone, she often legitimately thought of herself as a free and independent spirit, with a will of her own and a power to establish herself as a sovereign state within the universe. Life she found hard and embattled, but deeply as she suffered, she very rarely despaired and never surrendered. Her high personal courage becomes one of her outstanding characteristics. This courage proves in her both splendid and benign, and wholly without the desperate and sinister qualities of Melville's symbol for the uncontrolled will of Captain Ahab. As usual, Emily takes a position much in the middle of the road. Her ardent belief in the freedom of the will, inherited from long centuries of Christian controversy, places her with Western thought against the mysticism of the East; while her belief in will as exercised more persistently in the contemplative than in the active life places her with the contemplative East as against that Satanic West which Melville understood with such uncanny insight. But it is not with the cultural bearings of her position, however significant these may be, that our present argument is concerned. Rather it is with a brief recreation of her own optimistic view of the sovereign self, as a key to her own personality both in life and literature. These are the dominant chords on which she prefers to conclude her own poems, and are, accordingly, points of view to receive similar position and emphasis in any account of her literary character or of her picture of man as considered in terms of the singular number.

In still another sense Emily stands in the middle of the road. While she never emphasizes the desirability of renouncing the will and seeking a mystical union with the universe, neither does she believe in the exploitation of the will to a degree of egoism or eccentricity. While well removed from the pantheistic mystics who strive to rid themselves of the will, she stands still farther removed from the extreme romantic individualists who worship self-expression. Her passionate aim is not to diversify but to unite mankind. Her choice of the lyric in preference to the dramatic form is here significant. Although she wishes to assert and to sustain her own character, she shows small interest in characters in the plural. Her utmost will is employed in a spiritual quest for the attainment and expression of whatever is profoundly and centrally human. Her active quest is to shuffle off restricting bands of time and space, merely local customs, pedantic fields of knowledge, and all specialized learning, in order to attain instead the bedrock of humanity.

Emily has at times been praised as a nature poet, but it can hardly be too much emphasized that she reveres far more than nature the human mind, which by will and imagination grasps nature and achieves personal integrity. Her first love is for people. Nature supplies her the materials and tools with which to fashion her human ends. Her emphasis upon human love is also a part of her belief in the individual. Emily writes almost nothing about the love of mankind. That luxurious and romantic sentiment, that democratic and expansive affection, she left to Walt Whitman and similar spokesmen of spiritual democracy. Although believing in the rights and the sanctity of every human being, she asks affection only for the few. A group of her poems is addressed to her friends, a much larger number to her lovers. Regarding the latter, it is of interest that she almost certainly had more than one object of her warmest affections, that she wrote in hyperbolical terms to several men whom she extravagantly admired, and that she married no one. Her strictly amorous attitudes may easily be overemphasized, as Mrs. Bingham warns us in her *Ancestors' Brocades*. Whatever may have been her love-life in actuality, a mystery still unsolved and not likely to be solved, it is certain that her belief and practice agreed in accentuating personal affections. For father, mother, sister, brother, for her dear friends who were by no means few in number, she had the warmest heart. She believed in the narrow circle, in the domestic circle. In this social sense, as well as in the metaphysical sense, she extols the individual. Whitman believed in the plural, she in the singular. He boasted, not without some warrant in fact, that he loved mankind; in a revealing lyric she arrogantly asserts that on the many she has closed the valves not only of her love but of her attention, and given her devotion solely to one.

Her poems comprise a long autobiography of self-discipline, for which her metaphysics supplies the foundation. When writing of the song of the oriole, she refutes the "skeptic" who holds that the reality of the song exists in nature, maintaining instead that it exists within the mind of the individual listener. Hence, too, the plurality of meanings, since for her there are obviously as many songs as listeners. Only, she would add, some know how to listen better than others. But she is not dogmatic about the superiority of understanding. Strictly intellectual truth is hardly her ideal. Beauty, she declares, cannot be known in the sense that it can be argued or defined, but can only in an imaginative way be apprehended. Since the individual cannot fully communicate or explain his experience, there is little cause for his boasting of his intellect. The individual stands out all the more prominently, since his grasp of reality is in one sense incommunicable. Taste itself remains a baffling mystery.

Emily's aphorisms abound in statements of the importance of the soul to itself and of the prime importance of human identity. She states this condition as a necessity, a law that may or may not be a blessing, but that must be acknowledged. Life condemns us to this personal adventure, causing each of us to be pursued by his own identity, as if by a pursuing hound. The soul, another epigram asserts, is "the Emperor of Men." For each individual the most enthralling romance she finds to be his own. The greatest battles are fought within. The soul is its own best friend or worst foe. "Each life converges to some center", states another poem, with fundamentally the same point of view. Emily rarely discusses the problems of selfishness or altruism. Self-sacrifice she apparently defends primarily in those closest of friendships enlisting her ardent conception of love. Self-consciousness is her fundamental assumption. Her first principle of knowledge is self-knowledge.

Believing most ardently in activity, change, and the unexpected, she believes also in self-development. The self is not only the prime fact in life. The self changes, and by exercise of its own will should change for the better. Emily considered that her own life showed a ladder of ascent; that she gained strength by repeated victory over successive difficulties which circumstance, thought, and passion evoked. Life was a long learning, experience the truest teacher. Many of her poems deal with this theme of self-education. In one lyric, "A solemn thing within the soul, To feel itself get ripe", she employs the interesting metaphor of fruit growing on a tree. God she imagines as owner of the orchard, carefully noting the growth of each individual fruit and plucking it at the strategic moment of its highest potential ripeness. Emily had faith that in the end even the most tragic and grueling experiences could be mastered, digested, and made to serve their part in this personal growth. From this point of view she traces the course of her affairs of the heart. Nothing, she holds, is lost; or in any case the wise man can force any event to serve his ultimate needs. The first fervent glow of a passion is not its fullest meaning, but the deposit of wisdom, the strengthening of the spiritual sinews, which is left with us. The deaths of friends and lovers are precisely such hard lessons, conducive to an indwelling power in the end. Emily remains in a sense a puritan, for she champions austerity, advocating growth the hard way. She notes how hemlocks thrive on winter storms, northern winds their nutriment, and their "best Norwegian wines". Ultimately this hard doctrine begets a species of optimism, a faith and confidence all the firmer for having a foundation upon rock and not upon the moist bogs of sentimentality.

Emily never flatters life. For the pink and precious world of sentimental ladies, with their "dimity convictions", she entertains only scorn. Yet beyond her astonishing portraiture of suffering, is her still more remarkable picture of fortitude, courage, and faith. She has no tolerance for "a modest lot, a fame *petite*". Her whole inclination is that of a gambler. "Trust in the unexpected", she declares resonantly. She will push on to ever new adventures, anticipating storms, confident that in some way or other they can be weathered. Of course she will fail in many of her specific goals; but in one respect she will never fail. Her bows may plunge beneath the mightiest of waves, but they will also emerge, undaunted and undefeated. "Finite to fail, but infinite to venture", begins one of her most revealing poems.

Emily knew herself a good fighter. She also rightly appraised certain of her achievements. She felt herself morally and spiritually strengthened by the emotional trials which she had survived. She felt that she had drunk of certain of the waters of immortality, and had reached certain definite heights in the progress of her mystical experience. She generally declared herself to be happy. A tonic quality makes itself strongly felt in her poems. Her immense vitality in itself ensured a resilience and optimism. Reference to a few of her more spiritually invigorating pieces helps to sustain such conclusions.

A relish for winter proves revealing. "Winter is good, his hoar delights Italic flavor yield", are the opening words of one of her resilient little poems. She loves the "Sweet skepticisms of the heart". In the same lyric she notes "the delicious throe Of transport thrilled with fear." In a moment of special exuberance she begins a poem: "I'm sorry for the dead today". The lines continue with a glowing account of the farmer's life at harvest time. Similarly in her exhilarating mood she writes:

> We like March, his shoes are purple . . . .
>   Bold it were to die
> With the blue-birds buccaneering
>   On his British sky.

What a picture this gives of the gallant little birds of early
spring catapulting their blue bodies against the red of a
windy March sunset! Much of Emily's true temperament
is revealed in her fondness for audacious and daring birds
or animals. She especially loves the blue-bird, not because
he has occasionally been used as symbol of happiness, but
because of his audacity. Such delightful poems on the
bluebird as, "Before you thought of spring", or "After
all birds have been investigated and laid aside", tell more
of the poet's own character than many of her most clearly
introspective pieces. "Fortitude stanched with melody",
the last line of the second of these poems, affords an excellent epitome of Emily's own career. She shows special
gusto and understanding in her accounts of the bluejay:
"A prompt, executive Bird is the Jay", and "The joy his
castinet has struck". Poems on the bobolink, one of her
great favorites, belong in the same category. "Brave bobolink!" she pointedly exclaims. In one of her high-spirited
lyrics, "The bobolink is gone, The rowdy of the meadow",
she openly likens herself to this particular species, opposed to the duller sects of Calvinistic birds.

Emily's courage includes stoical fortitude, but progresses far beyond such a passive philosophy. She is compact of will, highly aggressive, a spirit constantly on the
assault, a bird of prey. "We like a hairbreadth 'scape",
she revealingly declares. She enjoys windy days, stormy
weather, an atmosphere that has a "maritime conviction".
In her infinite sympathy and with her spiritual powers of
microscopic discernment, she even extends her view of the
courageous to include plants and vines. So one lyric begins, "The blackberry wears a thorn in his side", and
ends with the typical exclamation, "Brave blackberry!"

Few poets have expressed suffering more powerfully or more poignantly than she, yet few have risen so far above morbidity, pessimism, or despair. The courage expressed in *Moby Dick* is somewhat desperate and grim. Nothing remotely to be called optimism can be construed from the flag flying from the masthead of the sinking "Pequod", or from the rescue of one so nearly drowned as the unhappy Ishmael. With Emily Dickinson the case is altered. Not in a last moment defiance amounting almost to an afterthought, nor in a rescue that might virtually be termed posthumous, but in the warp and woof of all her thinking we find the substance of high courage and hope. An ardent believer in the integrity of the individual, she interprets the word in its two senses, to mean both identity and rectitude. For her, to stand alone signified axiomatically to stand upright. Emily believed in the rectitude of the human soul; she had no truck with the orthodox Christian doctrine of the fall. Her faith clung to the individual man, with all his inherent or potential beauty and integrity. In this life she knew immortality, eternity, infinity, heaven, and God. She had suffered and overcome. Her dominant chord is one of personal triumph. Like Dante, she had during her mortal life and walking upon her own feet traversed the long spaces of hell, purgatory, and heaven. She had, according to her own terms and desires, received the mystic vision. No wonder, then, that her final tones are affirmative. Emily believed in mankind. Her poems are a celebration of the dignity and noble functions of Man in his universal aspect.

PART II
REPRESENTATION OF MEN

1 *LITERARY ANALOGUES*

According to the scheme of this study, borrowed from a favorite distinction in nineteenth-century thought, the First Part offers a glimpse of Emily's poetry from the psychological point of view, that is, in terms of the properties of the individual mind and soul, whereas the Second Part affords a glimpse of her work from the sociological viewpoint, or in terms of literary, philosophical, religious, and social movements. One view depicts the poems as an expression of Man, the other, as an expression of men; one relates them to the ego, the other to the corporate organism of mankind.

Since the poems are indubitably literature, it is with literary traditions and movements that one naturally begins. Taking the poetry as a pivot, one turns both backward and forward, retreating well into the past and advancing as far as possible into the future, or, in other words, covering the time from the publication of the works to our own day. It is relatively unprofitable to linger over Emily's own present time, for in an ideal sense there is no such time. It is only necessary to consider that some books were written before and some after her own compositions. The former may possibly have influenced her; the latter may have been affected by her. Particularly as concerns Emily, the present dwindles in importance, since, however much she derived from her contemporaries —and it is certain that she eagerly read current books— she by no means represented the prevailing taste of her own period; her poems remained for the most part unpublished in her own lifetime; and they much more nearly resemble work done long before or considerably thereafter than any contemporary products. Moreover the dating of many of her lyrics is uncertain; they may belong to any time within a period of thirty years.

The chief object of the present survey is not to determine what books influenced Emily's own writing, but to state what books may best influence and aid our own understanding of what she wrote. One is naturally interested in Emily's "sources", but in so original a poet one is much inclined to hold the only true source to be the spring of her own poetic inspiration, the well of her own life's experience. Properly there is only one source for any true poem, namely, the Pierian Spring. Undeniably it is useful and important to know what books helped to form Emily's mind and art; it is at least of equal value to know what writings they have helped to shape. Such approaches constitute the core of any comparative studies in literature. Encompassing a smaller circle lies a larger and still more enlightening circle, comprised not of the sources or derivatives but of analogues. For purposes of understanding, analogues are often more useful than sources, for they are commonly closer in points of comparison. In the ensuing pages both are indiscriminately mingled, but since this is a philosophical and aesthetic study rather than a textual or biographical one, emphasis falls strongly on the analogues. The question is, simply, whom does Emily most closely resemble among the masters of the past, and who among the masters of the present resemble her?

Regardless of how unusual and isolated a figure the recluse of Amherst may seem, she does not stand alone.

Most of her American contemporaries, warming themselves in each other's company to keep off the chilly lone-
liness of a New World, were destined in the eye of history to stand very much alone. If we are to believe certain
scholars of just repute, the American pioneers represent
a unique culture. Emily, however, comes close to many
great poets of the most diverse culture and periods,
especially to masters in the metaphysical lyric. Professor
George F. Whicher, my old teacher, has with much skill
placed Emily in her local setting; with what I feel sure
is his cordial approval, my own aim is to take her out
of it. This broader view should help the reader to grasp
her contribution more firmly, to appraise her stature
more justly, and to appreciate her more warmly. Her
seclusion notwithstanding, Emily desired fame. This fame
was not mere praise for herself, but entrance into the
goodly company of truly great souls. Her search was,
properly speaking, not so much for fame as for immortality. The rightfully ambitious seek most not isolated
greatness but membership in that ideal society of the great
who, according to ancient myth, cluster in the company
of the Muses about the aforementioned Pierian Spring.
At Amherst stands an empty sepulchre. The poet is not
there. If we are to find her with all her flashing liveli-
ness of soul, we shall—according to my own judgment—
find her only in Parnassus. Let us, then, consider figures
analogous to herself, those persons who in the Elysium
of the poets would be the most delighted to exchange
cordial words with her and clasp her hand.

Fragmentary as are the remains of Sappho's verse, and
dissimilar as her morals and those of her friend Anacreon
doubtless were from those of the "nun of Amherst", the

terseness, directness, and fervor of the first great lyric
poets of Greece suggest like qualities in Emily's lyrics.
Certainly her poems come much closer to Sappho's than
most of the hybrid pieces in English vainly imitating the
Sapphic versification. Like the chief Greek lyric poets,
Emily was an epigrammatist, and a large proportion of
her works may profitably be considered in close connection with the Greek Anthology. Her brief lyrics on
joy, love, and nature approximate many of the less
familiar of the anacreontic poems. Both Anacreon and
Emily wrote on grasshoppers, perceiving the fitness of the
small poem for celebrating small creatures. Both possessed the microscopic eye. Meleager in turn, the first
editor of the Anthology, wrote exquisite little pieces on
the grasshopper, the bee, the cricket, and the gnat, all
in some respects anticipating Emily's delightful trifles on
the same creatures. The severely studied perfection of
her form and her rigid economy have the classical ring.
She in herself includes much of the entire scope of the
thousand year old Greek collection, inasmuch as she can
be fervent with Sappho, blithe with Anacreon, sublime
with Simonides, metaphysical with Plato, trifling with
Meleager, and withering with the sad singers who concluded the anthological tradition, as Palladas and Glycon.
She, too, in minute, fastidiously carved gems depicts the
human story of love, death, heroism, and despair, celebrates the beauty of flowers, mirrors the consolations of
nature, relaxes in mirth, contemplates the graver matters
of religion, and worships beauty. A large number of her
best known pieces may easily be imagined as adaptations
from the Greek. Among them, for example, are "Elysium
is as Far". "I Died for Beauty", "The Heart Asks Pleasure

First", "This Quiet Dust Was Gentlemen and Ladies",
"Ample Make This Bed", "The World Feels Dusty", and
"The Mountains Grow Unnoticed". Emily would unques-
tionably be at home with the Greek masters in Elysium.

In her more satirical or relatively less emotional pieces,
her work surprisingly resembles certain Latin masterpieces. Thus in a little poem of twenty-two words she
gives one of the most familiar of the Latin conceits: "The
show is not the show, but they that go." The entire
thought and expression closely parallels Martial. The
breadth of her achievement can be fairly measured by her
occasional close approximation to the most disciplined of
the Roman poets with whom in general she may truly be
thought to have little in common. All terse, sententious,
and didactic verse is likely to resemble Horace. In some
instances, even to the nuances of image and rhythm, Emily
can be extremely Horatian. The following lines afford
an instance:

> On a columnar self
> How ample to rely;
> In tumult or extremity
> How good the certainty
>
> That lever cannot pry,
> And wedge cannot divide
> Conviction, that granitic base,
> Though none be on our side.

Both the thought and art of Emily Dickinson's poetry
belong in their essence to the literatures of the most remote and ancient peoples. They signify an advanced
civilization rather than any qualities fundamentally American. Her reverence for the sun, for example, has its

parallels in the Hebrew psalms, which, of course, she
knew in her Bible, as will as in the hymn of the Egyptian
Pharaoh, Iknnaton, from which the passages in question
in the psalms appear to be derived. The fascination which
immortality and allied theological concepts held for the
New England poet help to place her in the company of
masters of the religious lyric in the most distant times.
Again, to travel still further afield, her transcendentalism
as well as her aphoristic and oracular style often strongly
suggests the writings ascribed to the greatest of the
Chinese mystics, Lao Tse. It will be found stimulating
to place beside her more metaphysical poems passages
from Lao Tse's work as translated by the American poet,
Witter Bynner. By virtue of her laconic and imagistic
style Emily Dickinson comes much closer to the classical
masters of Chinese and Japanese poetry than the Imagists
of the early twentieth century who over-fastidiously imitated the oriental. So far as can be seen, there is no direct
influence. No one has as yet discovered whether or not
she read translations from Asiatic poets, though she may
have done so, as Emerson and Thoreau certainly did. We
do know that on one of her visits to Boston she went to
"The Chinese Museum", but what she looked at there
and whether any of the highly sophisticated oriental
masterpieces in art, so similar in spirit to the oriental
lyrics, attracted her, remains impossible to say. In any
case her metaphysical or mystical insight has many
analogues in Chinese lyrics. Her extraordinary delicacy
and succinctness are even more clearly paralleled in translations of the Japanese hokku, such as the striking versions
made in recent years by Arthur Waley and Harold
Henderson. With Near Eastern masters of the verse

aphorism she enjoys much in common, as with Saadi and Omar Khayyam.

Her highly individualistic, emotional, and metaphysical poetry has many analogues in the rich poetical literatures of Spain and South America. In both form and spirit the chief Spanish poets traversed long before her the paths which she knew well. The great and austere mystical poet, Luis de Leon, anticipated much of her vision. The ancient Spanish practice of couching reflective poetry in "couplas", or brief aphoristic stanzas, likewise created a verse and a verse movement very similar to hers, as may be seen in the celebrated couplas by Manrique, much diluted in the translations by Longfellow. That Spanish poets have by no means lost their gift for a deeply introspective and metaphysical poetry is indicated, for example, by the lyrics of the contemporary, Georges Guillen, much of whose finest verse, especially that rich in nature imagery, belongs in strictly the same tradition which Emily cultivated.

Illustrious Italians are also her rightful companions. The historical roots of her idealistic love poetry inevitably go back to Petrarch. Her homely and biting realism has arresting parallels in the racy, popular lyrics by Lorenzo de Medici. In moments of her most towering idealism she approximates Michelangelo of the grand and somber sonnets, or Bruno with his fiery neo-platonism. More intimately, her heroic stoicism and scorn of the more sordid values of the world very closely resemble the thought and expression of the greatest of all Italian lyrical poets, Leopardi. At the height of their powers these two meet.

Foreign as Emily's forthright and yet subjective poetry may be to the classical tradition of the French, there are

French masters who share much with her. This leader of the American Renaissance may be described as an Heloise transported into the crucial moment in history when Calvinism is painfully dying and modernism is in the equally agonizing process of being born. The shrewder and less metaphysical of her didactic aphorisms resemble the quaint trifles of the chief Frenchman who stood between Medieval and Renaissance traditions, Clement Marot. Her profound aphorisms rival Pascal's. In her imagery she clearly anticipates the lyrics of the symbolist, Verlaine; while in the most pregnant passages of her symbolism she rivals a more powerful poet than Verlaine, Êmile Verhaeren. Like Poe, Emily Dickinson strangely anticipated French poets of whom she was never to hear and who, at least until the most recent years, have not heard of her.

Her inwardness and spirituality place her nearer to the Germans than to the French. There is, perhaps, no closer parallel to the metaphysical side of her verse than afforded by Angelus Silesius, the German mystic and gnomic writer of the seventeenth century. His masterwork is a collection of several hundred of these brief rhymes, many of them much in Emily's style and temper. One of his quatrains, for example, sums up the paradox of Emily's way of seeing:

> Two eyes our souls possess;
> While one is turned on time,
> The other seeth things
> Eternal and sublime.

I am availing myself of a fair translation of these poems, but it is only right to observe that the "sublime" in the last line is sheer padding for the sake of rhyme. The translator treats Silesius much as Mrs. Todd as an editor occasionally treated Emily. Silesius wrote merely: "Hin in die Ewigkeit." Using prepositions as substantives, Silesius anticipates not alone precisely Emily's thought but her intensely realistic manner of dealing with abstractions. His little poem beginning, "Es ist kein Vor noch Nach", may be rendered as follows:

> Not after nor before:
> What shall to-morrow be
> In its true essence God
> Sees in eternity.

This is exactly Emily's idea expressed in the twelve lines beginning: "Forever is composed of Nows". Her idealistic metaphysics are stated by the German as follows:

> They say that time is swift.
> Whoever saw it fly?
> Within our world of thought
> Unmoved we find time lie.

The same principle applies, of course, to space:

> Thou art not in a place,
> The place thou'lt find in thee.
> Discard it, and e'en now
> Appears eternity.

Emily in one of her moods would heartily have agreed with the further paradox expressed by the mystic:

> In spirit senses are
> One and the same. 'Tis true
> Who seeth God he tastes
> Feels, smells and hears Him too.

She would have unequivocally endorsed his comment on God and man:

> A man beholdeth God,
> A brute the clod of earth;
> Hence every one may know
> His nature and his worth.

Emily's sense of identity and aloneness is stated as succinctly as she could herself have stated them;

> Who not with others bides
> And always lives alone,
> If he's not God himself,
> Must into God have grown.

The two see virtually eye to eye in the all important matter of love and death. Emily's own spiritual biography is stated in the simplest terms:

> Young love storms like new wine
> In wildest fermentation.
> Old love is still and clear,
> Strong through tranquilization.

The lofty place of love in the scheme of things is equally asserted by German and American. Silesius wrote:

> The nearest way to God
> Leads through love's open door;
> The path of knowledge is
> Too slow for evermore.

Finally, Silesius, like Emily, briefly and forcefully states the beneficent place of death in life.

Death is a blessed thing!
The stronger death chastizes,
The much more glorious is
The life that therefrom rises.

The well-known and profound aphoristic lyrics by Goethe, containing but a few lines each, are in much the same category of art and of lyrical merit as the many perfect short poems by Emily Dickinson. Her more feminine and naïve lyrics stand close, also, to the brief songs of the eminent lyricist, Möricke. But the German of the nineteenth century whom she most frequently resembles is undoubtedly Heine. A large number of her short lyrics are as simple, magical, and tender as his. The same romantic sensitivity begot them. One truly wonders that this relationship has not been commonly observed. Of more recent poets writing in German, Emily Dickinson most nearly resembles Rilke, whose evolution from a writer of simple, romantic lyrics to a poet of much more profound and difficult thinking resembles her own spiritual history. The two are, perhaps, of much the same stature. Lastly, in her vigorous, masculine, and unsentimental imagery she stands by no means far removed from the best of Stefan George. Emily would have understood also the wholly unpedantic realism of the chief Slavic poets, as of Pushkin, for example, in his tender and affectionate lyric in honor of his old nurse.

It may not seem strange that analogues have seldom been noted between her work and the leaders of continental poetry; but that her English analogues have so rarely been mentioned may cause some surprise. One naturally begins with Shakespeare, since she herself once extravagantly observed that for literature Shakespeare

alone would suffice—a remark that looks almost like a
knavishly impious reference to the puritan notion of the
all-sufficiency of the Bible. Her admiration for Shakespeare has several times been remarked, though its implications appear not to have been observed. It seems certain that he was actually one of her chief masters, whose
methods as a poet she carefully scrutinized for purposes
of her own. Like Shakespeare, she took the maximum of
liberties with language consonant with an adherence to
the basic principles of expression itself and the demands
of a dramatic clarity. Like him, she passes lightly between
extremes of starkness and eloquence. After the pattern
of the Elizabethan, she employs a most flexible syntax,
repeatedly uses one part of speech as another, and builds
a language of positively orchestral range and power. Her
frequent references to *Antony and Cleopatra* indicate that
even the most opulent Elizabethanisms attracted her.
Often where a relationship cannot definitely be proved,
one may well feel a strong probability. Such a phrase, for
example, as Emily's, "The admirations and contempts of
time", appears to me remarkably Shakespearean. In Elizabethan fashion Emily expends much of her finest eloquence, at once poignant and sententious, in utterances on
the "democrat" death. The thought and language of
Antony and Cleopatra is surely indicated in this quatrain:

> This latest leisure equal lulls
>   The beggar and his queen;
> Propitiate this democrat
>   A summer's afternoon.

A few entire poems read like paraphrases from Shakespeare. Thus her twelve-line poem, "When I see not, I

better see", is a deliberate and almost line for line translation of the forty-third sonnet beginning, "When most I wink, then do mine eyes best see." Emily merely drains off Shakespeare's baroque eloquence, leaving the terser New England statement, twelve short lines taking the place of fourteen long. Her poem beginning, "A tongue to tell him I am true", derives from a number of Shakesperean speeches wherein a lover sends messages of adulation to the beloved, each image piled upon another in half-humorous extravaganza. That the parallels in these two cases have escaped scholarly comment must be laid chiefly to their first appearance in print in Mrs. Bingham's volume, 1945. But from the beginning it should have been clear that the relation of Emily's language to Shakespeare's was of more intimate and vital meaning for her poetry than the accidental coincidences in subject matter and imagery between her work and the metaphysical poets of the school of Donne. That her realistic and rebellious poetry shares something with Donne's lyrics is, of course, apparent; but the relationship is not so close as that with Shakespeare, and there is no evidence that she knew Donne, whose fame remained more or less quiescent until revived in the early years of the present century.

There is, however, an ancestor of John Donne with whom Emily, if transported to Tudor times, would have had much to say. That jesting martyr, John Heywood the epigrammatist, who lived and labored during the reigns of all the English monarchs of the sixteenth century, was her predecessor in being one of the greatest English masters of the racy or eloquent aphorism, a deeply humane spirit combining a flashing wit with a fervently religious soul. Emily would have well understood the quaint old humorist and fabulist who gave neat and permanent literary form to hundreds of the canny proverbs of the medieval folk.

But to return to the metaphysicals, with whom her relations should be neither exaggerated nor forgotten. Although a much less pedantic poet than Donne, she occasionally allows herself the elaboration of a figure after the manner of Donne's extravagant ingenuity. Presumably few of her readers have overlooked her approximation to Donne's technique in one instance. Her poem, "My life had stood a loaded gun", is thoroughly the equal of Donne's celebrated lyric wherein parting is compared to the movements of a pair of compasses. She has something akin to each member of the Cavalier school. Externally, Emily's poems resemble no book more closely than Herrick's *Hesperides*. As master of little poems exquisitely carved, she may well be described as a puritan Herrick. In other words, she is Herrick with one quality added which may be variously estimated according to our various temperaments, namely high seriousness. Hence, while her form bears closer relationship to Herrick, her content comes much closer to the austere Vaughan, a great poet with whom we know her to have been to some extent familiar. In her, as in Shakespeare, extremes meet. Her homely and unaffected imagery often suggests one of the most pleasing and distinguishing features of Thomas Traherne; her exuberant and religiously profane love poetry sometimes suggests the super-baroque laureate of the Counter Reformation, Richard Crashaw. Her proximity to the School as a whole is symbolized in her relation to the most popular of its figures in the literary mind of approximately 1850. For her own pleasure she copied eight lines from George Herbert, beginning, "My God, what is a heart." By a perfectly natural and pardonable error Mrs. Bingham included them as Emily's in *Bolts of Melody,* an error first noted in the well-informed columns of *The New Yorker.* Emily's own favorite seventeenth-century author was, however, only incidentally a poet. Very naturally she fell under the spell of Thomas Browne's powerful imagination, by which her poems are influenced much as by Shakespeare. Too original to be a mere copyist, she fully assimilated her own reading in both authors. The "influences" were not so much on her page as in her blood. Long graduated from the servile position of being a parodist or a copyist, she stood on an equal plane with her more illustrious predecessors, who are now better regarded as her companions than as her teachers.

Even among poets of the Augustan period notable analogues and "sources" exist. It should not be forgotten that despite her ecstatic lyrics Emily on her worldly side is author of many short pieces of light verse shaped and polished with a neo-classical art by no means far removed from the chief master of the light lyric as written in England, Matthew Prior. Going to another extreme, in versification, imagery, and feeling her ecstatic, hymn-like lines, "Bring me the sunset in a cup", intimately resemble that classic of poetical and religious enthusiasm, Christopher Smart's *Song to David.* These remain coincidences, however striking; but one eighteenth-century poet Emily both loved and imitated, namely, Burns. She was, albeit slightly, afflicted even with the Scottish dialect, and in an early poem could use such an expression as "the bonnie souls". She captured Burns's habit of lilting repetition of phrase as expressive in pathetic passages. Only naturally she responded to one of the greatest masters of humor and emotion in English verse and one who, like herself, living in a provincial region well removed from the more sophisticated literary conversation, turned to the spoken language of the people for certain basic and strengthening qualities of verse.

As complete master of the mystic or metaphysical aphorism and as a natural rebel against the conventional insincerities and sentimentalities bedevilling English thought and verse, Emily has close kinship with Blake. One must not be misled by the glaring differences in their personalities, or by the maidenly quality of one and the frank eroticism of the other. At their highest level the two stand side by side; indeed some of the closest parallels in English to the more philosophical of Blake's lyrics, notably those in *Songs of Experience,* are to be found in the American poet. Both were peers and fellows in the mystic way; both uniquely gifted with the art of combining a philosophical insight with a warm, glowing, and lightning-like poetic expression. "Bolts of melody" describes with almost equal accuracy the most memorable work of each.

Nothing can be more apparent to the reader of Emily Dickinson than the divorce between her own poetry and the typical products of the British romantic school, although she herself was apparently hardly aware of the extent of this divorce. A few of the Victorians she much admired. Very fittingly, a noble lyric by Emily Brontë was read when she was laid in her grave at Amherst. For Elizabeth Barrett Browning she entertained a fervent admiration under the circumstances not so readily understood, but none the less worth remembering in estimating some of the tints of her own background. That her devotion to nature occasionally reminds one of Wordsworth or that her ecstatic lyrics in rare moments approach Shelley's verse-rhetoric are notable not so much because these parallels exist as because they exist so seldom. She is not a follower of the romantic poets. It is much truer of her to say that she anticipates the revolt from them which has reached full force at the present time than that she shows a timid conformity to the ways of her contemporaries. In all essential respects she lived not for time but for eternity. To be sure, in certain broad attitudes toward personalism, nature, love, religion, and society she does conform, but the essence of her poetry, its art and its manner of envisaging life, was her own achievement fundamentally aided far more by older traditions, mystical, classical, medieval, renaissance, Elizabethan, Cavalier, and Puritan, than by Romantic taste.

She simply does not resemble any of the nineteenth-century romantics closely. Her religiously tinged nature poetry is, for example, more trenchant and fervent than Wordsworth's contemplative rhymes. Her realistic and intimate love poetry stands almost as far removed as possible from Shelley's vague neo-platonic idealism. Her style is entirely divorced from the deeply traditional neo-Miltonic eloquence of Keats. Byron's best work, his expansive satire on manners, proceeding from a strongly objective view of the world, is as remote from her typical vein as is Byron's atrocious sentimentality. With Scott, Campbell, and Crabbe she shares nothing. Suave Arnold, Tennyson steeped in a provincial British traditionalism, and Swinburne, infatuated with the gushing fountain of his words, all belong to far different worlds of poetry from her own. There are, to be sure, a few nineteenth-century British poets whose command of the imagination in secondary aspects resembles hers. She shared Coleridge's magical, supernatural touch, Gerard Manley Hopkins' penetrating sense for the value of passionately laden word and phrase, and, at times, Lewis Carroll's abandoned, childlike humor. But all likenesses here remain tangential. Nor did her fondness for current romantic novels vitiate her verses. She remained free.

Her profound and undeclared freedom from immediate British models was partly her rightful heritage as an American. That she unconsciously derived something from such imagistically realistic and profoundly religious poetry as that of Anne Bradstreet and Edward Taylor has been rightly urged. The likeness of her homespun verse-mottoes to the racy verse aphorisms of Emerson has likewise been well noted. It is even more pertinent that her spiritualized realism finds fairly close companionship in the briefer poems of Thoreau and Melville, only recently coming in general critical favor. Many of the poems in question by Thoreau remained, like her own, unpublished. So did many of those by Melville, although his admirable volume, *John Marr and Other Poems,* was privately printed. Yet even with these analogues in mind, the most compelling comparisons thus far mentioned are with the distant past rather than with the period of her own life. Emily was a reincarnation of masters long dead and a prophecy of masters to come. To use one of her own telling images, the garment which she wore was fitted not to the limbs of time but of eternity.

2 *POETRY AS PROPHECY*

It has been shown that Emily Dickinson affords an emphatic refutation of the commonly received opinion that an artist is best understood by reference to his own times and environment. Helpful as a familiarity with the society of Amherst and the state of the Western World approximately a hundred years ago may be for the interpretation of her work, this is much more fully grasped through specific reference to the centuries which preceded her and the decades that have followed. With conclusive power she exhibits both the independence of genius and the breadth of a classic, faithful to the opposite poles of the self and the centuries. And from precisely the same causes she illustrates the conception of true artists as prophetical. All such are prophets, for however much or little they may be understood or acclaimed during their lifetime, their strongest impact is upon posterity. No artist can be preëminent whose total work merely recapitulates the past in learned fashion, or serves the present with a skilful opportunism. The realm of the spirit follows in this regard virtually a biological analogy. Whatever is most valuable biologically marks an adaptation to new conditions, exhibiting the power of growth not only in the individual but in the species. So is it with works of art and culture. Scholarship concerned merely with the task of placing a genius in his age and environment is therefore not even good history, not to mention good criticism. The zest of life flows from its dynamic qualities. Sources and contemporaries are well enough, but as the Christian Church with a biologically and an historically sound intuition has perceived, the liveliest part of the story concerns posthumous miracles. None has performed these more effectively than Emily Dickinson.

The meaning of a writer becomes best clarified by his influence upon others. So the centuries accumulate the significance of Shakespeare. But careful scrutiny usually discloses that the foremost artists are no more the founders of new schools of taste than mere adherents of schools which have preceded them. It is more important for a creative artist to be a force among his successors than a model for them. The artist who is too easily imitated is presumably below the highest station. Raphael could be imitated but not Michelangelo, Beaumont and Fletcher but not Shakespeare. Pope had fairly successful disciples, whereas the followers of the greater Chaucer merely betrayed their own banality and by contrast still further magnified the stature of their master. This does not, of course, mean that the greatest artists fail to influence mankind; it means only that just as their commanding genius has risen above the commonly accepted taste of their own times, they leave masterpieces in no strict or literal sense imitable. They guide the spirit, not the letter, of the age to come.

Emily Dickinson did not really die; she merely slept for a generation to awake and find herself young. She complied in all respects with the pattern of the major, not the secondary, artist, for she became the force and not the model. That she escaped the less fortunate fate deserves special note. Much merely on the surface of her life and art argues her to be a narrow genius. And where genius is narrow it runs to a few formulas definitely in-

viting imitation. The most readily imitable artist is one,
like Pope, who perfects a few relatively simple manner-
isms, whose art is the fruit of formulas. Emily lived and
worked in seclusion but not by rule, monkish in her retirement but not in her practice. We have seen that she confined herself to her house in Amherst in order to enjoy the
greatest advantages for seeing the larger world of the
spirit. She avoided fellow townsmen in order to make
neighbors of mankind. Similarly, she chose a simple,
basic metrical pattern for the greater part of her verse,
and wrote only short poems, often mere epigrams. This
represents what she conceived as the microscopic phase
of her vision. The seemingly small proved, however, to
be the vast. She worked almost exclusively with gems,
but with gems of many kinds and colors. Her ascetic restrictions were virtually humorous deceptions by which
this wily and enchanted maiden captured the unicorn of
the absolute. Her strategy of humility was her subtle net
to trap infinity. The puritan virgin proves to be a sister
of Cleopatra. Who was to imitate or to capture such
fecundity? What in general her poetry spiritually and
aesthetically signified could be readily perceived; but like
the snake which she so vividly describes, her art moved
too elusively ever to be captured by followers. Realizing
how far her own inspiration stood above formulas, she
taunted potential imitators in her little poem, "Beauty
is not caused,—it is." To capture beauty by reason is as
difficult, she declares, as to overtake the creases in the
meadow when the wind runs his fingers across it. Ideally
speaking, there are no limits to the beauty that may be
created, whereas the mere copying of it dooms itself to
speedy sterility. To write as Emily did, it is merely neces-

sary to become a complete master of the English tongue.

The world's capacity to profit creatively by Emily's verses has inevitably been based on its capacity to understand them. The readiest key to the problem is the unique story, already summarized, of the publication of her poems. Those of an emotional and therapeutic value— or, in other words, those at least subject to a sentimental interpretation—were among the first which Mrs. Todd selected for publication. The public taste, and doubtless to some extent her own, determined the choice. Gradually we have been privileged to read more and more of Emily's more mature and austere pieces, the pieces which are the most imaginatively worded, and to read them in faithful texts unsentimentalized by too solicitous editors. Taste and criticism have caught up with the more difficult qualities of her verse. Her true meaning has been increasingly felt, but this influence shown less in any close imitation of her finest art—which remains inimitable—than in the gradual triumph of the aesthetic ideals for which she stood and for which she singlehandedly waged so brave a battle, till in due time a host arose in defense of her posthumous fame. Just as in the study of Emily's relations to her predecessors, the critical eye looks primarily for analogues, not for imitations.

Imaginative individuals in private shared feelings familiar to Emily considerably before their writings achieved public recognition. It is of some interest that the chief painter to express American transcendentalism, Albert Pinkham Ryder, in close relation to his pictures composed many poems of a highly symbolical or mystical nature which in their general conception and technique are by no means far removed from Emily's much more

skilful verses. The two had kindred minds. Ryder in his
garret in New York painting tiny pictures loaded with
mystery and poetic symbolism followed closely upon the
footsteps of Emily in her second-story room secretly com-
posing tiny poems equally rich in the golden ore of
mystery and metaphorical implication.

The new age demanded a new inwardness and subjectivity of which Emily had been so distinguished a fore-
runner. Far less lyrical and succinct than Emily, but
equally a poet of the spirit, Edwin Arlington Robinson
offers attractive features of contrast and comparison. Although Robinson never possessed Emily's refined diction
or acute and feminine eye for the outer and visible world,
he followed Emily closely in being a spokesman for New
England. It is true that she expressed a still vigorous
New England, when economic capitalism was at its height
and the spiritual capital of the Calvinistic faith had by
no means been wholly exhausted, while he expressed a
profound malady in the social, economic and religious institutions of the region wherein his spriit was so thoroughly acclimatized. But powerful inwardness existed in
both poets, proceeding from much the same historical
source. Their inwardness was their unfailing strength.
And just as the public failed at once to plumb the depths
of Emily's spiritual life, the public even as yet, apparently, has failed to recognize the profundity of the great
narrative poems which the leading poet from Maine wrote
in the last years of his life: *The Man Who Died Twice,
Cavender's House, Matthias at the Door, The Glory of
the Nightingales, Amaranth,* and *King Jasper.*

Although not a New Englander to the manner born
as Emily and Robinson, the highly gifted Robert Frost

well understands many of the stylistic and lyrical qualities distinguishing her verse. In keeping with the movements of his times, which have admired Emily increasingly, his own art has steadily tended to share more with hers. He commenced his brilliant career with special fondness for narrative poetry at least in the general manner of Robinson's Browningesque verse monologues. There is at least a basic likeness between the poems in *North of Boston* and in *The Three Taverns*. With time Frost has grown less dramatic and more lyrical, less diffuse and more succinct, less objective and more subjective. He has increasingly polished the surface of his stanzaic verse. Many of his finest lyrics enter at least into the same world inhabited by the earlier poet of Amherst. In *Tree at My Window* he uses the same symbol for subjectivity employed by Emily in lines beginning: "By my window have I for scenery Just a sea with a stem." His fine lyric, *To Earthward,* has much of Emily's intensity, with a symbolism carrying an extraordinary weight of thought and feeling. *Stopping by Woods on a Snowy Evening* has something of her magic and simplicity. And such epigrams as *Fire and Ice, Nothing Gold Can Stay,* and *Bereft,* share her power of compression.

Although Sandburg is usually far less personal and intense than Emily, he too at times rivals her gift for verse epigram. His justly famous little trifle, *Fog,* shares imaginative qualities with some of Emily's more naïve poems. But Sandburg and most of the American poets who exploit a social subject matter derive from the tradition of Whitman, not that of Emily Dickinson. One turns for closer analogues to poets of the metaphysical stamp.

Emily's poetry has been praised by Mark Van Doren

in the Foreword to Mrs. Bingham's collection; it is not surprising to find so searching, spiritual, and idealistic a poet as Mr. Van Doren, further possessed with a disciplined sense for literary style, among those who express the warmest admiration for Emily and most nearly approach her manner. The progress of his art may be seen as one contrasts the Wordsworthian spirit of his first volume, *Spring Thunder and Other Poems,* with the Dickinsonian quality of his latest collection, *Our Lady Peace.* He has passed from poorer to better models, from a diffuse to a succinct style. Even earlier than Van Doren, Hart Crane realized the power of Emily's terse and imaginative phrase, and while paying her eloquent tribute in his own verse enriched his poetry with inspiration caught from her.

Almost all our more imaginative poets are to some extent in debt to her and in some measure her followers, although at times we must look beneath the surface in the work of highly original or eccentric genius to perceive the likeness. Endowed with a plentifully active fancy, E. E. Cummings nevertheless has seen fit to borrow the title of his most recent book, *1x1,* from a lyric by Emily: "One and one are one." Although Wallace Stevens has usually been more indebted to French than English or American masters, and more given to affected eloquence or mystification than the forthright daughter of Amherst, in many of his best and simplest pieces Stevens comes not far from Emily's lyric style. Younger poets than he are likely to come closer still, as the profoundly metaphysical José Garcia Villa, the virile and succinct Richard Eberhardt, and the only too chaste classicist, Yvor Winters, who preaches a puristic criticism as a metaphysical equivalent of virginity. Just as one of the best essays ever to be written on Emily appears in the volume by the poet-painter, Marsden Hartley, in some of Hartley's own strongest poems the influence of Emily's style is clearly discernible. There seems, indeed, a tendency for poets to be at their best as they come closest to some of Emily Dickinson's familiar practices, and at their poorest as they move in the opposite direction. Thus the finest of Archibald MacLeish's work is to be found not in his pretentious poems of public propaganda but in such a severely built, stanzaic lyric as *You Andrew Marvell;* while the finest of John Crowe Ransom lies in charmingly direct verses, such as the trenchant *Lady Lost,* rather than in his occasional excursions into fields of literary surrealism.

Although Emily as poet to a great extent stands beyond sex, having passed through marked femininity to universality, it is natural that those who most often appear her followers should be women. She has received many sincere tributes from women poets, as from Genevieve Taggard, who wrote a glowing and romantic biography. Naturally Miss Taggard came under Emily's spell, as may unmistakably be traced in such poems as the forceful and direct, *Try Tropic,* and *Dilemma of the Elm,* the latter piece resembling the same poem by Emily which Frost approaches in his *Tree at My Window.* The subjective and metaphysical school of modern women poets has had few leaders more forceful than Elinor Wylie, whose lyric in the ascetic mood, *The Eagle and the Rock,* and whose delicately worded lyric on snow, *Velvet Shoes,* may profitably be compared with many analogous works by Emily. Such pieces as Léonie Adams' highly magical

April Mortality, and Louise Bogan's trenchant satire, *Women,* are in a manner that Emily would certainly have liked. Finally, that gifted poet, Marianne Moore, when escaping eccentricity and achieving the fine verse of which she is capable, often approximates Emily's work, as may easily be seen in Miss Moore's recent and most thoughtful volume, *What Are Years.*

The poets of Great Britain and Ireland repeat much the same story. First of the leading innovators laboring in behalf of standards comparable to Emily's is the already mentioned Gerard Manley Hopkins, who, if he was her predecessor in the sense that he wrote before her verses were published, was also her successor in the sense that his own works first saw print considerably after the larger part of hers. The romantically eccentric Hopkins was a bolder virtuoso and experimenter than Emily; accordingly he achieved more surprising effects (though not, it is generally thought, so profound) and made more serious mistakes. Like most poets on the British side of the Atlantic, Yeats, leader of the progressive movements of two generations, inherited too much traditional eloquence to follow in the path of Emily's puritan frugality; but the deep sincerity which he shared with her resulted in a very similar directness of speech. This cleansing quality is found more often in his satirical and political pieces than in his better known lyrics, eloquent or sentimental. His volume, *Responsibilities,* exhibits this forthright attack; while the terse symbols of short lyrics in his later books, as the songs to Crazy Jane, share Emily's gift for a pregnant imagery.

In the group of recent poets who hailed Yeats as their living master, W. H. Auden is commonly regarded as the most richly endowed. One of his best lyrics, *In Memory of William Butler Yeats,* concludes with strict and forceful stanzas in much the temper of Emily's severe writing. *A Christmas Oratorio* affords a more extended example of economical and emotional verse on metaphysical and philosophical themes. It presents an extension of Emily's basic principles of poetry into new and ampler forms. But as a whole Auden has grown closer to Emily only as he has become increasingly the master of poetic form; he seems never to have been truly intimate with her art; and, to borrow from his own statement in the matter, his greatest debt to her seems to have been the initial impulse which she gave him to devote his life to poetry. His friend, Stephen Spender, possesses a lyricism and idealism closer to Emily's, and by virtue of a singularly resilient personality and clear, incisive language. C. Day Lewis probably comes closest of the three to achieving what Emily demanded of a poet.

Other Englishmen have come closer still. First of these is W. J. Turner, one of the foremost masters of the compressed metaphysical lyric since Blake. Skill in verse epigram associates A. E. Housman, W. H. Davies, James Stephens, and Humbert Wolfe with one notable phase of Emily's craftsmanship. And women in England, as in America, have shared Emily's more feminine qualities, such as poignantly direct speech and singularly spontaneous expression of feeling. Sylvia Townsend Warner should probably be mentioned first in this group, followed by Anna Wickham, Dorothy Wellesley, and Charlotte Mew. These, in brief, are some of the men and women who have advanced those standards of taste and directives of the imagination initiated by Emily Dickinson in the previous century. Most of the aforementioned American poets read her work with enthusiasm; a lesser number of the English knew her also. Whether they knew her or not, all were advancing her sound literary ideals and furthering also her own fame, since they prepared the public for a steadily growing appreciation of her achievement. To judge by the momentum of time, there is good reason to believe that these developments even now stand at their beginning, and that both her own reputation and the popularity of the kind of poetry which she represents will increase throughout the second half of the twentieth century, as it has already progressed during the earlier period.

3 *PROBLEM OF RELIGION*

Emily Dickinson embodies in a heightened form the fatality of her age, wherein religion became less a normal function of the human soul than an agonizing problem in human morbidity. Throughout the civilized world, and scarcely more among Christians than among Moslems, Chinese and Jews, the foundations of faith were shaken. Persons retaining their orthodoxy did so as a rule with a struggle and with diminishing conviction and success. Foes of orthodoxy showed a hectic zeal and no slight unrest within. Finally, most thinking men and women vacillated with considerable spiritual discomfort between moods of zealous belief, ardent disbelief, and, worst of all, skepticism, confusion, and dismay. Emily, herself a universe, expressed all these moods repeatedly and with unique poignancy. To seek for an ingeniously articulated body of thought would presumably be unwise in the instance of a poet and a woman whose reports of life issue so directly from her own experience. Poetry, she declared, had first of all to be alive; she was not primarily concerned with whether or not the productions of a single poet in themselves presented a philosophical system. Her extreme fondness for writing very brief lyrics and aphorisms, with little technical vocabulary, indicates her pragmatism. Thus she resembles neither Aquinas nor Blake as regards the organization of thought. Her poetry may lose something in masculine and philosophical strength; it also retains its purity, incisiveness, and spiritual reality. No one was ever less of a pedant. Her favorite abstract terms in theological thinking, as God, eternity, immortality, heaven, infinity, and the absolute, appear for her at times almost interchangeable. In a celebrated lyric she declares that truth and beauty are one. Although theological speculations fascinate her, she is not to be caught in a net of dogma; God is at once God, Adam, Eve, and the serpent.

That this singular lady living in virtual seclusion should add any definitely new concepts to theological or religious speculation would scarcely be expected. There is nothing in the general argument or direction of her poetic thought unknown to her own times. Yet it would be too cavalier by far to hold that she contributes little or nothing even on an intellectual plane. Her trenchant words and bitter emotional experiences frequently have a unique qualitative shading. With the making and the unmaking of gods, the human male seems to have been chiefly concerned; the gods owe women fewer major services and can hold fewer injuries against them. Women seldom break lances in theology. But Emily was neither an ordinary woman nor a docile believer. Like no one else, either man or woman, she stuck pins in God. Voltaire presumably bruised God more; but Emily snared the throne itself with thumbtacks.

Her relation to orthodoxy is a strange story. As already observed, she at times accepted it, at times undermined it, and at times frankly expressed a bewilderment ranging from the humorous to the tragic. No fundamental position can be found in her poetry concerning the faith. And here it becomes much more than a metaphor to note that she never outgrew her childhood. The God whom as a child she came to know from her elders, she never forgot. This educational experience must have resembled in its abiding significance her first walks with nature, her earliest family affections, and her first girlish loves. Clearly she read the Bible often and with enthusiasm. For her it constituted a supreme poem. As a girl and young woman she was subjected to much persistent religious instruction. Her father, though only for a part of his life an active member of the Church, possessed and taught a severe piety. As a young woman she heard many preachers, falling in love with at least one. She knew far more about religion than about science, history, politics, art, or perhaps any other phase of human activity except literature. Indeed, it might be argued that the larger part of her reading was distinctly religious. Her family was barely removed from the age of the New England theocracy. Religion itself appealed to her as one of the deepest and most fruitful aspects of man's life. But she acknowledged no leader. No preacher or doctrine in the public religious life of Amherst or of the world won her allegiance. To use her own metaphor, on the seas of life and religion, which at times seemed to her virtually one, she embarked in her little boat alone. Needless to add, it proved a voyage perilous. By the very definition of her condition, all the world was in a sense against her. Religion, like truth and beauty, signified the utmost development of the personality. Ultimately, her quest for God was identical with her battle for personal integrity. Her vision even of the divine—perhaps even chiefly of the divine—had to be her own. Indebted to all and enslaved to none, she pursued her quest of eternity.

Many times with ultimate and religious problems in mind she asserts that no definite answer or solution is available in this life. She knew that she could not accept her father's religion. They pray to an eclipse, she said, which they call God. But she, too, knew the God of religion only in eclipse, since this was the inevitable condition of humanity. Religion became for her the language of the soul, but not as yet the salvation. This, so far as she discovered it at all, came to her not through the tradition of the churches, but through that of mysticism. To this mysticism, intimately connected with her religious thoughts, we shall turn presently; but it will be well to linger at least briefly over her relation to orthodox practices and creeds.

A considerable proportion of her finest verse contains a religious imagery without any serious implications either positively or negatively for religious belief. Admittedly this constitutes a delicate problem, to which contradictory answers have been given. Thus in her book on Emily Dickinson, *In the Name of the Bee,* Sister Mary James Power holds that Emily's words, "In the name of the bee, and the butterfly and the breeze, Amen", comprise a reverential allusion to the Trinity, and that at heart she accepted the orthodox doctrine. The reference is incontestable; but the interpretation remains, to say the very least, debatable. Another commentator may with equal plausibility argue that in this poem Emily was attracted merely by the rhythm of the religious phrase and deliberately turned away from Christian worship to the worship of Nature. Neither of these extremes seems in fact the best solution. The most plausible interpretation of all such passages is that in the thoughts, words, symbols, and images of religion the poet spontaneously found the aptest lauguage for the expression of her metaphysical, subtle, and at times mystical ideas. Such expression incontestably proves her extensive familiarity with the Christian religion. It usually offers no conclusion as to her attitude toward it, whether friendly, hostile, or merely skeptical.

Poem after poem contains such imagery. The sacramental usages of the Roman Church are the most commonly suggested by her verse, as indeed they are the most poetical and imaginative forms achieved by Christianity. This daughter of Calvin has a remarkable aptitude for ritual. "O last communion in the haze", begins one of her most exquisite passages. "There came a day at summer's fall", abounds in imagery like that of Catholic poems of the Spanish Renaissance. Allusions to the Crucifix and Mass comprise the substance of which it is made. In another piece she writes of how "priests adjust the symbols when sacrament is done." She readily invents such curious phrases as "one mitred afternoon." All this may argue a certain aptitude for the older Church, but nothing more. Such imagery must be seen for what it is, in due proportion against the background of her work. Of great psychological and aesthetic importance, it makes no decisive contribution to the interpretation of her thinking and feeling as regards the Christian faith. In this regard it signifies little more, for example, than the irresponsible and therefore idle use of profanity.

As so frequently noted in this book, Emily herself explains even her more difficult riddles when her poems are read in sequences appropriate to whatever question comes to hand. Amidst the comparative chaos of riches presented by the two major books now containing her work, readers should be helped to discover a number of small topical anthologies. Many of her strongest poems deal specifically with religious faith—not with the mystical element, but in one way or another with the orthodox theology of the Church. From her extensive work may be culled three minor anthologies, each unsurpassed in its own kind during the nineteenth century. She offers in turn anthologies on skepticism, on the acceptance of the orthodox faith, and on the condemnation of it. The orthodox poems are the fewest and the least impressive, the skeptical pieces more moving, numerous, and brilliant, and the antagonistic pieces by far the most numerous and imaginative of all. She gives an anthology of Reason or Urizon, a booklet of Heaven, and a much more colorful Book of Hell. Such are her Blakian gospels of Innocence, Experience, and Wrath. Not being a synthesizer or a man, Emily does not attempt the grotesque impossibility of the marriage of heaven and hell. Or if she envisages such a marriage, it proves an unhappy and a contentious one. God she occasionally describes as the God of goodness and light, but much more often as God of terror and anger. Here she speaks of the God of the Churches. Her own faith seldom evokes the name of God. Heaven, eternity, immortality, or the absolute serve as her passwords to mysticism. God remains another matter.

Many types of skepticism and conditions of irony are expressed in her anthology of doubt, those poems which show the soul caught between conflicting tides of faith and disbelief. One of the most remarkable is a series of three hymn-like stanzas beginning: "Behind me dips Eternity." Here Emily is convinced that mystery surrounds life, whereas the solution of the mystery lies beyond her. Immortality is the most instinctively attractive to her of all religious beliefs. On death she will enter a world unknown. "They say", as she remarks, that this realm is a "perfect pauseless monarchy"; but Emily cannot be sure. At death she will merely launch upon further explorations. Eternity lies behind her, immortality before, as sunset and sunrise, west and east. To the north and south stand the kingdoms of nature or of menace. The sea is a crescent:

> With midnight to the north of her
> And midnight to the south of her,
> And maelstrom in the sky.

In short, much as religion haunts her, nothing in it has power to fix or console her mind. Another poem declares bluntly that she goes to Church on the Sabbath with nature and not with the pious company of Churchgoers. She, too, meets God. Sadly she acknowledges that, "To lose one's faith surpasses the loss of an estate." Without faith, being itself is reduced to beggary. The inference is that her own faith remains to say the least precarious. In one mood she accepts the faith in a future heaven and at the same time imagines it less satisfying than earthly life. "Their height in heaven comforts not", she declares. In still another mood she considers herself unfortunate from childhood, ever seeking, never finding, and convinced

> That I am looking oppositely
> From the site of the kingdom of heaven.

In still another piece she wonders how God's children can follow his precept, "Come unto me", when there are "firmaments between." "I prayed at first—a little girl—", is a lyrical lament that prayer, doubtless a true blessing to many, remains a closed book to her. "'Tis whiter than an

Indian pipe", records her doubt as to immortality itself. Although she will not definitely conclude the high argument, she wonders if the future world is somehow not a further tragedy and frustration. One of her closest approaches to a solution of the problem of God appears in her lines, "A little over Jordan", retelling the wrestling of Jacob with the angel who was God. The inference here is that man must wrestle against the non-human god if he is to reduce God to humanity and lift himself into Godhead. This thought offers a gateway to her mystical belief asserted in such an aphorism as that, "The brain is just the weight of God." Emily well knew that in such opinions she was retreating from orthodox Christianity. Indeed she felt it with burning intensity, and as usual expressed her feelings most forcefully. So she once exclaims:

> What triple lenses burn upon
> The escapade from God!

Occasionally her desire for affirmation, her imaginative power, and her heritage from a phenomenally sensitive childhood enabled her to write in full confirmation of Christian attitudes and beliefs. She can describe her own soul, somewhat exuberantly to be sure, as

> Given in marriage unto thee,
> Oh, thou celestial host!
> Bride of the Father and the Son,
> Bride of the Holy Ghost!

There are expressions which at least appear on the surface as pure piety. Such is her doubtless fanciful poem, "Only a shrine," where she imagines herself a nun petitioning the Virgin Mary. Once she briefly addresses Jesus on the Cross: "Jesus, thy crucifix." "No crowd that has occurred," rivals the finest hymns in English, new or old, on the thrilling theme of the day of general Resurrection. "Life is what we make it," is her warmest address to Christ, this time as the great pioneer in the exploration of death. "Through the straight pass of suffering," is, at least outwardly, an orthodox panegyric upon martyrdom. Finally, "Unto Me," proves so conventional an address of God to the soul that one wonders whether the poem has not a definite source in seventeenth-century verse, or whether indeed it should not better be regarded as a mere copy.

In Emily's realm of religious thought, both doubt and belief occupy minor places beside a direct and hostile attack upon the orthodox position. Often with a fine irony, yet with unmistakable intention, she reviled her ancestral God. No one thought of bitterer gibes: even Blake appears vague and indefinite beside her. Thus in reviewing the story of Abraham's obedience to God as related in the story of Isaac, she concludes:

> Moral: with a mastiff
> Manners may prevail.

"Burglar, banker, father," she addresses the diety, in a memorable line hinting at a relation in her subconscious between her father on earth and in heaven. She cannot absolve God for veiling his face behind the ruthlessness of life and nature. "Shame is the tint divine," she concludes, in a remarkable aphorism. God has vainly sought to envelop himself in a pink shawl. A brilliant poem begins with the seemingly innocent and orthodox statement, "I know that he exists." The argument is that God plays hide-and-seek with his creatures.

> But should the play
> Prove piercing earnest,
> Should the glee glaze
> In death's stiff stare,
>
> Would not the fun
> Look too expensive?
> Would not the jest
> Have crawled too far?

Sometimes her irony can be directly insulting, as when she returns God's promise of blessing with an almost gratuitous gibe:

> "I will give," the base proviso.
> Spare your "Crown of Life"!
> Those it fits too fair to wear it—
> Try it on yourself!

The same thinking inspires a poem which commences:

> "Heavenly Father," take to Thee
> The supreme iniquity,

and concludes:

> We apologize to Thee
> For Thine own Duplicity.

In a lyric of ethical implications, she declares that she could easily climb a wall and steal strawberries, but only if she stained her apron and offended a scolding God. It all seems so unfair:

> Oh, dear! I guess if He were a boy
> He'd climb, if He could!

The last phrase, as usual with Emily's highly feminine satire, contains the sharpest sting. The memorable effusion, "Who were the Father and the Son'," clearly states her lifelong resentment at the religious instruction of her girlhood. Even to her childhood she ascribes the withering observation that at least the three Persons of the Trinity cannot possibly be worse than they are described! It will be noted that all her instincts lead her to believe in the reality of God, and equally induce her to doubt the reality of the preposterous monster proposed to her by conventional religion.

Like a lawyer for the plaintiff, she cherishes all available evidence against God's providence. A remarkable poem states that Moses was not fairly used. The same she finds true of Ananias. The snow and frost which the psalmist declared to glorify God she finds to be his disgrace. Of the latter she observes:

> The blond assassin passes on,
> The sun proceeds unmoved
> To measure off another day
> For an approving God.

God, she discovers, is the most colossal of hypocrites: he instructs men to pray, without any intention of answering their prayers. Even as a child, Emily states in one poem, she discovered this supernatural swindle:

> Of course I prayed—
> And did God care?
> He cared as much
> As on the air
> A bird had stamped her foot
> And cried, "Give me!"

She finds that no one really wishes to know God or even to see him, else why do men naturally fear death? A terse and bitter poem on drowning enforces this point. Three times the drowning man rises in his effort to escape:

> The Maker's cordial visage,
>   However good to see,
> Is shunned, we must admit it,
>   Like an adversity.

The whole instruction of the Church displeases her. Like most puritans, she prefers the Old Testament to the New, yet finds the God of the former especially revolting: The Bible, she discovers, is "an antique volume" full of fairy tales and lies. Faith, she scornfully observes, is "a fine invention for gentlemen who see." As for herself, she prefers the microscope of truthful, private observation. Throughout all nature she discovers God's "marauding hand." Life on earth would doubtless have been very tolerable without his uncalled for intervention. The conventional heaven she does not desire, since it suggests to her the dreary puritan sabbath. She has no use for God's "posthumous" medicine; and since she has been no party in any agreement with God, she logically denies his moral jurisdiction over her. Once in a hasty and irate parenthesis she declares of God, "I don't know him." Especially the drumming up of enthusiasm in the pulpit offends her. It is all to no real purpose, and is moreover basically dishonest:

> Much gesture from the pulpit,
> Strong hallelujahs roll—
> Narcotics cannot still the tooth
> That nibbles at the soul.

Such is Emily's vigorous attack on religious orthodoxy, which she finds both morally and intellectually repugnant.

Her many skeptical poems and her relatively few orthodox ones, as well as the total complexion of her work, reveal the essentially religious and spiritual nature of a woman eager for religious experience; but she was as clearly dissatisfied with all churches and creeds. Her own soul and body shaken by an earthly love, she instinctively felt how close this human love stood to the divine and how each in a measure interpreted the other. Both naturally and supernaturally she found a redeemer. A new experience in love obviously resembled for her a conversion in faith. Yet the tradition of the churches offered her only the raw materials. These, refined through a mystical tradition, came ultimately to give to her vexed life some consolation and stability. The story accordingly turns from the failure of the outward and visible churches to the partial success of the inner and spiritual life privately cultivated, in turn not without analogy and reference to familiar doctrines in mysticism. Emily, to use the terminology of her own day, preferred transcendentalism to Christianity. The latter she utilized, only to pass quickly beyond.

4 *THE MYSTIC WAY*

Revolting from the harsh Calvanism of her immediate environment, Emily Dickinson discovered in an amateur and homebred mysticism much of the consolation which her neighbors found in orthodoxy. At the very heart of Christianity, especially in the Fourth Gospel, lay a potent mysticism ultimately oriental. This factor as centuries advanced, however, became overlaid by a Hebrew or a Roman legalistic theology, a rigid ecclesiasticism, a neo-classical morality, and a large number of influences which, operating in unison, subordinated, distorted, and at times actively opposed mysticism within the Church. While it became clear that the two traditions intersected within a certain area, it was still more apparent that in larger areas they remained opposed and suspicious of one another. The Church was founded on the supernatural but not upon the mystical. Distinguished mystics might or might not win sainthood; as a rule they did not. While they generally conformed outwardly to the powerful religious system, their hearts remained elsewhere; and while this system occasionally looked upon even advanced mystics with favor, it not infrequently viewed them with a frown, or even burned them as heretics. Wild as the vagaries of the mystical mind might be, a certain core of mystic tradition became ever clearer; the Western World was not destined to lose a potent vision drawn fundamentally from the East. Protestantism and the Counter Reformation aided its cause. The mystics constituted a powerful minority party within Western thought, intellectually somewhat like the Jews, a part of society yet outside orthodox society. With alliances on the one hand to the metaphysical philosophies and on the other hand to sects of outlawed, vulgar, or turbulent fanatics, the mystics made their strange and indefinite progress through the centuries of European civilization and even through the virgin lands of the New World.

To view Emily in their company raises a challenging problem. As already noted, her mysticism, if the term is rightly used, was homebred and amaturish. She belonged to no mystical sect, is unlikely to have read widely in mystical literature, and was herself, perhaps, even unfamiliar with the word. Mysticism is not, like the Church, an institution; and clearly her own mystic life was founded upon no system of thought or discipline comparable to the theology and practices of the Church. In her dealings with the Church she appears in relation, even though hostile, to an institution; in her participation in mysticism, on the contrary, she appears as an individual secluding herself from society and from tradition in the strictest sense of the word. But all mysticism begins with the personal life. It transcends individualism only as it progresses to its fruition through the personal to the universal. The leading aspects of mysticism prove strangely recurrent. Even though Emily herself may have thought little of her place in one of the most venerable movements in the history of the human spirit, such a role she does play. Her mystical tendencies are the sequel of her break with orthodoxy. She moved, almost imperceptibly to herself, along roads travelled at virtually the same time by leading spirits in America, as Emerson, Thoreau, Melville, and Whitman. Accordingly her mysticism provides a topic in her representation of men rather than in her representation of Man.

She herself recognized the distinction between the Christian theology, with its emphasis upon the atonement through an objectively conceived Savior or Deity, and the mystical vision, with its preference for development and growth within the soul. To Emily as a mystic the brain was "just the weight of God." At an early age she knew that her poetry carried another religious message than that of the Church:

> Not such a strain the church baptizes
> When the last saint goes up the aisles,
> Not such a stanza shakes the silence
> When the redemption strikes her bells.

Bluntly she argued against the conformists:

> Our Lord indeed bore compound witness,
> And yet,
> There's newer, nearer crucifixion
> Than that.

The God whom she addressed was beyond all else a "God of width." She states her difference with the Church most tersely when she observes that her aim is not merely to sight the Savior but to be the saved. The Church commonly accuses mystics of pantheism. Emily plays perilously with this heresy when in describing the glories of the sun at dawn, noon, and evening, and the splendor of the stars, she exclaims that "in the zones of paradise the Lord alone is burned."

The Church bases its teaching upon Scriptures regarded as documents of more or less historical validity. Both the New and Old Testaments are so interpreted. But mysticism is first of all to be distinguished as a state of mind superior to time and place, and hence beyond historical reference. The life and vision which is the mystic's fruition consequently lies, ideally speaking, in a transcendent present only. "Forever is composed of Nows," as Emily writes in one of her most revealing aphorisms. With the same thought she insists that her only news lies in daily bulletins from immortality. "Eternity is now," she declared. And elsewhere:

> Eden is that old-fashioned House
> We dwell in every day.

In the same spirit she insists:

> We felt how neighborly a thing
> Was the invisible.

She holds that "earth is heaven, whether heaven is heaven or not." With similar meaning she declares:

> The Infinite a sudden guest
> Has been assumed to be,
> But how can that stupendous come
> Which never went away?

Truth, in other words, is intensity, sufficiency, the complete aesthetic experience. Truth and eternity are merely full realization, the soul completely poised:

> I stand alive to-day
> To witness to the certainty
>   Of immortality
> Taught me by Time.

The lover, like the poet, shares in this perfect experience. This she indicates in abrupt phrases:

You constituted time.
I deemed eternity
A revelation of yourself.

Mystics throughout the world have enjoyed likening their
vision to the perfected hour of high noon. None states
the case more brilliantly. Emily writes of the enlightened
soul:

> Whose summer set in summer till
> The centuries of June
> And centuries of August fuse
> And consciousness is noon.

Emily grasps all the cardinal features of the mystics'
dream, as its privacy, quietism, anti-intellectualism, uni-
versalism, and super-naturalism. Writing of the mystic's
cherished privacy, she observes:

> A Soul admitted to itself:
> Finite Infinity.

The mystic way belongs to the contemplative rather than
to the active life. Its quietism Emily many times expresses
and defines, often with charming naïvete:

> The grass so little has to do,
>   I wish I were a hay!

The pearl lies within:

> But when all space has been beheld
> And all dominion shown,
> The smallest human heart's extent
> Reduces it to none.

The familiar world of human activity, buying, selling,
arguing, travelling, does not appeal to her.

> Earth at the best
> Is but a scanty toy,
> Bought, carried home
> To Immortality.

Elsewhere she drastically asserts:

> In thy long paradise of light
> No moment will there be
> When I shall long for earthly play
> And mortal company.

And, finally, the soul should be superior to the normal world of time, space and emotion:

> This world and its species
> A too concluded show
> For its absorbed attention's
> Remotest scrutiny.

Here is the familiar platonic image of the physical world as a mere dramatization or expression of the ideal world of the spirit. In such a world death as death loses its pang. Ideals of the mystic in mind, Emily interprets the teaching of Jesus: "He told me death was dead."

With unusual acumen Emily analyzes her own soul and especially those experiences casting light upon her allusive ideal, to be captured, if at all, not by reason but by metaphor. With strange felicity she describes the mystical experience in terms of light. One of her most revealing lyrics begins:

> It's like the light,—
>   A fashionless delight,
> It's like the bee,—
>   A dateless melody.

In short, the experience is like music, but like a music un-contaminated by fashion, in unfailing, deathless, luminous harmony. In another attempt to hint at the mystery she asserts: "Light is sufficient to itself." In a typical poem she states that she would rather guess than know the riddles of the world. Guessing is more fun. Her unrelenting search for an art and an imagery beyond time's contamination shows her comprehensive allegiance to the metaphysical ideal. Moments and aeons become for her almost interchangeable, depending solely upon the sovereignty of mind and imagination. Mere size signifies nothing: the bee is equal to the elephant, the molehill to the mountain. The entire outer world is thus dedicated to relativity. Science must not usurp the upper hand in the mystic's universe. There is a stern but unwritten law of discipline to which the enlightened adhere. As she, with most mystics, asserts, the difficult goal stands remarkably close to the once familiar land of childhood.

Emily nicely contrasts the mystic light, which is truly the light of discipline and not that of chance, with various types of opportunism. The opportunist is at once near the goal of the mystically enlightened and yet subtly removed. He stands, as it were, upon the brink of eternity. The atheist may be closer to the mystic way than the orthodox believer, but he is still deficient. Nature does not know the supernatural light, nor is it disclosed to the genial lover of the casual and the idle. In Emily is nothing of the spiritual anarchy to be found in Whitman. These thoughts receive chiselled expression in her verses:

The dog, the tramp, the atheist,
Stake an entire store
Upon the moment's shallow rim,
While their commuted feet
The torrents of eternity
Do all but inundate.

From what depths of experience Emily drew her insight remains hardly more answerable a question than from what casual reading in the mystical and metaphysical thinkers she enriched her understanding and expression. Although psychology and scholarship are all but impotent today to answer either doubt, something at least may be concluded. Parallels to her thought and phrase occur in virtually all civilized literatures, from China, India, and Persia, to Italy, Germany, France, Spain, and England. Elsewhere in this book have been quoted, for example, several quatrains by the German mystic, Angelus Silesius, closely resembling Emily's poetry in thought and word. It would be equally fruitless to pursue all possible literary sources for her work and to overlook her rightful place in the mystical tradition. She probably read more theological than mystical writers, but the latter were spiritually her closer companions. Emily achieved universality without the aid of prosaic instruction in comparative literature. It is essential that we should see her today beside her peers whom she truly resembles, whether in mysticism or in stoicism, instead of envisaging her in the parochial society of her New England village.

5 *STOICAL DISCIPLINE*

Against the slings and arrows of fortune, of which Emily's tragic lines report so much, she opposes two principal weapons, the spear of a traditional mysticism and the shield of a no less traditional stoicism. Her combative and high-spirited nature led her on the whole to prefer the aggressive weapon. A large number of her poems are inspired by the creative mysticism of which she became so remarkable a mistress. Employing this strategy, she opposed material evil with mental action. She drew from the deepest impulses of the human spirit. Only vaguely aware of her indebtedness, she inherited the most profound spiritual wiles of Indo-European culture, the wisdom of the East and the mystical elements continuously associated in greater or lesser intimacy with Christianity. But this inspiring doctrine and brilliantly allusive fencing was not enough. Her mind might dart spears of burning gold, with a colorful and electrical brilliance keen as the aurora, and yet her heart be still exposed to daggers of pain. A shield was needed in her spiritual armor. After all, Saint Paul, himself a Roman and half a Stoic, demanded both spear and shield in the accoutrement of every man. Emily herself clasped to her arm a shield modelled essentially on the Greco-Roman pattern. It was the tough shield of stoical self-sufficiency and spiritual pride, whose contours are drawn in the uncorroded and metallic words of Epictetus, Cicero, Horace, Seneca, Marcus Aurelius, and Boethius. Once more the ancient

weapon received a new burnish, flashing its lyric gleam
in our eyes.

Among the penetrating comments on Emily's mind in
George Whicher's biography, is the observation that many
of the aphorisms found in her letters during the last years
of her life resemble the grave and weighty sayings of
Marcus Aurelius. The sentences which he quotes, however, resemble the comments of the stoical emperor rather
in their imaginative and eloquent style than in actual
content. Several are of an essentially mystical import. If
we start with the hint given in the biographer's introductory remark, it will be useful to note more closely precisely what poems by Emily come nearest to the Stoical
pattern, and in what measure she follows not merely the
manner but the matter of the sententious ancients.

Stoicism is no more inconsistent with mysticism or
Christianity than the foundations of a house are with its
superstructure. It is true that the profound and oriental
pathos in the utterances of Jesus strongly contrasts with
the cold Roman fortitude preached by the Stoics. But
the essence of Stoicism is no more its mood than its morality. Beside so eclectic a religion as Christianity, it appears
stark and simple. Its core is self-sufficiency, self-discipline,
and self-restraint. The more positive and vastly more
various elements in mysticism or Christianity make Stoicism by comparison almost negative. It should be recalled
that even if certain Stoics violently opposed the rise of
the seemingly vulgar, outrageously romantic, and sentimental religion emanating from Palestine, other Stoics
showed no such hostility, and the Church itself all but
beatified Boethius, who, with Cicero, became one of the
foremost moral preceptors of the so-called Dark Ages.

Neither in the history of thought nor in the poetry and psychology of Emily Dickinson is there any fundamental break between the more romantic and the more classical ways of feeling and thinking.

The aphorisms and poems of the older Stoics have left, it seems, an indelible mark upon Western culture. The power of the tradition has been commensurate with its continuity. The rhymes of Boethius and the minor Stoical poets from the patristic period firmly established the tradition within Christian culture; the rising popularity of Seneca, Horace, and other Romans aided during the Renaissance in confirming, broadening, and perpetuating the same tendency. What Epictetus, Cicero, and Aurelius contributed in prose was supported by analogous offerings of the poets. Virtually throughout Europe, and accordingly in the New World as well, the steady pressure of influence was felt. Grave, philosophical, and didactic poetry, ranging from work of hymn writers to that of secular versifiers, retained unmistakable coloring determined by the long stream originating from a high classical source. Even a literary figure, such as Emily Dickinson, appearing well in advance of her times and virtually contemporary with ourselves, might prove a part of the long procession.

Distressed through her romantic sensibilities, Emily was precisely the person to feel the need of expressions of the Stoical spirit. If relatively few works by the ancient fathers of the movement, and comparatively few by their most direct heirs, actually came to her hand, she was all the more tempted to create such expressions for herself. In a score or more or her poems the Stoical spirit clearly predominates; in many others it supplies a strong undercurrent. As we read the verses by the New England recluse, we may fancy ourselves perusing free translations of the ancients, of their imitators in the early Christian period or during the Renaissance. Here, again, is an instance of her work falling readily into an older cultural pattern, whether or not her own somewhat limited historical perspective envisioned herself in such a light. In any case, she must have recognized the exceptionally strong proportion of didacticism in her lyrics seasoned with a stoical flavor. Much as they express her own spiritual needs, they are also designed for an audience. Even if Christianity crowded Stoicism to the wall and gradually attenuated it as a School of Philosophical thought, while the attitude of the aging Christian world toward mysticism became on the whole friendlier, the modern stoic is likely to be less given to self-expression than to moral generalization. Both represent schools of individualism; but even more than the mystic, the Stoic speaks of and for men, and becomes so much the less concerned with the celebration of Man.

Reference to a few of Emily's poems pertinent in this connection most readily shows the existence and quality of her provincial Stoicism. One such poem has already been cited, the peculiarly Horatian lyric which begins with the classical phrase: "On a columnar self How ample to rely!" The same idea approached from a slightly different angle constitutes the kernel of her lyric: "Superiority to fate Is difficult to learn." A little poem still more deeply embued with the austere Roman spirit begins: "Fate slew him, but he did not drop." Another commences with a boast typical of the stoic pride: "No rack can torture me, My soul's at liberty," and comes full circle in a no less classical conclusion: "Captivity is con-

sciousness, So's liberty." Stoical self-sufficiency rather
than romantic introspection characterizes a number of her
poems. "Who court obtain within himself," is a brief
didactic poem giving a severe expression to the equally
austere doctrine of the ancients. "Know thyself," the
axiom passed down by Socrates to the Stoics, receives
new emphasis in her most Senecan lines:

> Never for society
> One shall seek in vain
> Who his own acquaintance
> Cultivate.

"To know the art within the soul, the soul to entertain,"
is the theme of another lyric. A similar thought attains
poetic form in the aphoristic lines, "My soul accused me."
Here the poet moralizes on the relation of the one to the
many. With an unquestioning arrogance, self-judgment
is pronounced supreme, either to approve or to condemn,
while the judgment of the crowd is declared folly.

An interesting and more psychologically acute variant
of the familiar pattern appears in the poem, "The Malay
took the pearl." Here two characters are contrasted. An
Earl desires a pearl, but fears the dangers of the sea too
keenly to dive for it. A Malay native who neither cares
at heart for the pearl nor fears the perils that invest it,
dives for the prize and secures it as his own. The essence
of his success is his superciliousness to fate. He neither
covets riches nor dreads danger. Such a man is armed in
an impregnable self-sufficiency.

> To gain or be undone,
> Alike to him, one.

No reader can mistake the ultimate inspiration of this poem as drawn from the mines of Stoicism.

Typical emphasis upon the fortitude that is also patience distinguishes the poem commencing, "Through what transports of patience I reached the stolid bliss." Both the language and experience closely resemble those of the Stoics. Many times Emily employs such revealing phrases as "fortitude incarnate." According to the view characteristic of her more ascetic hours, she holds that the chief end in life is not pleasure but one or another form of relief from pain. Such is the sober philosophy of her powerful lines: "The soul asks pleasure first, And then, excuse from pain." No wonder Emily's critic finds her aphorisms resembling those of Marcus Aurelius! Extended demonstration of the view might in pedantic hands prove exhaustive indeed; but sufficient indication has been given to show how rightly she may claim her place among the long procession of writers following the Stoical schools of Greece and Rome. Emily is plentifully eclectic. In more ways than one, both in form and content, she proves surprisingly classical.

6 *ROMANTIC SENSIBILITY*

The contrasted seeds of mysticism and Stoicism took root in Emily's mind not only because of her own personality, but through a congenial ground prepared for them by romantic sensibility. From a remote past ultimately came the two of her most precious heritages. But from her own cultural age she prudently drew what it had best to give. In view of her total accomplishments she is neither a mystic nor a stoic poet, though she undeniably is both mystical and stoical. Neither can her total achievement be labelled or confined by such descriptive epithets as classical, romantic, or modern. In some degree answering to each specification, her total stature can best be described in the phrase shrewdly noted by her biographer: "this was a poet." Nevertheless for a rounded appreciation of her art, recognition of its definitely romantic quality is essential, since no major aspect of her work can be properly grasped while others are disregarded. Her mind was integrated at least to the extent that such qualities as her peculiar mysticism and Stoicism are themselves properly explained only in the light of her romantic environment and soul.

Just as it is true that Emily remains far from wholly romantic, so it is clear that the whole of Romanticism in the historical sense is not to be traced in her own work. Singularly free from many of the qualities of her contemporaries or immediate predecessors, she has little specifically in common with the romantic poets, either of her own time of Tennyson, Browning, Swinburne, and Arnold, or the earlier period of Wordsworth, Coleridge, Keats, and Shelley. That she revolted from a Calvinistic training which she could never wholly forget, by no means makes her a follower of Byron, whose thought thus far, at least, followed hers. That she devoured Scott's tales, in no way allied her creative mind to the acknowledged master of the early nineteenth-century novel. She well knew that she followed her own star. Yet the popularity of her poems when first published, far surpassing the expectations of her editors and publishers, proves her to have been in some respects indigenous to her age. The woman who confessed that, whether with or against her will, she perforce saw "New Englandly," must have known that she also saw to some extent in the light of her age, coincident with the height of the Romantic Movement. Her conscious aims to retain the fresh imagination of childhood, to celebrate the self, to praise nature, and to indulge freely in fancy, stood among the most conspicuous ideals in the literature of her century. Although in the last analysis both her spirit and her style break violently with leading cultural patterns of the century, she was still its child, however naughty and rebellious. In no respect did she comply more closely than in cultivating the richest and most conspicuous vein in romantic thought as a whole, namely the new sensibility.

This sensibility is a mental state both in life and art accentuating the emotional life. Under circumstances which would at any time evoke strong feelings, romantic theory and practice made them still stronger; under conditions which would hardly be expected to elicit emotional responses at all, this sensibility begot an ample flow of sentiment. To the romantics, feeling became a badge of distinction, just as in the Restoration world "wit" was so regarded. Artifice became social practice, or, in Oscar Wilde's words, life imitated art. The familiar story requires no retelling here, but should be at least recalled. Women kneaded their emotions into a refined state of sensitivity, while men affected effeminacy. Soft phrases and melting airs grew to be marks of polite society. It was ingeniously contrived to man's temporary comfort and lasting discomfort that as industrial society grew uglier the personal life grew more refined. This hyper-development of purely personal reactions accompanied the rise of revolutionary individualism and *laissez faire* at the same time that it soothed the old or more conservative regimes into a forgetfulness of social ills known only too well. Radicals and conservatives differed on almost all scores save one, but in that one respect happily concurred. Virtually all men and women loved the poem or novel of sentiment. Sensibility was the cultural slogan of the age. The man of feeling became the man of distinction. Whereas Aristotle, arch-master of the classically minded, advocated the stern elimination of pity and fear, romantic leaders in poetry and fiction founded their art upon a shameless exploitation of these very emotions. Sympathy and terror ruled the imagination of the Revolutionary Age, and even governed much of its practice. Sympathizing with the conditions of the poor, revolutionaries aimed to relieve their poverty and reduce the hard inequalities of opportunity. Conservatives found social utility in focussing in private life the emotionalism indulged by the reformers in their attitudes toward society. Both dwelt with fond sorrow over their own misfortunes. Art and literature evolved into a vast hyperbole of passion; effeminacy, or at best a literature more appropriate to the feminine boudoir than the masculine forum, gained ascendency; sentimental clichés distorted style; in time it grew even more fashionable to pity one's self than to pity the poor; and, finally, with so many forced, affected, and abnormal attitudes disfiguring a fundamentally morbid society, neurotic elements tyrannized in art and poetry, and very nearly dominated all fields of aesthetic expression. Shelley's career perfectly represents the usual course traversed by the romantic author, and—what is more important— epitomizes the evolution of the entire movement. He began by pitying the poor and ended by pitying himself.

All these too-well-known qualities, for better and for worse, inevitably leave some marks on Emily's verse. Though never sentimental to the degree of hypocrisy, nor extravagant to that of vulgarity, she utilizes her age for the best interests of her art, and occasionally commits the inevitable mistakes. In no other period, perhaps, could her writing have acquired such warmth; in none could it have fallen victim to the peculiar lapses which at times prevent it from attaining greatness.

Certain passages are the most conspicuous in betokening her romantic background. A number of her poems offer particularly apt illustration of the romantic tendency to indulge an hyperbole of emotionalism. "Dare you see a soul at the white heat?" is, for example, a lyric admirably in key with its first line. There is a touch of self-consciousness here, not as yet precisely a weakness, but indicative of the true romantic spirit. Certain of Emily's verses show a keen awareness of the physical states of the body induced by extremes of nervous excitement. They are par-

alleled by her account of true poetry itself, which, as told
to the incredulous Colonel Higginson, she identified as
an experience making her "feel physically as though the
top of my head were taken off." Her verse abounds in
trembling, freezing, and burning. The following is indicative:

> It was not frost, for on my flesh
> I felt siroccos crawl,—
> Nor fire, for just my marble feet
> Could keep a chancel cool.

The verse of this tightly restrained New Englander contains many images drawn from volcanic fires. Significantly
enough, volcanoes fascinated and haunted her. Their
"reticent" ways, periodically giving place to violent irrup-
tion, paralleled her own experiences and the behavior of
her friends and family.

> A crater I may contemplate,
> Vesuvius at home.

One commentator has somewhat boldly equated this Vesuvius with the outbreaks of her father's anger. Although
some of her most moving love poems are majestically impersonal, or, in other words, come nearer to Sappho or
Dante than to Browning or Tennyson, a number by no
means of her least impressive pieces are stamped with
marks of peculiarly romantic sensibility. One of her best
known lyrics, "Although I put away his life," is very
much in Mrs. Browning's equally sentimental and realistic
manner. Emily dreams of a connubial happiness that has
failed to be realized. She might have been the faithful
and devoted servant of a husband, sowing the flowers he

preferred, soothing his pains, pushing pebbles from his path, playing his favorite tunes, or fetching him his slippers. The more fanciful of her love hyperboles also tend to follow current patterns. One of her longest lyrics, "I cannot live with you," proves a more concise version of the romantic theme of love and immortality as handled in Rossetti's *Blessed Damosel*. Emily vividly describes her own sensitivity in language unmistakably romantic, as when she asks the rhetorical question why a bird at daybreak

> Should stab my ravished spirit
> With dirks of melody.

She is even critical of her own romantic excesses. In finely romantic diction she voices the fear that her lines may drip overmuch and have too red a glow:

> Sang from the heart, Sire,
> Dipped my beak in it.
> If the tune drip too much,
> Have a tint too red,
>
> Pardon the cochineal,
> Suffer the vermilion,
> Death is the wealth
> Of the poorest bird,

Without losing high merit, Emily's verse occasionally steps down from a high and impersonal dignity to assume the consciously feminine manner especially admired in the mid-nineteenth century. Though the poetry is more than commonplace it is less than universal. The feminine note grows unmistakable. This is heard most clearly in the poem describing a girl's excitement on receiving a message from her lover: "The way I read a letter's thus." In a manner which Samuel Richardson would have approved, she tells how she locks the door, fingers the envelope, glances nervously about to assure herself of absolute privacy, and, finally, reads the words of a lover whose identity she coyly declines to disclose. "I am ashamed, I hide," describes in some detail a bride's bashfulness according to the most familiar romantic ideals. "Wert thou but ill," similarly describes the bride who romantically protests that she will follow her lover through a series of the most trying misfortunes. Much of the sentiment in Emily's nature poetry also betrays the age of sensibility. This shows clearly in a little poem, "To lose, if one can find again." The poet tenderly covers over her garden, hopefully awaiting springtime resurrection, as she confidently expects reunion in heaven with her beloved.

Even though Emily never descends to the baser moods of self-pity, it would be superficial to overlook the romantic poignance which her verses occasionally attain through a tendency in this perilous direction. "I was the slightest in the house," she writes, in an autobiographical poem somewhat exaggerating her own social limitations. With similar self-consciousness she addresses herself as, "the favorite of doom." "Don't put up my thread and needle," she writes, in a tender and genuine piece descriptive of her own hopes and fears in time of dangerous sickness. In several of her poems, as the notable, " 'Twas just this time last year I died," she indulges the melancholy fancy that she is dead, and wonders how gravely or how lightly the family will cherish her memory. Such poetry affords a nice contrast to the same theme treated in the witty and cynical Augustan manner in Swift's remarkable lines, *On the Death of Dean Swift*.

After the unabashed fashion of romantic poets, Emily
at times unhesitatingly exposes the more neurotic features of her personality. Such writing falls into the emphatically self-conscious romantic idiom. With powerful
imagery she describes the gingerly walk of the neurotic
genius through the terrifying jungles of experience: "I
stepped from plank to plank." She discloses the painful
tensions within the pathological soul. In one poem, "The
body grows outside," she describes the soul as hiding
behind the flesh. In another, "Me from Myself to banish,"
she reveals the agonies of the split personality, pains of
which she must herself have been poignantly aware.
Briefly, at least, she probes the tragic abyss of her own
sub-conscious: "The subterranean freight, The cellars of
the soul." In a tragic poem, "Had we our senses," she
suggests that men would become even madder if they saw
clearly into their own madness. Sanity is merely the in-
tegument of an invincible stupidity. Baudelaire himself
could have proposed no more cynical a view.

These various romantic attitudes Emily shares and explores, without as a rule falling victim to the typical ban-
alities of her times, either in meaning or expression. In
other words, her poetry shares the deeper and grander
qualities of her chief contemporaries without sinking for
any length of time into the commonplaces of romantic
thought, sentiment, and style. In this regard it becomes
appropriate to note a few instances in which her language
or her images come close to losing the sharpness and distinction of her own literary personality. "Glee! the great
storm is over!", for instance, approximates the style of the
typical, undistinguished romantic ballad. The rhymes are
commonplace: "land—sand"; "souls—shoals"; "door—

more"; "eye—reply". The meter is painfully regular.
The symbols of sailors shipwrecked or saved hardly
achieve distinction. Longfellow himself might have written the final line: "And only the waves reply." The poem
has a saving irony which is Emily's own and preserves it
from bathos; but it remains extremely romantic. Another
lyric, "Good night! which put the candle out?" is comprised of a series of all-too-familiar romantic images
drawn from home or the sea. In still another, "Forever
cherished be the tree," the image of two robins as two
angels has the customary nineteenth-century extravagance
with little assurance of Emily's better genius. In short,
to her contacts with the Romantic Age she owed a small
but very definite part of her artistic success; and much
the greater part of her by no means fatal faults. Her devotion to "eternity" may have been due in part to a dis-
trust, at times latent and at times highly conscious, of
the dominating fashions of her times. Although she distrusted Romanticism, she was too shrewd to discard it
altogether.

7 *SCIENCE AND POETRY*

Despite a life that outwardly seemed narrow and an excessively shy attitude toward the public, Emily wrote poetry of true breadth. Either we must conclude that she was sensitive to much beyond her personal life, or that this life was itself of extraordinary scope and implications. Although her experiences were all intensely personalized, she knew much of what passed in the intellectual and social world about her. Far from isolating herself from thought and society, she became keenly aware of them. She was an integrator of the world. With what agility this woman who claimed to be without formal education explored her way into realms of philosophy and theology has been shown in earlier pages. Of at least as curious interest is her positive relation to the great ferment of scientific activity taking place about her. In her singularly precise descriptions of nature she approached the development of natural science in America as symbolized by John Audubon; in her equally precise accounts of mental states she anticipated the rise of psychological science under the leadership of William James. A passionate student and believer in the arrival at truth through exact observation of phenomena and equally exact statement, she remarkably reflects some of the leading intellectual tendencies of her times. Although to some extent conscious of this relationship, she can hardly have known the facts clearly. Educated in an intellectual climate which even she must have taken to some extent for granted, she can scarcely have realized the full measure of her indebtedness to her age or her own contribution to it.

Her avowed attitude toward the new science is as interesting to record as difficult to envisage coherently. Somewhat as in the instance of her attitude toward Christianity, she was alternately hostile and cordial. For the pedantry of classifiers she clearly had nothing but scorn, although with the romance of exploration and research this spiritual explorer had instinctive sympathy. Pedantic names especially offend her. Even the common names of flowers she realizes as more or less empty symbols, for she is vitally concerned only with emotional reality struggling for expression in poetry. "If the foolish call them 'flowers' ", she argues, the scientists who merely boast more learned names should offer no objections. Her boldest frontal attack on science is contained in the lines, "Arcturus is his other name,—I'd rather call him star!" Science, she finds, replaces a lively joy in nature with a barren and deadly pedantry. A monster with a glass is busy computing and classifying the blossoms. Butterflies sit erect in cabinets, transfixed with pins. Heaven is turned into zenith. She prefers the old-fashioned religion and the old-fashioned girl, naughty and unregenerate as she may be. The practical applications of science bulk less in her mind than its lamentable weakness to distinguish the subtle human qualities disclosed by daily observation and by the arts. Yet such are to some extent merely lyrical bursts of a satirical petulance. The lyrical poet records the mood of the moment, fearless of inconsistency and innocent of system.

In other of her pieces it appears that science may even yet have some positive meaning for the life of the spirit.

One of her many revealing phrases describes herself as "the scientist of faith." Read in the context of its poem, "The lilac is an ancient shrub", this phrase implies that even in the more spiritual activities of man there is a place for the methods and ideals of pure science. In still another poem she turns to science in complete friendship for spiritual aid in her own quest:

> The chemical conviction
> That naught be lost
> Enable in disaster
> My fractured trust.

Thus, instead of destroying faith in life, science comes to its support. "Gentlemen," she writes in a famous aphorism, may be content to invent faith, but she leans in an emergency upon the microscope. The word "microscope", is, of course, used symbolically; but this is hardly the language of one willing comprehensively to condemn science, or even to prefer it to religion. Emily's partiality for science is owing in great measure to her deep and sincere regard for fact. Beauty, she declares, she has pursued all her life, and in another place she states that beauty and truth are one. In a striking lyric, "A dying tiger moaned for drink", she recounts a number of sufficiently harrowing incidents in the last hours of the beast as she observes them. (There is here, I suspect, either consciously or unconsciously stated, an allegory of one of Emily's lovers.) None of the earlier incidents or feelings vie in importance with the statement in the last line of the poem: "but 'twas The fact that he was dead." In final analysis this poet is captivated by facts. However she begins, she ends a friend of science, not a foe.

Emily holds much the relation to pure science held by
some early American naturalists, more distinguished for
their aesthetic tributes to nature in descriptive art and
literature than for contributions to pure science and scientific theory. She has kinship with a long line of amateur
naturalists; she observes widely, takes little or nothing
from the books, notes details with the utmost precision,
and sharpens the finest instrument within her reach to
record her researches. Almost all Emily's little nature
lyrics have a quality of research. They are field studies,
fresh and unconventional. Sentimental or traditionally
literary views of nature she generally scorns and escapes.
Neither in respect to nature nor society is she the typical
romantic introvert, transforming the seen into objects unknown to reality. When she deals in fancy, she does so
openly and honestly. Her interpretations of outer reality
are exact and capable of deceiving no one. That her
images of nature commonly have an inner and emotional
meaning, by no means invalidates the truthfulness of the
images considered as such. Moreover she takes acute
pleasure in their accuracy. Frequently, as in her impres-
sionistic descriptions of reflections in moving water, the
image may seem fantastic; but this holds merely for the
ill-trained and ultra-conservative, who think of nature
as taught to think of it by books, and who have failed
to look at actuality for themselves. Were they more
honest, they would more often be amazed.

Emily's descriptions of mountains and sunsets, of clouds
and landscapes, are commonly figurative, and, though
fundamentally very faithful, possess a lush verbal imagination foreign to scientific statement. It is in her far
more numerous close-ups of flowers, small animals, birds,

reptiles, and insects that she distinguishes herself most, and best approximates a scientific vision. Since there are literally hundreds of such pieces from her pen, it is unnecessary to specify them in detail. Of more importance is the fact that among these poems are some of her most popular and surprising compositions. Nearly all her readers carry away a vivid memory of her poem on the bird who came down the walk. To Emily we owe an uncannily vivid picture of this bird of unspecified species cutting his angleworm in half and eating him raw, drinking "a dew from a convenient grass," glancing with hurried eyes, and calmly flying away when the observer offers him a crumb. Emily's bird and insect paintings have an astonishing clarity. After reading her pages, one can scarcely see a robin, a jay, a bee, a butterfly, a spider, a beetle, or a worm, without recalling that one has met the same creature in the poet's verses painted on the mind with a more indelible pencil than nature's. Her creatures are not the dull specimens in museum cases, nor the relatively lifeless prisoners of zoological gardens. They move naturally in their habitual settings and their unrestricted tasks. Thus we see every motion of the snake in the grass, until it glides even less in the grass than in our own chilled soul. So precisely does she describe the long sigh of the frog on a summer's day, that we have not only heard the frog as never before; a new psychological or emotional experience has been achieved.

Her inclination to intimate and personal life aids her frequent images from human physiology. In a remarkable poem, "A clock stopped—not the mantel's", she proves how closely she has listened to the beating of the human heart. Her accounts of her own bodily sensations

are equally convincing. She has looked steadily, even if
with frigid limbs, at the sick and dying in their beds,
capturing every significant gesture and expression. Her
imagery grows virtually medical. Several striking lyrics
deal with the medical theme of crises in illness. It should
suffice to quote in part that beginning, "Crisis is a hair."
The description appears to be of an impending stroke of
paralysis:

> Let an instant push,
> Or an atom press,
> Or a circle hesitate
> In circumference,
>
> It may jolt the hand
> That adjusts the hair
> That secures eternity
> From presenting here.

The atomic minuteness of this observation shows as well
as any other feature of Emily's verse her kinship with the
scientific approach.

It seems unnecessary to educe further evidence of her
cordial cooperation with the scientific spirit of her age
by citing her approaches to a field even more congenial
to her own nature, the psychological. Emotional states
she repeatedly describes with uncanny accuracy, as in the
harrowing poem, "After great pain a formal feeling
comes." Not unnaturally her imagery has attracted the
attention of psychologists, and especially of persons familiar with Freudian points of view. Perhaps as notably
as any author of her age, she dissects the heart of the
lover, probing the lover's pains and faithfully recording
his ecstasies. Particularly remarkable are revelations of

the kinship between experience of the earthly and of the heavenly lover, he who loves man or God. In each instance occur much the same symptoms of yearning, dreading, doubting, rejoicing, grieving, despairing, and surrendering. In each occurs the same violent and soulwrenching experience of conversion. Her poetry records these curious adventures of the soul with unflinching fidelity. Very definitely was this woman a bold predecessor of the author of *Varieties of Religious Experience.*

8 *THE SOCIAL SCENE*

The life and reputation of Emily Dickinson easily promote a misconception of her attitude toward people and society. Her emphatic gesture of seclusion, her dread of publicity, her love of nature, and her passionate devotion as poet to themes of love and personal immortality, all lead to the abrupt conclusion that her thinking is altogether personal or metaphysical and that her introspective art is confined to a narrow expression of self. According to this view, one can understand her poetry fully only as one neglects the outer world. Not alone the literary tradition and traditional human quests in religion, science, and philosophy may safely be neglected by the critic, but the entire complex of human society with its characteristic institutions has little or no relevance for her work. The briefest scrutiny, however, shows such a view to be a hasty error of extreme superficiality. Deeply personal and highly individualistic as her thinking is, it by no means loses touch with society. People in the mass and in their public relationships concerned her less, to be sure, than the more intimate chambers of the soul. But the former did concern her. Many romantic writers were actually far more advanced than she in their divorce from social consciousness. Free from the egotistic variety of sentimentality, and, if one of the most elusive, at the same time one of the least evasive of mankind, what she saw she looked at honestly and clearly. If she was not an active member of society, neither was she taken in by it. She saw through its shams more clearly than the sentimental optimist, Whitman, and almost as trenchantly as Ibsen. Although her thirst for the universal discouraged her from any persistent considerations of manners and public affairs, she was far from holding a closed mind to these subjects. Some study of her relations to institutional society, then, should supplement that more extensive consideration of her researches in the private soul.

There is real danger that this salutary alloy in her writing be overlooked. She does not preach the doctrine of the many, as Whitman did, nor does she lean toward any variety of socialistic doctrine, either sentimentally soft or toughly realistic. Because she flourished as an artist in a distinctly virulent phase of capitalistic society, and by virtue of her stubborn individualism seems to constitute almost a grotesque exaggeration of the doctrine of *laissez faire,* the twentieth-century apologist for socialism is tempted to point to her poetry as the morbid swan song of a morbid capitalism. He sees in it a retreat from reality into a metaphysical and religious fog, as well as an apotheosis of the selfish and decadent romantic ways of sexual sublimation. Thus she becomes the apex of all that the socialist most heartily despises. There is some reason to fear that this viewpoint may in the near future temporarily obscure her reputation. In reality it is a doctrinaire and very fallacious viewpoint, a caricature of her actual position. It is true that she turned primarily to the personal rather than to the public life. But on occasion she was keenly objective and socially minded. Just as her descriptive poetry affords an unsurpassingly honest picture of nature, free from romantic sentiment and distortion, so her glimpses of society, however rare, are clear-sighted and on the whole revolutionary. Circumstances over which she had little control made her admittedly a specialist in the personal life. This life, however, has always been lived by man, and however political institutions may change, will always comprise a large part of his existence. No changing tides in public affairs will therefore wash away her major accomplishment. Meanwhile, as a minor part of her achievement her realistic and objective social outlook must not be underestimated or obscured. It is in fact an important and indicative part of her literary character, throwing light into all other chambers of her soul and revealing what manner of woman this singularly fearless and outspoken poet was. Above all, she was no mystagog. The pins which she stuck in God were more than mere playthings or the equipment of a feminine workbasket. They were tipped with poison. Lenin and she might have been much in agreement as to the actual functioning of organized religion.

Entirely apart from the exposition of her own views, the history and general contours of her poetry lend themselves especially well to an economic interpretation. Had Lavinia Dickinson not been covetous of pin money, it is a grave question whether Emily's poetry would be known to a single reader today. And had Lavinia not feared for the safety of her financial interests and so felt it necessary to please her rapacious lawyer, she would presumably never have broken with Mrs. Todd and all of Emily's verse manuscripts would long ago have been published in a single, ably-edited, and scholarly volume. Both our possession of any of the poetry whatsoever and our embarrassment in possessing the poems in a condition so distressing to scholars we owe to economic motives.

The general character of this poetry is that which the social position of the daughters of New England capitalists in the mid-nineteenth century largely determined. Emily's father, scarcely capable of thinking in other than the inhumanly harsh terms of ownership, kept his daughter in his house as men keep bonds in a bank vault. She was his best investment, costing least and yielding highest interest. Her education was curtailed, her circulation in society restricted, her life reduced as far as possible to personal terms. It was rumored in the gossip of the town that at least once she planned a violent escape from her imprisonment. She did not escape in the flesh. Her escape was in the mind, and in some respects more successful than any flight in the body could possibly have been. At the same time that she contrived to love her father, she succeeded in despising the culture which he so completely represented. Remaining at home in Amherst and in America, she put into words destined for posthumous release many a charge of explosives that have since aided in the destruction of the walls once her prison. No social conservative or reactionary has ever confirmed himself in his opinions by reading her verses. And if too few radicals have noted the carefully concealed charges of social dynamite in her poetry, that is their fault, not hers. Time is the test of true friendship, and even an increasingly socialist society must discover in time that Emily Dickinson was at least more its friend than its foe. To the body of *laissez faire* capitalism she clings like the worm to the flesh of Cleopatra, lovingly stinging it to death.

To dwell upon Emily's poetry as propaganda would undoubtedly be farfetched. The primary question pro-

posed is not the political implications of her poems, but
her awareness of society. One may begin with the most
shocking public event in America during Emily's lifetime,
the Civil War. Her position as poet may best be envisaged
here by use of a contrast. The importance of this calamity
for the poetry of Walt Whitman has frequently been remarked. Although he treats the war both realistically and
symbolically, a vague cloud of romantic emotionalism
floated between Whitman and the actualities before him.
Too often he expressed an egotistical reaction rather than
an objective vision. He tells us what he himself felt,
rather than what the men and women immediately concerned felt. His longest elegy on Lincoln is a desperately
subjective poem; many pieces in *Drum Taps* express
sheer war hysteria, wholly divorced from intelligent understanding. Emily approaches such subjects differently,
and both more forcefully and frequently than her critics
have cared to note. "When I was small a woman died,"
is one of the most poignant war elegies in our language.
When placed beside Whitman's famous poems on Lincoln, both "When lilacs last in the dooryard bloomed,"
and "Oh, Captain, My Captain", her work appears remarkably free from vague impressionism or forced sentiment. It is a truer war poem, perhaps, than any that
Whitman ever wrote.

Whitman never condemned war with the drastic language used by Emily, nor penetrated so far into its ethical
sophistries. The woman looked more deeply into war's intrinsic baseness. Whitman was scarcely masculine enough
to have written Emily's quatrain:

> The popular Heart is a cannon first,
> Subsequent a drum;
> Bells for an auxiliary
> And an afterward of rum.

These are sharply etched words for the America of 1860, or for any imperialistic country at any time. "War seems to me an oblique place," Emily once wrote, with an acute sense for its ethical ambiguities. She perceived at the same time the divinely heroic sacrifices of the soldiers and the diabolical forces of the public economy which compelled men like puppets to fight for an invisible Mammon:

> It feels a shame to be alive
> Where men so brave are dead. . . .
> Do we deserve a thing—
> That lives, like dollars, must be piled
> Before we may obtain?

As regards flags, Whitman had many violent emotions and almost no thoughts, whereas Emily had both thoughts and feelings. In one of the most tender and beautiful of her lyrics she writes:

> Flags vex a dying face,
> But the least fan
> Stirred by a friend's hand
> Cools like rain.

With similar thought she observes that flags make a bold sight, but that no true eye ever passed one steadily. In one poem she cries, "Bless God, he went as soldiers!", thus paying her rightful tribute to military valor; but in another she exclaims ironically, "How martial is this place!" and with an unwonted burst of anger declares that had she a gun she would shoot the whole belligerent human race and promptly rise to heaven! Her critical awareness of war, which meant in a very real sense to her the war in which her relatives and friends fought and died, appears in several poems where a military image outweighs the symbolic value which it nominally contains. The first lyric in *Collected Poems,* "Success is counted sweetest", is aimed to voice the psychological notion that we extol most the values beyond our attainment. The avowed conclusion of the lyric is its moral. Actually, the poem owes its power to its image of the defeated and dying soldier who hears in the distance the shouts and rejoicing of the victors. The lyric shows a psychological insight into war questionably equalled in any of Whitman's poems. By contrast, *Drum Taps* skims the surface of its theme. The above poem is far from unique in Emily's collection, although one more example must suffice. "To fight aloud is very brave", owes its strength chiefly to its military imagery, drawn from a cavalry charge.

Emily's poems of social protest are companion pieces to her bitter gibes at orthodox theology. The most ardent nineteenth-century rebel could hardly have stated his position more boldly than she:

> I took my power in my hand
> And went against the world.

With the revolutionary spirit of Jefferson supported by a more seasoned philosophical vision than most thinkers nursed in the eighteenth-century commanded, she observed that, "Revolution is the pod Systems rattle from." On all sides she struck out against the chains binding mankind. Typical of the most radical thinkers of her times, she called schools jails. A poem on the customary

half holiday on Wednesday afternoon commences: "From
all the jails the boys and girls Ecstatically leap", and continues with unequivocal protest against an inhuman system. The adult world itself pleased her no more, not
even that of the railroads and factories, in which her father
played no inconspicuous a role.

> Oh, could we climb where Moses stood
> And view the landscape o'er,
> Not Father's bells, nor factories
> Could scare us any more!

She disliked both trade and imperialism. Thus in one
poem when wishing to express a change for the worse she
likens the alteration to an encroachment of trade upon
a sacrament. In a lyric to be read with regard for critical
overtones, she says that her foreign trade is with the
splendor of evening clouds, not with the stuffs of mer-
chantmen reaped from Oriental lands. Her profits come
from the Yellow Sea of the sunset, not from exploited
orientals. Contrast is inevitably inferred between the lover
of beauty and the lover of wealth. In short, she instinctively hates the pride of the wealthy and the great. Her
entire aim in life is to attain a dignity "passing pomposity."
Assaults on a pompous deity are accompanied by assaults
on pompous men. "Burglar, banker, father", almost certainly refers both to her father on earth and in heaven.
She is sickened by people who "care about careers" and
little else. She is led to exclaim, "How happy is the little
stone", in comparison with such hardened mortals.

In an America blindly striving for sudden riches, certain of her utterances were violently heretical, as, for
example, her declaration, "There is a shame of nobleness

Confronting sudden pelf." Throughout her poetry the word "gentleman" is used with a tart and ironical meaning. Such is the case in her well-known couplet praising the truth of the microscope as opposed to the too facile faith of "gentlemen who see." In a poem full of social bitterness, she notes how easy it is to die not only when nature continues unperturbed, but when trade and commerce flourish, when stocks are quoted high in the market, even though the dead lie among daisies, and when "gentlemen so sprightly Conduct the pleasing scene." For public leaders she has little but rebuke. A crow reminds her of a pompous consul, perhaps of some official whom she remembered meeting in Washington. A faded boy in sallow clothes driving a lonesome cow to pastures of oblivion—such is her figurative representation for a statesman. In a lyric with obvious reference to her own life as repressed by the conventions of a ruling class, she observes, " 'Tis true they shut me in the cold." She found small reason to love the rich. Once she describes life's treasures as parcels which the poor watch as the rich take them from stores. And she had definite sympathy with the poor. "The beggar lad dies early", is a more or less typical romantic poem of social protest. It has only rebuke for "The cruel smiling, bowing world That took its cambric way." Another representative poem of romantic protest, "Upon the gallows hung a wretch", is directed against both capital punishment and the morbid society that permits the depravity of the criminal. On social customs regarding death, Emily also harbors revolutionary opinions. In a realistic aphorism she advises her sentimental contemporaries to "Endow the living with the tears You squander on the dead."

Emily Dickinson listened carefully to preachers from their pulpits and found words to describe them, both cordial and hostile. "He fumbles at your spirit," is a sincere tribute to a leading church orator, while "He preached upon 'breadth' till it argued him narrow", consists of telling satire upon ecclesiastical speciousness. Both poems prove that Emily objectively studied the public aspects of religion, however much her poetry as a rule treats directly with the inner life.

Her objective and social comments deal not only with institutions and classes of men but with individuals critically observed. A few "italic faces", or telling portrait sketches, emphatically vary the more lyrical work which she generally preferred. Most powerful of her portraits is that of the ruthless and successful business man: "A face devoid of love and grace." This merciless attack asserts that the face and a stone thrown at it would at once recognize their common quality. Emily herself casts the stone and precisely hits the mark. "She dealt her pretty words like blades", affords the companion picture of a woman heartless not in public deeds but in private inuendos, "I wish I knew that woman's name", asserts that the poet's hatred of social hypocrites will extend even beyond human burial. She will hate even from the grave. In much lighter vein is the vignette on the woodpecker who with his cap and frill and his industrious quest of worms in wood is recognized by the careful reader as more than a real bird—as a caricature of some academic bookworm whom Emily observed on the streets of her college town.

This woman was no weak social critic. She had her eyes about her. The weakness of individualistic New

England she whimsically epitomized in a single sentence: "Maybe Eden ain't so lonesome As New England used to be!" Her lines on the stars of the American flag show that she had rightly appraised the idealistic movement in transcendental America as contrasted with the materialism dominant in British thought. Her images when merely read for themselves reveal an observer of the world. In one poem, for example, she alludes to floods that have "blotted out the mills", in another, to telegrams from the Civil War battlefront; in a third, to the circumstances of Major André's death and the fashionable customs at Saint James'. In short, much as she tended to concentrate upon the life of the spirit and the problems of personal development, she never directly disparages social effort, as certain later Romantic friends of Fascism have despicably done in bad verse, nor gives aid, direct or indirect, to a blind or indolent defense of the status quo. On the contrary, Emily Dickinson had exceptionally clear social understanding on those few occasions when she cared so to direct her attention. Her poetry, which is no evasion, contains certain fiery particles definitely of tonic value for reformers, if not even for revolutionaries.

PART III

THE POETRY IN ITSELF

1 *A POET'S AESTHETICS*

Thus far the content of Emily's poetry has been reviewed with only supplementary references to its art;
henceforth the whole subject will be approached from the
reverse angle, and the art reviewed with no more than
supplementary references to its content. In the instance
of Emily Dickinson it becomes especially important to
stress the poet's own views on the interrelation of form
and meaning. Highly as she valued art and the imaginative life, she was by no means an aesthete holding art
detached from meaning. No such prolonged analysis as
that of the foregoing pages is required to show her strong
emphasis upon content, for she places a high value on
the emotions and ideas which her lyrics express. In her
mind, life and art are organically related, much as leaf
and flower. To pluck the flower from its leaves is merely
to hasten its death; to detach art from life is a murderous
process of which her imagination was barely capable. She
acknowledges the two factors within her universe; there
is no problem of their confusion. So far are they mutually dependent upon each other, that they cannot even
be wholly segregated for purposes of discussion. The
thinker in either of the fields turns for aid to the other.
Nevertheless, dialectical strategy does invite some division,
and at a given time any critic speaks primarily from the
point of view either of content or of form.

The fortuitous manner in which destiny has delivered
Emily's poetry to the world, as sea treasures casually
washed on wide beaches, has tended to conceal the per-

sistence with which her own mind actually pursued certain well limited fields of thought and experience. That she wrote a few poems about poetry itself is generally known; but small attempt has been made to show how persistently, widely, and profoundly she thought on problems of art and technique. Although largely self-taught, she was well taught; her life refutes that arrogant neo-classical maxim of Ben Jonson, chief Elizabethan dramatist after Shakespeare, who declared that whoever had himself for a teacher had a fool for his master. Jonson, a product of the schools, simply could not conceive the measure of self-discipline attained by such a poet as the most singular heir of the New England puritans. Equally intellectual and self-conscious, she was anything but the natural, spontaneous, and untutored singer for whom the London romantics of the eighteenth century looked so longingly to the provinces. This American provincial by a series of miracles acquired the wisdom of ages. One of the most celebrated pictures today on public exhibition in New England represents a Taoist poet, a woman, walking in the snow; the Sung painting of centuries past unconsciously provides a spiritual portrait of Emily Dickinson; there can be no question of the ripeness of her mind. Shakespeare's "ripeness is all" applies no more adequately to any man or woman, for she contrived her education with aid of the maturing process of experience. Moreover her thoughts on art arise from this body of experience. They are not only practical and pragramatic; they afford an almost inevitable introduction to a discussion of her own poetry. In stating her thoughts on the imagination, on art, and on style, she indicates not only her own ideals but a faithful key to her own practice.

Art was to her the simplest and noblest reality in life. The very content of her poetry is largely concerned with the imaginative faculty from which art springs. She becomes an advocate of the imagination as a way of living. The thirst for beauty seems to her as natural to the mind as thirst for water is to the body. Training may improve art and the artistic sense, but nature has created it. In this sense, science and philosophy are far more the products of education than art and poetry. As she declares in one of her aphorisms: "Estranged from beauty none can be, For beauty is infinity." Her conception of beauty as mother of art is indicated in another maxim: "To see the summer sky Is poetry." Behind all completed works of art, whatever their technical perfection, Emily recognizes an imaginative understanding which is beauty and truth even without formal expression. From this reservoir of the imagination all art flows.

Her mysticism and her homebred metaphysics encouraged her to find virtually a religion in art. Here she discovered a god, having lost the God of the churches. Her poem, "I reckon when I count at all", frankly prefers poetry to heaven, to nature, or to God. "This is a blossom of the brain", another lyric, refers to a poem, or other work of art, as a seed mysteriously fructified within the spirit. A few persons rejoice in it. The wise carry it home, since other flowers, that is, other works of art, may spring from the same source. A lost poem signifies "The funeral of God." In short, Emily in this instance, as elsewhere, specifically makes a god of art.

One of her most cryptic and charming verse aphorisms, "I died for Beauty", states that truth and beauty are one, and further implies that they are alike in being unobtainable in perfection. Translated into a much less poetic form, the aphorism may be taken to propose that much beauty is contained in truth and much truth in beauty. Emily does not mean that philosophy and art are the same, but rather that they have much in common. Thus, according to another poetic maxim, Euclid "looked on beauty". According to Emily art gives a faithful record of experience. In short, to her the meaning of art is generally of great importance. Indeed art's power to record is, by her own words, at least equal to nature's power to create. "The one that could repeat the summer's day were greater than itself", begins a revealing lyric. The ideal world simply is that of beauty and of art. Here her idealistic metaphysics comes into play. To live, it is necessary first to die. True knowledge follows the completion which is death. Count no man beautiful till his death, Emily might have said, in variation of the Greek proverb. So in another poem on the death of Summer, whose funerals are observed by Autumn, she notes that, "Our summer made her light escape Into the beautiful." True beauty is, then, the reality behind the appearances of the physical, where the physical has itself been superseded by the creative power. Other poems strikingly show the degree to which she pushed her neo-platonic idealism. The visible world remains to her merely reality in the bud, to be ripened, disclosed, and revealed solely by the sun of the imagination. This is a familiar idealistic concept and image, to be found also, for example, in William Blake. Emily states the view in her poem, "Essential oils are wrung", where she writes of the rose as "expressed" by the sun. All the world blooms for the human spirit only through the wamth of imagination, the power which in its highest manifestations creates the masterpieces of poetry, music, and painting.

Although Emily's speculations in aesthetics are generally concerned only with essentials in thought and craft, she occasionally glances aside at secondary views or even at popular misconceptions. She perforce knew something of that degenerate and sentimental art especially popular in her own times and known to all times wherein the artist is primarily concerned with offering compensations or substitutes for reality instead of serious expressions of reality. "Make me a picture of the sun", is a playful and an ironical lyric with undercurrent of satirical intention. Deliberately using an imagery befitting the nursery, Emily proposes that we have pictures of the sun on our walls in winter to keep us warm. Let us avoid reality by living in a picture world of undisturbed pleasure and ease! Let us forget the frost, the storms, and the decay of autumn: "Let's play these never come!" Emily not only knew the austere principles of great song; she knew, it seems, the wiles of the tempter who with his specious charms and soft promises is forever driving mankind from art's legitimate paradise.

Emily thought long and hard about her own activity as poet. She knew the painful labors of artistic creation and accepted the burden, with the realization that the true artist wins his chief fame after his own death. And she continually worried about her own work, at bottom believing in it, but never believing in it lightly or thoughtlessly, and forever calling it before the strict bar of her best judgment. A remarkable poem too seldom cited by her critics, "I fit for them", describes her labors as directed entirely to the future. In a dark obscurity she struggles to suit the mind of posterity, enduring a long abstinence that she may create "a purer good for them." She cannot be sure of success, but she has at least enjoyed "The transport of the Aim." In another lyric she asserts that all beauty is painful, yet even so, she wishes to die in its presence. The strict inquisition to which she summoned her own art is witnessed in, "I cautious scanned my little life." This piece states that her life has been an attempt to gather into a barn a harvest available to the future. Has she succeeded, she asks querulously? Has she winnowed the contemporary from the unfading, the local from the universal? Sometimes, she tells us, on going to her barn she imagines it empty. In moments of cynicism and disillusionment, she always puts the question, is her heart in her work? Is it in the barn which love (love of life, or love of lovers) has provided for her? This becomes her ultimate test. Where the heart is, there is the treasure of art also. The one lasting element in human nature proves to be the heart. Poetry comprises the form or spiritual body preserving the divine heart of man long after his physical heart within his mortal body has disintegrated in dust.

With her idealistic faith as her support, Emily emphatically believed in the role of enthusiasm in art. One of her most charming fancies, already quoted in another connection, shows the esteem in which she held this essential factor in the aesthetic experience. "I cannot dance upon my toes," describes a troupe of toe dancers which the poet had somewhere seen. From one angle her account is both worthy of Degas and remarkably close to that great painter's customary cynicism. Emily was not over favorably impressed with the antics of the dancers, which she found often to be awkward, stiff, and affected. Yet she did perceive in their aim a recognition of a quality that the New England arts too often forgot, namely, true ardor. Such *esprite* she had seldom, perhaps, witnessed, and it impressed her. Recognizing a certain puritan austerity as a surface quality of her own verses, she knew also that their reticence quietly held fires far fiercer than any which the ballet dancers had remotely conceived. Within her own soul, she concludes, "It's full as opera!" Emily trusted enthusiasm.

Although her mind commonly thirsted for an ideal truth, dwelling rather on the eternal man than on specific relations between the poet and his readers, she did occasionally glance at the relation of one poet to another and of the poet to his public. "Let books renew of books, But wells of failless ground!" she wrote in an aphorism contrasting the second-rate and derivative author, whose works are a mere tissue of borrowings, with the truly creative artist, who relies primarily on the fresh, unfailing spring of his own inspiration. "The poets light but lamps" snipes from another direction at the same giant of pedantry. This unusually realistic statement of art in action represents poets as matches, soon in themselves burnt out and very properly forgotten. Their value lies not in themselves but in their work, not in the transient spark that began the blaze, but in the light which they have lit. Successive centuries Emily likens to a succession of shades surrounding the inner flame. Each casts its own peculiar refraction from the light within, without the least assurance that any one shade marks an advance over the preceding. Her modest pebble kills the giant of pedantry without the giant being in the least aware that the pebble has been thrown. Emily well knew that although truth is a sword, nothing is so merciful as ignorance. The finest satire is for the initiated only.

Her comments deal with the skill and practice of her art as well as with the fundamental principles of her aesthetics. Although the two are obviously mutually related, experience teaching theory and theory experience, emphasis may properly fall on one or the other side; and throughout the remainder of this discussion attention falls chiefly on the more practical considerations. In the beginning for Emily is the word. Her greatest single contribution to the art of poetry was a rediscovery of a truth, well known to Virgil and to Pindar, that the art of poetry is primarily the craft of bringing the greatest possible weight of meaning to each word used. Poetry is power, and power compression. Consequently Emily handled words as cautiously as though they were slender wires charged with a high voltage of electricity. In a singularly searching aphorism she observes that, if we were fully conscious of the consequences of any word, awe should reduce us to silence. Not even so much as a syllable would be spoken. Because she revered brevity most, she had an almost equal reverence for the individual word and for silence. Her object, declares a brief aphorism, is to speak words in such a manner that they shall rise from death into life. In another piece she says that whenever her words are fluent she knows them to be false. She instinctively distrusts all save her most vigorous economy. "Your thoughts don't have words every day", she confesses in a poem declaring that true poetic inspiration comes rarely. We may speak at any time, but to speak with the intenser truth of art and poetry becomes quite another matter. Even the greatest poet can do that only at rare intervals. Emily dreads lest the fluency of entertaining conversation prove the fatality of true literature.

However shrewd or learned one's strategy may be, the proper word, she holds, comes only by inspiration. " 'Shall I take thee?' the poet said", relates in a brief allegory the nature of the poetic process. It represents the true poet as at once self-critical and inspired. He keenly realizes the difficulty of finding the right word; proposes to himself many possible choices; and only after he has laid aside his labors and his critical debates, does the true one come to him purely by intuition. This poem proceeds directly from Emily's experience. Her manuscripts show that her common practice was to write several choices for certain crucial words, and to wait apparently for days, months, or even years till the final word or decision came. She admirably grasped the place of both labor and inspiration in artistic composition.

That success in art lies ultimately beyond either explanation or appraisal, she several times maintains. "Beauty is not caused, it is", begins one of her trenchant pieces; "The definition of melody is That definition is none", she asserts in another. This conception of the imagination is strongly conditioned by her instinctive tendency toward lyrical form. Massive constructions or systems appeal to her no more in art than in philosophy. She sees reality in sharp flashes of intuition. One of her poems in particular gives a singularly vivid and direct statement of the case: "Glory is that bright tragic thing, That for an instant means Dominion." The poem continues with the observation that the recipient of these occasional visitations of insight often stands among the most unhappy and unrewarded of men.

Because art is at best a mystery, it becomes a fatal folly to pursue it as though it were a science and to make all seem logical and clear. The imagination and emotions contained within it are aroused not by prosaically exact statement but by indirection, by intimation, and by symbol. Here, too, the principle of brevity makes itself felt. In a famous epigram Emily holds that a prairie may best be represented by one clover and one bee, plus revery. With a charming inexactness, she observes as afterthought that revery alone will serve if bees are few. The principle of all highly suggestive poetry, from the ancient Chinese to the modern "Impressionists", cannot be better stated. This vital factor in her own work is likewise indicated in the first line of another very helpful poem: "Tell all the truth but tell it slant." The growth of any truly imaginative conception, she realizes, always owes more to overtones and developments than to its main symbol. She does not minimize meaning; she enriches it with hints and intimations vastly beyond the possibility of merely direct statement. Her art, like that of a great painter, depends on delicate inflections of line, color, and texture. One of her noblest lyrics, "The tint I cannot take is best," expounds and exemplifies this ideal.

Her own style is intimate, realistic, surprising, earnest, flexible, and rich in a dramatic sense for climax. Concerning all these qualities her verse comment proves specific. In her well-known lines, "This was a poet," she defines the best poetry as that casting a new and revealing light upon aspects of life familiarly but too superficially known to all men. Her art never strains for the

grand style, the rhetorical, the baroque, or the artificially
ornate. References to shades in her more somber elegies
on the grave remind us that she shares more in common
with the homely grave-diggers' scene in *Hamlet* than with
Shakespeare's great oratorical harangues gorgeous with
Renaissance aristocratic eloquence. So when she writes of
Elijah's chariot she insists on calling it just a plain wagon.
Her realism bears strong marks of her inherited New
England frugality.

In place of the more specious ornaments of art, she
turns to the basic elements of all emotionally moving
writing. Her poetry, to use her own phrase, again and
again shows "the garment of surprise." "To pile like
thunder to a close," is her maxim for the art of climax,
in life, love, or art, an art which she thoughtfully extols
and assiduously practices. She, too, in her own fashion
believes in deep seriousness, though hardly in Matthew
Arnold's "high seriousness." Her most cherished ideal
is a tragic earnestness conveyed with the fewest possible
words. The thought she expresses most forcefully, though
somewhat indirectly, in the following epigram:

> The words the happy say
> Are paltry melody;
> But those the silent feel
> Are beautiful.

Nevertheless, in nothing will she be rigid or doctrinaire.
"Touch lightly nature's sweet guitar", she advises in another aphorism, praising variety, resilience, and lightness
of touch. Emily, in short, believes in aphorisms, but distrusts all rigorous rules.

The study of the art and technique of her own poems,

the adventure on which the concluding pages of this book are embarked, is, ideally speaking, a vast and intricate enterprise to which her own words afford much the happiest introduction. Emily herself equips us with our compass. As always, her intellect was put to useful service. She thought in order to act. The necessities of poetic composition brought her keen intelligence face to face with certain critical and philosophical problems which she accordingly tackled vigorously and with the brilliance for which she was everywhere distinguished. Emily was far too honest with herself to fail to strive for the goals which her critical insight disclosed. With her own comments, therefore, in mind, one proceeds well fortified to some analysis of the remarkable scope of her poetic attainments considered from the more technical point of view. We shall see at once how well she profited from her own mind's counsel.

2 ART OF THE VERSE EPIGRAM

Too often we are prone to mistake the talent of a second-rate artist confined within a highly restricted field for the force of genius actually or potentially effectual in many fields. In creative genius there is almost always something generous and broad, in a specialized talent, something pedantic and confined. Truly great power, not merely a severe channelling of average powers, is obviously required for major achievement. Outstanding leaders commonly excel in many phases of their art, if not even in more arts than one. Shakespeare wrote the finest lyrics as well as the finest plays, and showed his mastery equally in verse and prose; indeed it is difficult to conceive a form of literary expression beyond his range. Similarly Dürer excelled in all types of painting and drawing. The genius of Beethoven enabled him to conquer the problems of virtually all types of musical composition. Degas was both sculptor and painter. Flourishing in an age especially conducive to versatility, Michelangelo triumphed in nearly all arts. Extreme narrowness within the liberal arts should beget a suspicion of weak powers too carefully husbanded. If we fancy ourselves in the presence of a superior genius but at the same time fail to recognize a display of genuine scope, the probability is that we are either deceived in our initial feeling, or as yet unappreciative of the range of his accomplishments. In the instance of Emily Dickinson the careful reader discovers far greater versatility than appears at first sight. Within a sphere outwardly limited and strangely unShakespearean, her work remains in breadth fascinatingly comparable to Shakespeare's.

Nothing in Emily Dickinson's theory of the principles or techniques of her art can be construed as promoting illiberal narrowness. Her relations to tradition and to posterity, to the past and future of literature, also suggest her range. Although a certain threat to the broadest humanism may be detected in her intense subjectivity, this concerns her social vision rather than the soundness of her artistry. As already seen, this somewhat rigid figure in New England gothic casts about her a surprisingly wide arc of light. Despite her retired life and the severe restrictions which she deliberately placed upon the length and construction of her poems, she attains great sweep and variety. The true scholar in Emily Dickinson differs from the beginner chiefly in his growing awareness of her scope. All phases of her art are highly developed. She proves master of language, word harmony, imagery, and constructive power, and capable of admirable work in widely divergent types of composition. Three types or genres of poetry in particular she made completely her own: the verse epigram, the light or familiar style, and the high-spirited lyric. Most of the spacious territory covered by her modest art may conveniently be triangulated by successive views of these sharply distinguished species of composition. Actually, there is danger that any of her work be misunderstood if the broad compass of it is not fully realized. Her poems must not be read in one spirit, as that belonging to the epigram, the light verse, or the pure lyric of romantic enthusiasm. The reader must be prepared for rapid shifts in his point of view to match the shifts by Emily herself, and to overcome difficulties proceeding naturally from the conditions under which the poems are commonly read, where distinct species of verse jostle each other in bewilderingly rapid succession. The history of critical comment upon her work shows that these errors are actual and not merely theoretical.

Her shortest poems fall into a class by themselves. She is particularly fond of pieces of eight lines, although in many cases these lines are so brief and so arbitrarily arranged on the page that four lines would constitute a better description. Almost all these poems have but two parts or rhymes: aa: bb. At times Emily even compresses her epigram into a single quatrain as presented on the page. Poems of one or two quatrains, in short, constitute virtually the entire bulk of the pieces now under consideration. Her longer compositions share something of the feeling achieved in these shortest ones, since in all her mature writing Emily maintains a high degree of frugality and compression. Moreover, the shortest pieces, remarkable to say, share much of the emotional intensity of her major lyrics or of the charm and wit of her merely light verse. Nevertheless, the octaves and quatrains do constitute a class in themselves. Here the maximum of verbal compression is felt. The poem is virtually contained for the reader within a single sentence or for the speaker within a single breath. Its structure, as Emily conceives it, almost ensures a bilateral symmetry, with the caesura in the center. Poetic ornament or elaboration become virtually impossible in such brief compositions. These are the very atoms of poetry, and Emily may be said to be the most representative of modern poets in that she most successfully reduces poetry to the atom. Here the spirit of the epitaph or inscription is fully achieved; in longer form it becomes either difficult or impossible. Yet even so brief a work has its form and development, its introduction and climax. But it has a pure and severe unity unobtainable elsewhere. This constitutes poetry in its virginal form. The genre proves perfect for the statement of an idea (which gives us the aphorism) or for the evocation of an emotion in its simplest possible state. Here is more than a mere theme, but less than an ingenious development of one or more themes. We have a phrase comparable to the briefest possible song, or to an actual inscription, where each word, syllable, and letter is meticulously measured.

One need not be over-troubled with definition, where, the subject being art, definition remains really impossible, and, above all, where literary history provides the most copious of concrete illustrations. Poetry of this nature is almost completely ubiquitous. How thoroughly traditional Emily's field in this respect is, has been summarily noted in an earlier chapter dealing with her literary analogues, which may easily be educed from China, India, Persia, England, France, and Spain. The subject, however, must be examined more thoroughly, from new angles. Most illustrious of modern names to be associated with the verse epigram is Goethe, whose epigrams, like those by Emily, combine a lyrical warmth with a marmoreal smoothness. Many close and highly suggestive parallels can be traced between the epigrams left by Emily in verse manuscripts, and pieces similarly left by her contemporaries and fellow countrymen, Emerson, Melville, and Thoreau. The chief recent authority in English to whom one naturally turns for real enlightenment in this field is the late Humbert Wolfe, whose translations from the Greek Anthology have often been described as unrivalled, whose translations of the shorter poems of Heine are almost equally distinguished, and who not only translated these materials but wrote attractive pieces of his own in the same genre. Asia has presumably composed the finest epigrams; but the basis of any study in this field, even where the approach of comparative literature is not primarily employed, is unquestionably the foundation for the art firmly laid in the West by the thousand-year accumulation of the Greek Anthology, one of the most delightful and undecaying gatherings of verse ever assembled by mankind. An examination of Emily's technique in her own pieces should be preceded by at least a glance at the congruous achievements of the ancient world, primarily in Greek, but in part also in Latin.

In all the subtler considerations of style, imagery, and content, the ancient Anthology represents the very antithesis of Emily's work and presents perhaps the most formidable evidence that could possibly be advanced against it. The Anthology, the very flower and quintessence of the Greek spirit, is an unrivalled monument to the perfection of humanism and restraint. Life is everywhere depicted in social relationships. Even the epigrams most brilliantly colored by nature imagery prove essentially human, for if the most important allusion is not to the all-too-human gods, it is likely to be to men. Thus a beautifully situated spring is recommended as a pleasant place for a traveller's repose; an attractive hillside affords an ideal meeting ground for shepherds. If the ocean trembles beneath a cliff, it trembles with delight through all its myriad waves at the thought of the goddess who arose from its foam. No magic, beauty, nor charm deflects the epigrams from their normal, sociable, and friendly spirit. They are as strictly contained within the neighborly borders of a sociable humanity as within the reticent confines of a most modest art. There is no religious or metaphysical extravagance, no unnatural or supernatural straining toward the divine. To the old poets the religious world of myth is even more relaxing than the easily accepted world of man. The poems are further conditioned by the custom that they were actually used for inscriptions or written with the requirements of inscription in mind. They are public declarations, not private meditations. Their fastidiously chosen words are such as may be read rapidly under an open sky. Thus they become the practicable currency of poetry, fit for frequent popular quotation. Above all, they are concerned with simple and direct statements regarding the here and now of space and time. The metaphysical idealism of Emily's poetry, with its exalted emotions, far-fetched images and cosmic implications, belongs, then, from one point of view to a totally different domain. The old poets represent a profoundly pagan and secular culture, as Emily represents a deeply Christian or in any case a deeply religious culture. In content there is as great a difference between Simonides or Meleager, leaders in the Greek Anthology, and Emily Dickinson as between Sophocles and Saint Francis. They stand almost at the antipodes of the human world.

Compared with the ancients, Emily explores a vaster though less attractive and engaging sphere of consciousness. But however great may be these differences in content, as artists the new and old meet in close alliance.

Although the classical epigram as a rule lacks the bilateral symmetry so common in Emily's work, it shows many of the formal elements which she also cultivates. The practice of gaining epigrammatic sharpness by special emphasis upon the last line, or even upon the last word, was directly passed on from the Greeks to the Romans, especially Martial, who in turn bequeathed this technical mastery to imitators in the Renaissance, as, for example, to Ben Jonson, chief master of the neo-classical epigram in English during the Elizabethan period, while Jonson in his turn taught that Cavalier Emily Dickinson, the accomplished epigrammatist, Robert Herrick. The sharp, epigrammatic quality of the opening line, the rigorous passages of development, so conspicuous in a brief poem open to microscopic inspection and obviously intended to be memorized, and the high pressure of the poetic atmosphere due to the rigid economy necessarily practiced within so confined a space, are found in both the ancients and the New Englander. Minor devices, as the use of dialogue, question and answer, or sharp dramatic paradox enliven each. Little poems, when skilfully handled, give, like small creatures, an impression of extreme neatness. This is equally true of the best of the Greek work and the best of Emily's. The pithy maxim or the poignant feeling is almost equally successful in old poems and new. Although Emily certainly did not studiously imitate the classics as did Jonson or Herrick, basic principles underlying art and the human mind cause her again and again to follow in the footsteps of the imaginative Greeks. Hence her art, both in character and worth, comes close to theirs; closer than to the masterpieces of her great romantic contemporary and master of the smallest lyrical forms, Heine. The lyrical German, to be sure, stands nearer to her than the Greeks in so far as he was a romanticist and a modern, but Emily emphatically approaches nearer the ancients in her gift for compressing a maximum of thought, feeling, and imagery into a few words highly charged with poetic fire.

Her ability to make substantial poems out of words so few as to indicate only a trifle, appears not merely in those epigrams widely known for a generation, but in many of the most recently published poems. From the latter collection useful illustrations may easily be found. Three from the single section dealing with death will suffice. The following strikingly illustrates her ability to handle imagery, rhythm, and idea in such a manner that deep feeling is conveyed even in so few words:

> It knew no lapse nor diminution,
> But large, serene,
> Glowed on until through dissolution
> It failed from men.

> I could not deem these planetary forces
> Annulled,
> But suffered an exchange of territory
> Or world.

Success in the epigram, as in a short running race, depends largely on getting away to a good start. The epigram above, together with hundreds of Emily's other brief poems, reveals her mastery in this respect. Her skill in writing magnificent first lines for her poems virtually equals Shakespeare's in his Sonnets—at least two of which are paraphrases from the Greek Anthology. Emily's gift in this regard augured excellently for her epigrammatic art.

To convey a mood with the use of such a minimum of materials clearly argues a high degree of power. Moreover in these unassuming masterpieces by Emily Dickinson there seems a total absence of strain or laborious effort. Beauty descends as quietly as a snowfall. A fine instance of this masterly ease occurs in the same group of poems. The little epigram is a sigh arisen from the depths of the soul:

> Gathered into the earth
> And out of story,
> Gathered to that strange fame,
> That lonesome glory
> That hath no omen here
> But awe.

The haunting musical quality of these lines, their freedom from all conventional restrictions, even of the strict requirements of the prose sentence, the complete originality, and the extraordinary emphasis upon the last, breathless word, show how fully Emily controlled her form.

In other elegiac epigrams she retains the freshness and firmness of her art while coming nearer to the traditional decorum of classical epigram writing. This affords an instance:

> Snow, beneath whose chilly softness
> Some that never lay
> Make their first repose this winter,
> I admonish thee
>
> Blanket wealthier the neighbor
> We so new bestow
> Than thine acclimated creature—
> Wilt thou, Russian snow?

In the Greek are epigrams as tender as this, with only minor differences in phrase; as, for instance, in place of the Russian we read the Riphaean snows.

A tiny epigram outside the sphere of the social epitaph helps to indicate that Emily within her brief form commanded the versatility so conspicuous among the ancients. It will be recalled that scarcely a phase of ancient life or thought escapes the finely woven net of the Greek Anthology. Scores of classical epigrams accentuate the feeling for microscopic form by selecting as subject matter bees, crickets, grasshoppers, and similar minute creatures. It is a notable phase of this gem-like art, whether in ancient Greece, medieval Japan, or modern America. Emily also has dozens of such insect poems. They are not slight, and possess a truly exquisite beauty impossible to attain in more extended compositions. This poem contains a history of the bee:

> Upon a lilac sea
> To toss incessantly
>   His plush alarm,
> Who fleeing from the spring
> The spring avenging fling
>   To dooms of balm.

The extraordinary euphony of this piece, the lightness of the sounds at the opening, with the breadth of the vowels in the conclusion, where the voice seems itself dissolved in honey, prove how genuinely microscopic Emily's art became. She did indeed discover a universe within an atom.

Delightful as an anthology would be composed solely of the briefest pieces from Emily Dickinson's works, the economy of criticism rejects extended quotation here. Nevertheless a few of her more celebrated epigrams demand both mention and analysis. Frequently their delicate carving suggests the jeweller's art: the epigram closes with a line or two having the effect of a gem on the rim of a ring. This sharp, epigrammatic pointedness was, as previously noted, a formative principle in the ancient epigrams, notably those by Martial. The art is exhibited by Emily in such a piece as: "My life closed twice before its close," ending with the memorable words: "Parting is all we know of heaven, And all we need of hell," A use of the ending to accentuate the feeling, rather than to embody a pithy and gnomic saying, occurs in many poems, as, for example, in that delicate instance of poetic pathos, "New feet within my garden go." Here the contrast is made between the new generations of the living and the constancy of the seasons themselves. The former ironically remind the poet of her own loss, the latter of the eternal but inhuman patterns of nature:

> And still the pensive spring returns,
> And still the punctual snow!

Emily thoroughly explored the possibilities of design within her little eight line poems. No space was so small to her as to be other than vast. The simplest symmetrical division and that most often employed was to split the octave into two quatrains. But the fine art of balance was by no means exhausted so simply. Even in such small poems, patterns of alternation might be employed. Thus the poem could be divided into four parts, so that parts one and three would have one tone, parts two and four another. This scheme is forcefully used in a remarkable epigram, "Ample make this bed." Parts one and three have a humble, domestic imagery, concerning the daily art of bed making. Parts two and four contain a sublime imagery opening toward immortality. Their bed is the grave, and the grave the portal to eternity. Among Emily's other shrewd devices in poem construction, is her practice of beginning and ending her octaves with the same word, obviously a key word to the poem.

The Greek Anthology was, by the very derivation of its name, a wreath of flowers, and the poets were not hesitant in using flowers as subject matter. Emily, too, realizes the relation between the form of her epigrams and the concise beauty of a blossom. Some of her loveliest epigrams are flower poems; many were actually sent to her neighbors on cards with gifts from her garden. In "South winds jostle them," she contrives to give to her dipodic lines the very movement of the blossom in the breeze. The whole poem is the gesture of a woman picking flowers. The blooms are made the more ethereal by reference to winds, bees, and butterflies, and, finally, to the imaginary goal of the butterflies' journey in the flower haunted Vale of Cashmere. Such materials may not be unusual; they may in themselves seem even banal. But in the hands of a consummate artist they assume life hiterto undreamed. This poem is all motion. There are nine verbs, vigorous and carefully chosen in eight short dimeter lines. The bees, for example, "come, hover, hesitate, drink, and are gone." The poem is a flower of flowers. It does not stand in isolation. Equally terse is the little epigram, "I send two Sunsets". In this instance Emily pleasantly observes that whereas sunsets may be vaster than flowers, they are not held so conveniently in the hand. She hints at the distinction between epics and epigrams.

The latter form is known for its wit as well as for its serious use in the epitaph. Emily's New England humor at times combines the two, as when she writes on the democracy of death. In " 'Tis an honorable thought", she notes that on encountering the thought of the death awaiting all men, she feels like someone lifting his hat to gentlefolk in the street. While pompous tombs and pyramids decay, the poorest man lives on. True gentleness is conferred only by immortality, which belongs to all.—The humor lies here in the contrast between the pompous pretenses of mere celebrities and the modesty of real greatness. Emily deals a clean swift stroke of imaginative irony.

Even in her epitaphs, she introduces a lightness of touch arising from a humor dashed with pathos. This is seen in such a well-known epigram as the lovely poem which begins:

> This quiet Dust was Gentlemen and Ladies
> And Lads and Girls;
> Was laughter and ability and sighing,
> And frocks and curls. . . .

The lines remind one of that exquisitely unassuming Greek epigram on the singing girl by Callimachus: "The daughters of the Samians often require Crethis the teller of tales, who knew pretty games, sweetest of workfellows, ever talking; but she sleeps here the sleep to which they all must come." The brevity of the epigrammatic form permits a lightness of touch not capturable elsewhere. Its supreme difficulties were to the daring Emily merely a supreme challenge.

The most astonishing feature of Emily's epigrams, wherein she surpasses the Greek and suggests the Orientals, is her ability to create an impression of vastness by the use of only a score of words. Within the scope of four or eight lines she gives most imaginative expression to illimitable thoughts and spaces. Nothing in nature is so expansive as to discourage this epigrammatist. Sky, sea, and mountains become her home. Her poems on mountains prove in this respect especially noteworthy. From her window she pondered musingly while looking at the Pelham hills, over which, as seen from Amherst, the sun arose. "The mountains grow unnoticed", is an octave with calm and unsurpassable sublimity. Less serene and profound, but more brilliant, is the epigram "Ah, Teneriffe!" where in eight lines she gives a passionately personal account of the huge volcanic mountain sheathed in ice. Other poets have labored long romantic accounts of great mountains, as Byron, Coleridge, Wordsworth, and Shelley. Their lines seem almost dull and diffuse beside Emily's octave. Theirs' diminish with long inspection, whereas her uncanny little view enlarges itself to vast proportions within the mind.

Vastness and magic together play their part in a number of her most successful epigrams. In "Lightly stepped a yellow star", she describes the moon and stars with subtly veiled reference to her father's dining room. The moon is the lamp, the stars are the candles, and God is, as often, represented by her father. The poem is almost equally humorous, magical, and sublime. Her famous octave on the hummingbird proves no less allusive. "A Route of

evanescence," plays delightfully with the contrast between the size of the hummingbird and the vast migration
ascribed to it. The bird's presence is perceived by the
gentle vibration of a blossom on a bush. What can be
the cause of this almost unperceivable occurrence? Doubtless the mail from Tunis, the poet answers! Here in a
single epigram Emily toys most successfully with the scale
of size, from the immeasurably large to the immeasurably
small.

All epigrams thus far mentioned are octaves, by far
her favorite form. To achieve comparable results in the
simple quatrain, was obviously still more difficult, but she
at times made the attempt, usually with good results. Instances of the realization of genuine poetry in the quatrain
may be seen in, "To the staunch dust we safe commit
thee", and, "We never know we go when we are going."
True, some of Emily's epigrams, both longer and briefer,
fall short of great poetry, as do a large number in the
Greek Anthology or in any other extensive collection.
Undeniably she left unsuccessful fragments and trifles,
together with verse jottings not intended for publication
and of use merely to herself. Her briefest poems are at
times no more than light whimsies, quite without serious
emotional or imaginative substance. A considerable number of her short pieces are didactic. Among them are
dictionary poems, redefining abstractions, of worth chiefly
in supplying the reader with bricks from which to construct Emily's philosophy of life. In this instance, as
already mentioned, they may possess biographical value
while falling considerably short of high aesthetic value.
These qualifications notwithstanding, there remain at least
a hundred verse epigrams from Emily's hand which show

not only the quintessence of her art but the highest reaches of which this traditional form proves capable. They disclose how deeply Emily studied the varied possibilities of the genre.

3 *LIGHTER VEIN*

The range of Emily's achievement is most clearly measured by the extremes to which she is fond of going in her chief poems, shifting between light verse and the most intense lyricism. The general surface of her poetry becomes almost confusing, as in her books it appears indiscriminately dotted, like a Christmas tree lit with many colored bulbs, with poems of the most widely different emotional complexion. As a result, her critics show considerable disagreement. One of her biographers places special emphasis upon her charming light verse, for which he appears to have a marked preference, and warns against the danger of taking her too seriously. Another tends to overlook the light or even the humorous side, stressing instead her poems of the most fervent or romantic ardor. Obviously, everyone is entitled to his preferences; but the happiest reader will be the one who enjoys the most poems and best recognizes the opposite poles to which her spirit led her. Her writing at least becomes the more accessible in that her practices remain even in these contrasted fields wholly customary and orthodox. On one side of her genius Emily is an almost ideal exponent of the well established tradition of light verse, on the other side, of the purest lyricism. Just as her long and diligent pursuit of the verse epigram brings her directly in line with one of the oldest and most firmly grounded traditions in poetry, her inclinations to the lightly amusing and the rhapsodically ecstatic place her upon two of the main thoroughfares of poetry. To envisage her work in these comprehensive terms is to relieve it of the false stigma of eccentricity and to make it more approachable and more fully intelligible. It is to lift it from abscure byways to the broad highways of poetic expression.

Light verse as a conception is broad rather than indefinite. By the term is not properly meant the poetry of hilarious humor, downright parody or travesty, indignant satire, nonsense verse, or juvenile rhymes. Among its leading qualities are charm and grace, possibly with civility, and certainly with the capacity to entertain. It is a poetry observing a mean, avoiding equally the descent to mere triviality or the ascent to emotional heights. Its observance of a mean and its preference for a firm though cheerfully held control, usually the instinctive attitude of a well-trained mind and personality, made such verse one of the favorite types in the classical world. Especially as that world in its later stages attained the mature plane of ripe culture and sophistication, light verse grew one of the most natural modes of expression. In this manner is the style perfected by Theocritus in his Sicilian Eclogue, and by Horace and the larger number of the epistolary Romans. Although the aristocracies of the eighteenth-century Augustan period at times appeared to limit light verse to *vers de société,* this merely witnesses the peculiar limitations of the age. In the broader sense, light verse is ubiquitous. By no means all its finest practitioners even in the eighteenth century itself were courtly writers. One of the leading masters of true light verse in English, William Cowper, whose work we shall have occasion presently to note in some detail, is, sociologically considered, emphatically a spokesman for the Middle Class.

A large number of Emily's poems fall nicely within this category; to miss their charm in vain search for emotional heights which they do not attempt, or to miss their grace through failure to grasp the familiar aesthetic principles on which they are grounded, constitute most unfortunate errors. Their perfection of form and phrase becomes all the more accessible because none of this visible comeliness is obscured by overwhelming emotions.

By different roads she reaches this pleasant, inland country too seldom explored or enjoyed by readers of the strenuous years of the mid-twentieth century. Although capable, with Pascal, of thoughts that flame with passion, she frequently follows the guidance of an intellect bent merely on pleasing tours of curiosity. Not only does she take calm excursions through the inner and the outer worlds; she reports these expeditions of an amused intellect in verse of a type familiar enough in the broader annals of literature but not too well known to the romantic nineteenth century. "A thought went up my mind today", proves, for instance, one of her best known and most widely quoted poems, and remains nevertheless almost unique for its complete pianissimo. The lines give not the slightest suggestion of emotional stress. Emily is merely curious about her own mind. That she is able to investigate anything so intimately a part of herself with such complete absence of tremor, warmth, or self-consciousness, is really remarkable. She studies herself wholly objectively, with as little feeling as though her mind were some shell picked up on a beach in the South Seas. The poem is exquisite. Its total lack of an emotional climax or conclusion becomes one of its most novel characteristics. The last lines describe a thought passing lightly in and out of the consciousness, leaving not the slightest trace.

It just reminded me—'twas all—
And came my way no more.

The little masterpiece makes abiding art out of the utterly casual. The mastery lies above all in the lightness of touch. Emily can smite the chords of passion in truly withering words, or banish feelings in favor of the most placid observations. Each condition serves almost equally the interests of her art.

Psychological description characterizes a large number of her verses; description of nature a still greater proportion. Although some of her poems rich in nature imagery are clearly symbolical, ranking among her most impassioned and lyrical compositions, others are much reduced in emotional tone by their subject matter from natural history. Many of the poems on landscape and most of those on flowers, animals, birds, and insects, preserve a distinct lightness of touch. Some are humorous; others have gentle humor mixed with an equally delicate pathos. The numerous pieces clearly fashioned to the meridian of the child's mind may possess something of the naive excitement of childhood's fancy but nothing of the depths of mature seriousness and passion. A few references easily indicate the range within these lesser but yet artistically important provinces of her art.

As a match for the psychological, "A thought went up my mind today", might be chosen the remarkably literal and frank nature description, "At half-past three a single bird." The latter piece gives a dry, circumstantial yet delightful account of the movement of the dawn. The same theme inspires numerous other of Emily's works. "The fingers of the light," for example, the first poem in *Bolts of Melody,* affords an equally graceful but more fanciful

account of the same phenomenon. The poem is anything
but a rhapsody. In much the same detached spirit Emily
paints the various hours of the day and seasons of the
year. A delightful little poem, "Glass was the street, in
tinsel peril . . ." is comparable to the most informal and sociable of Dutch genre paintings. The lines describe gleam-
ing ice and vibrations of boys' sleds as they shoot past.

Emily's preference for the least pompous and imposing
of nature's creatures helps to reduce the tension of many
of her verses almost to a minimum. There are the score
of poems on bees, a remarkable piece on a beetle, and
little vignettes on thirty or forty of these minor species.
Occasionally, to be sure, she extracts strong emotions
from her minute particles, as in her magical lyric, "The
murmur of a bee"; more often she rests content with a
lesser ambition. "A single clover plank Was all that
saved a bee", provides a more representative example.
In "Two butterflies went out at noon", the poet's verses
rejoice in a lightness almost equal to that of the gay
dancers of the air themselves. "Bee, I'm expecting you",
is an epistle from a fly to a bee; epistolary verse could
hardly be lighter—or more delectable. Emily had special
fondness for the dandelion, generally regarded by poets
as a gay weed unworthy of note, though mentioned by
her under the resounding name, Leontodon. She toyed
with the thought of meeting Leontodon in heaven. Even
its ephemeral manifestion in the seed calls her to poetry
as delicate as the winged seeds themselves:

> Its little ether hood
> Doth sit upon its head—
> The millinery supple
> Of the sagacious God.

Since Emily's gift of fancy has been elsewhere discussed in these pages, recapitulation is unnecessary. Nevertheless, her many poems of wholly released and irresponsible imagination are always well worth remembering and should be recalled here. As an example especially useful in a review of her light verse may be cited, "The wind tapped like a tired man," where Emily imagines the breeze as an invisible guest whom she receives politely in her room, shows to a chair, and presently feels to be mysteriously passing out the door. The highly fanciful "Pigmy seraphs gone astray", a tribute to the colorful pansy, offers a comparison with her more imaginative and slightly more emotional account of the humming-bird in, "A route of evanescence."

In all her nature poems falling within the category of light verse, her work strangely resembles in spirit and distinction the products in the same field of the already-mentioned Augustan, William Cowper. He, too, was a recluse, a mystic, a quietist, a nature lover, and a master of almost impeccable taste within this particular sphere. He may lack that sterner greatness and more effectual spirituality possessed by the genius from New England, but in the lighter field the two prove close companions. The lesser birds and beasts attracted Cowper's tender and sincere love, winning from him lines naturally marked by the taste of his own century, yet also stamped with a genuineness and refinement shared only by the most felicitous poets of all periods including mid-nineteenth century America.

Emily, like Cowper,—who wrote a popular poem on the debate between the nose and the spectacles—is not above a few very successful efforts in what may properly be called society verse. If not truly representative, these do at least betray an important phase of her literary character. "The parasol is the umbrella's daughter And associates with a fan", is just such a trifle as British authors of *vers de société* would have delighted to have written for well over a hundred years before Emily picked up her humorous pen.

More significant for her mind and art as a whole is her fondness for dealing neither in heightened emotions nor with materials fundamentally non-emotional, but in those delicately suspended moods and moments when the emotional life is not dead but sleeping. Emily studied that most allusive of themes, an emotional truce or calm. In spheres of the feelings it resembles a fog wholly veiling a landscape of great potential excitement and beauty—such fog as doggedly clings to New England shores at Gloucester, Portland, and Mount Desert. The resultant expressions are light verse of an uncommonly subtle and even profound quality. As specimen may be cited, "A stagnant pleasure like a pool," where Emily analyzes the precise tone of a quiet not so ultimate as to be unapproachable to invading storms. Such is one of her most refined types of achievement in light verse.

Finally, she turns to light verse in the familiar jesting mood in which Hamlet indulged while in the graveyard near Elsinor, the mood of bantering away grief, holding it at arm's length with mirth. Here Emily deliberately probed depths of her own soul.

> The truth I do not dare to know
> I muffle with a jest.

This is the tragedy of the clown. A little way along this

route, and we are still in the realms of comedy and light verse. Then, while scarcely aware, the path crosses the frontier into tragedy, and we discover ourselves, where Emily also stood, upon the summits.

4 *LYRIC SPIRIT*

Although both the lyric itself as a literary form and Emily Dickinson's notable mastery of it might easily be thought too obvious to warrant comment, on closer inspection such proves not to be the case. The popular conception of the lyric is peculiarly loose, so that the term must really be redefined for each serious discussion, while Emily's success in this genre, though brilliant, applies to her work less widely than might at first be supposed. The major outlines of the problem are unmistakable, but some analysis in this important field should clarify the overall view of her achievement.

The broadest interpretation of the lyric as virtually any short poem, especially if written in stanzaic form, has little real utility, and chiefly serves to warn us of the lax and sterile condition of popular literary criticism. Terms in literature have at best not one thousandth of the edge possessed by tools of modern science. Many highly reputed authors have discussed the term in such an apologetic manner as to indicate their singularly casual use of it. This, for instance, became the case in Palgrave's preface to his celebrated anthology, where that venerable scholar implies that critical terminology in the ancient world was still firm and significant, whereas in the vague realm of romantic criticism no such precision can be expected. Palgrave broadly asserts that all the poems in his collection are to be regarded as lyrics, while he admits that the word has lost the greater part of its meaning. For the present argument it becomes almost equally profitable to note what is and what is not signified by the word. The verse aphorisms and poems comprising a large part of those pieces by Emily Dickinson just examined under the heading of the epigram, as well as her distinctly light verse and descriptive pieces, comprising altogether more than half her total work, are much better excluded from the category of the true lyric.

This species of verse may for the present be described as a short euphonious poem peculiarly appropriate to musical setting, concentrated in theme and emotional in tone. It is the poetry of lyrical afflatus, of the highly condensed and intensified expression of feeling. As partner to the heightened emotional pitch, the imagination itself is accelerated to a degree impracticable and impossible to maintain through a long composition. The lyric presents a domain of free and uninhibited feeling, where ecstasy and grief, aspiration and affection, play their strongest roles. This conception of the lyric is actually, of course, a most familiar one, though criticism too commonly relaxes into less definite and more lenient interpretations. We compromise with the values ideally signified partly to include under a flattering term minor versifiers in reality incapable of genuinely lyrical composition. For the lyric is the most deceiving of all poetic forms, in that it proves at once most tempting and most difficult. Many are called by "the lyric cry," and few chosen. Popular song and rhyme only speciously resemble an achievement soaring far above them. The true lyric is the fountain or the spire, lifted slenderly beyond the common surface or level lands of achievement. This is the pinnacle of poetry, within sight of all and reach of few. Its masters are the special favorites of mankind, as Sappho, Catullus, Petrarch, Villon, Burns, Keats, Heine, Baude-

laire, and Verlaine. By virtue of her peculiar contribution, Emily Dickinson lays just claim to stand among
them.

Not only is Emily's contribution to the lyric unusual
in quality; a surprisingly large part of her work lies outside of this category on more scores than have yet been
mentioned. Not all her long poems in stanzaic form outwardly resembling lyrics are properly so described. Her
analytic temperament leads her to an intellectual type
of writing alien to the lyric spirit. Such a piece as, "I
measure every grief I meet With analytic eyes", is representative of a large proportion of her compositions. A
penetrating, dignified, and tragic work, it can by no means
be described as an ideal lyric, but rather as a poetical
meditation.

In her use of two of the most important reservoirs of
inspiration for the lyric, Emily unhappily stood at considerable disadvantage. In a sense she was severely frustrated both in her religion and her courtships, in her love
for God and man. Although the result proved in neither
case desperate, and even shows Emily transcending her
difficulties, the height to which her poetry rose was not
in any customary sense of the words dedicated either to
religious or human love. In the usual sense she writes
very few hymns either of praise or of passion. While
occasionally bowing to orthodox religion, partly because
she appreciated imaginatively much that lay beyond her
realm of belief, quite by herself she found a sufficient
substitute for the usual religious consolation in her mysticism. Similarly, she proves almost equally unorthodox
in love. Passion she hardly experienced as by far the
greater number of the masters of poetry and art have

experienced it. Her victory lay in a transubstantiation of her unhappy human love into a metaphysical love. She dreamed of reunion in heaven, in eternity, or merely in the world of the ideal. Some of her best poems on love remain remarkably noncommittal on the subject. Thus "I had been hungry all the years", presumably, though not certainly, deals with a human passion. It remains quite possible to interpret the poem in a much more domestic light. Where Emily is franker and fuller in her love poems, she tends to lose the finest distinction of her poetic imagination, to forfeit her originality, and to fall back to some extent upon current romantic taste. "I cannot live without you", has been one of her most widely admired poems, but it is definitely Victorian. The likeness here to Rossetti has already been noticed. This is not the Emily Dickinson who will last best. Another dated poem, fairly elaborate for Emily and rather dubious in its aesthetic merit, is her pathetic and almost sentimental effusion, "Although I put his life away An ornament too grand." These lines of footless supposition relate how Emily might have attended to the humblest domestic wishes of her lover had the two been so happy as to be married. The great Emily is not here.

Without any predisposition as to the characteristics of the poems otherwise than that they should be striking and representative specimens of her true and inspired lyricism, let us select a score of pieces for close examination. Many of these are universally known, and the group would seem to be sufficiently large to give a fair cross section of her lyric art without the inconvenience of being over long. Of these it will be found that six are—at least so far as all outward and visible signs are concerned—pure nature lyrics. Three deal primarily with death. Two may best be described as psychological studies. Only two are frankly love poems, and these, dealing with immortality, have a distinctly metaphysical quality. The two remaining pieces defy simple classification, but admirably exhibit certain strengthening features in Emily's lyric art derived from her sense for dramatic climax, irony, contrast, and suspense. In order to give a firmer body of reference, it will be worth while to name and briefly describe these outstanding but representative lyrics.

As restitution for a lost religious faith, whose lack denied Emily the opportunity to write great religious or devotional lyrics, the rich imagery bequeathed to her by romantic tradition offered a symbolism and an emotional orchestration based on nature. A large number of her finest and most moving lyrics belong in this class. There is her biblically inspired litany of praise for the inexpressible glories of nature: "Bring me the sunset in a cup." Most entrancing of her lyrics is, "The gentian weaves her fringes", the little poem which ends with the magical blessing in the name of the bee, the butterfly, and the breeze. "The murmur of a bee", deals with the witchcraft of nature. It is one of her most magical and ecstatic songs. "These are the days when birds come back", treats exquisitely with the sacrament of autumn. Like all the preceding poems, it is essentially a hymn to nature. The inspiration is purely musical, purely lyrical. A much slighter poem with a stanzaic rhetoric clearly derived from musical analogues, "How mighty the wind must feel morns", if not a masterpiece, remains thoroughly typical of Emily's felicitous lyricism.

Her essentially metaphysical lyrics in an elevated and

austere manner disclose her greatest power. Among such pieces is, "Behind me dips Eternity", a hymn-like lyric in the melodic measures of the Latin chants by Saint Thomas Aquinas, a masterpiece that, so far as I am aware, has not as yet been reduced to those ultimate auctions of the mind of man, the anthologies. "It's like the light", achieves the distinction of being one of the most delightfully elusive of mystical hymns, whereas, "This dust and its feature", provides an extraordinary conjunction of intellectual clarity and mystical vision. Stanza by stanza it mounts from the human to the divine. "Under the light, yet under", is one of the most vivid of Emily's otherworldly visions, while, finally, with its grave and mysterious dignity, "Four trees upon a solitary acre", exhibits her full mastery of a solemn, andante measure.

It has already been argued in this book that Emily ranks among the poets most successful in deriving supreme art from the theme of death. In her hands the epigram became the epitaph with the glow and the lift of a lyrical ardor. But by no means all her great poems on death are epigrams. Schumann never composed a sadder or a lovelier song than Emily's, "Tie the strings of my life, my Lord", which quaintly depicts her ride to immortality. "Safe in their alabaster chambers", has the wonderful, musical euphony of a purest lyricism. No words of praise or appreciation, of exposition or analysis, can do the faintest justice to the recently recovered elegy that begins:

> Fortitude incarnate
> Here is laid away
> In the swift partitions
> Of the awful sea.

All such poems are stamped with the authentic lyric seal.

In certain happy instances Emily is not merely the intellectual psychologist or even the poetical psychologist; her power of exact observation becomes magically wedded to her deepest lyricism. A complete and wholly inspired investiture of lyric symbolism, music and language covers the naked strength of her acute analysis. Emily makes herself fully at home in such writing. Whatever the imagery, the content is intensely introspective. Such obtains in two incontestably major pieces, "There is a certain slant of light On winter afternoons", and "After great pain a formal feeling comes." The profoundly emotional quality of these compositions preserves them for the truest lyricism.

Rarely does Emily attempt the narrative lyric, or lyrical ballad; but the sharper, less romantic and more Elizabethan form, the dramatic lyric, she achieves often. Her philosophy instructed her to trust in mental action, in daring mental action, and even in a species of seraphic gambling. She believed in taking desperate chances in playing dice where the stakes were nothing less serious than the soul. This attitude confers a fine and spirited sharpness upon many of her lyrics which determines their outstanding quality. Such becomes the case with her ecstatic poem, " 'Tis so much joy! 'Tis so much joy!" assuredly a genuine lyric cry. Drama also means suspense, a psychological condition animating many of Emily's most dramatic songs. The quality appears clearly in, "Before the ice is on the pools," a hymn to an unnamed and as yet unfulfilled fate, where the entire emotion remains suspended in expectancy. It is one of the authentic hallmarks of the Amherst poet.

The most distinguished and least sentimental of her love lyrics are those which deal with her lover in heaven. They are, then, elegies as well as love poems, and songs of death as well as of passion. Remembering the mystical and metaphysical constructions placed by Emily upon death, it is immediately seen how rich and complex the thought and feeling of this group of lyrics becomes. They are not love poems in the manner of Sappho, Catullus, Villon, or Burns, but in a manner that Emily made peculiarly her own. Many as are her poems on love, surely none are more purely lyrical than "A wife at daybreak I shall be", and "Title divine is mine", two pieces exemplifying all the observations above. They afford an admirable index to the inspiration and imagination of Emily's lyricism. Yet even briefer material satisfactorily condenses the essence of her idealistic and metaphysical conception of the meaning of love as inspiration for her brilliant lyricism. Four lines from the poem, "While it is alive, until death touches it", give the clue to her genius in this regard:

> Love is like life, merely longer;
> Love is like death, daring the grave;
> Love is the fellow of the resurrection
> Scooping up the dust and chanting "Live!"

On the foregoing evidence, it may be concluded that her finest lyrics are among her most clearly transcendental poems.

5 _IMAGE AND STATEMENT_

The different types of poetry which Emily wrote, as epigram, light verse, and emotional lyric, to a certain extent define her aims and reveal the means employed to achieve them. But no approach as broad as this, dealing with her general strategy, comes to close grips with her art. The most intimate and detailed view of an artist is always the study of his technique. So far as any disclosure is possible, this reveals the inner workings and organism of his art, the veins, fibres, and tissues of which the body of his work is made. Since the technical problems of poetry fall commonly under four major headings, namely, imagery, composition or pattern, sound values, and the craftsmanship of words themselves, it is with a view of these phases of her art that the present analysis of Emily Dickinson's poetry concludes. As the most easily accessible of the four fields, that of imagery invites first attention.

"Tell all the truth, but tell it slant", Emily observes in one of her poems. Indirection becomes the cardinal strategy in imaginative expression, and indirection is imagery. The basic requirements of expression call for image or symbol, since this is the prime tool whereby the poet achieves universality. Life requires that all men have in a certain sense unique experiences within the concrete world. We have our singular adventures with love, death, happiness, and grief. By exercise of his imagination the poet discovers symbols which unite men by giving them as far as possible a common experience within the imaginative realm and thus proving to them their common share in actuality. In art, as in religion, the symbol is the outstanding device for unification. Moreover, the lyric poet in particular is prone to a legitimate and useful egoism leading him to see both nature and human life as images and as analogues to his own experience. He generalizes this experience by projecting it in metaphorical terms of nature and humanity, which entitles us to describe the greater part of his poetry as fundamentally imagistic. Always exceptionally shrewd in her analysis of herself and her work, Emily well understood these principles. In a remarkable aphorism she declares: "Nature is what we know But have no art to say." A more thoroughly subjective view can hardly be imagined. Another of her statements even more drastically and emotionally presents her eogtistical feeling for the world: "Creation seemed a mighty crack To make me visible." Much of nature and of life signifies to her no more than the materials for self-expression. This centering upon self happily does not imply any vulgar or socially destructive egoism, since Emily as a poet cherishes her personal experience only in so far as it enables her to speak with the most vital and intimate words of the general Man, of those primary feelings that all have in common.

Because Emily's poetry presents nature largely from a subjective point of view, using it as a common reservoir of imagery, the discussion of her attitude toward nature has been reserved for the present review of her imagery rather than segregated in a corner by itself. A good deal has been written by her critics on her relations with nature, though but little of this commentary, I think, warrants repeating. The superficial phase of the imagery lies on the surface for the casual passerby to snatch up, the real meanings lie below, shrouded in the symbolical content. Nevertheless, a brief statement of her occasional regard for nature in itself should prove not only a helpful digression but an indication of the subordinate place which such an objective attitude held in her thinking. The accuracy of her observations of the external world has already been noted as evidence of her kinship with the flourishing state of natural science in the nineteenth century in general and in her contemporary pioneering America in particular. Obviously, she loved nature dearly and found in it her chief preoccupation, apart from her reading and writing. She worked long hours in her garden and spent still longer periods in the enjoyment of natural scenes. The impersonality of nature pleased and comforted her, beset as she was in the human world with personal situations that stirred her too deeply, bored her too heavily, or made her difficult and shy. In particular she loved nature's silences. "My best acquaintances are those With whom I spoke no word", proves in this regard one of her more significant poems. Elsewhere she charmingly observes:

> We introduce ourselves
> To planets and to flowers,
> But with ourselves have etiquettes,
> Embarrassments and awes.

In her memorable lyric on her ride to immortality, she begs the Lord to stay his wagon just long enough for her to kiss goodbye to the hills. It is her last mortal wish. Such impersonal grandeur as that of the Northern Lights deeply stirs her romantic spirit, as may be seen by her lines: "Of bronze and blaze the north tonight!" Yet she proves much too inveterate a realist and skeptic to overlook the shortcomings of her friend, Nature. In all her work there is only one thoroughly sentimental and conventional view of the subject, an early poem, "Nature, the gentlest mother".

As she grew older, she became only too well acquainted with the underside of nature's divinity. In a little poem describing a storm, "The clouds their backs together laid", she concludes it a blessing to be safe in the tomb, beyond reach of nature's temper and vengeance. Her discerning poem, "The sky is low, the clouds are mean", tells how Nature is at times caught "without her diadem". In another epigram of equally sharp commentary, "Sweet is the swamp, with its secrets", she remarks that the snake is summer's treason, the very essence of guile. Remembering how affectionately Emily loved summer, one sees how sharply she was injured. Thus her views of Nature were skeptical, paradoxical, and inconclusive. The reality was man. Nature appeared to her as a kind of ghostly and fascinating riddle, far more attractive than the Calvinist God, but less appealing than humanity itself. Her creed was the subduing or conquest of nature, not by science but by art. In last analysis nature proved to be a mystery, like a fog, or like that elusive flower, the Indian Pipe, exquisite but cold. She symbolized it as an unfathomable well, where men stood precariously at the brink. Such is the conclusion of her notable lyric: "What mystery pervades a well!" The last lines assert that the scientists, who talk most glibly of her, know her least; that she is indeed baffling, since we all know her less the nearer to her we come. In the end, then, nature fails us. We must turn to man, or to the divine. In a revealing poem that might well conclude this entire argument, Emily observes, "I thought that nature was enough Till human nature came", and then proceeds to assert that she was similarly absorbed by human nature until that, too, passed into the spiritual. Experience she envisages, therefore, as a confluence of streams. Nature flows into the larger river of humanity, while humanity in turn flows into the divine. Each experience serves as a symbol to mirror the greater that lies beyond.

Any prolonged excursion into Emily's view of nature, accordingly, returns the investigator to the field of her imagery, since nature is transmuted by art into an all-too-human image of humanity and of God. Imagery becomes natural to poets, who are, as Emily says, "prone to periphrases". In the little elegy, "There's something quieter than sleep", she remarks that while homely neighbors on the occasion of the death of a child speak of "the early dead," the poet entertains some such airy image as that "the birds have gone." Her invisible soul becomes visible and articulate through imagery. Her typical wedding of image and emotion may be seen in so representative a poem as, "There's a certain slant of light On winter afternoons", when she depicts her own grief by reference to the austere face of a declining landscape. Even her more social and objective verse turns to nature imagery, as when in the quatrain, "His bill an auger is", she seems to depict a woodpecker while in actuality she describes a pedantic Amherst scholar. Of course she makes no discrimination between the natural and the artificial as reservoir for imagery. "You've seen balloons set, haven't you?", tenderly allegorizes the life of a tragically fallen human being as the story of a balloon, cooly watched by heartless eyes of boys and tradesmen. Her strong tendency to draw by powerful symbolism even the major aspects of social life into the crucible of the personality appears strikingly in her lines, "I never hear the word 'escape' ". Here she admits that she cannot hear of prisons liberated by soldiers without feeling a tug at the bars of her own life. With all industrious imagists, she at times even fuses the natural and the artificial, as in her many poems dealing with ships tossing on rough seas. Her spiritual imagery of boats and seas closely parallels the work of a great American genius, already mentioned in this book, and perhaps more closely akin to her in her spirit and in symbolism than any other person, the transcendental painter, Albert Pinkham Ryder. Ryder wrote poems for his tiny, lyrical, and spiritual pictures that read like the work of an awkward and clumsy Emily, a man who proper medium was not words. He easily said in pictures what she hardly more felicitously said in rhyme.

With the philosophical basis of her imagery already sketched, and the application of her art in its more technical aspects still to be considered, the question of the actual quantity of the imagery arises. The great majority of the poems are strongly figurative, and so are almost all of her masterpieces, though a certain number of poems by no means failures are direct statements strikingly devoid of imagery. Emily can be as economical and frugal in this respect as in any other. Her realistic interest in nature and especially in psychology on occasions dictated notably bare productions. But the scarcity of such poems only serves to emphasize the unusual importance of figurative speech in her work as a whole.

The outstanding quality of Emily Dickinson's imagery is boldness amounting almost to the fantastic. These fancies account for some of the happiest moments in her poetry, a pleasure and an inspiration to review. Imagery proves the most flashing sword wielded by her genius. "Split the lark and you'll find the music", is the startling beginning of one of her poems. Another, devoted to the sunset, commences, "The largest fire ever known Occurs each afternoon." The sky led Emily to peculiarly fantastic and splendid figures. Evening clouds she once describes as "listless elephants" straggling down the horizons. In a brilliant account of a thunderstorm, she writes of "the doom's electric moccasin". A singularly bold and effective image declares that "shadows hold their breath." Emily depicts a sparrow in the act of flying off a branch. Alarmed by human approach the bird:

> Turned easy in the sky
> As a familiar saddle
> And rode immensity.

The success of all these figures depends on their insolent boldness.

In many cases her radical and experimental imagery points the way to modern impressionism. Her fancy accepts the challenge flung it by the more fantastic aspects of nature. She achieves a new realism by faithfully recording some of the more evanescent and startling of appearances. Colorful reflections around a wharf suggest to her fantastic sailors. The little poem begins, "Where ships of purple gently toss On seas of daffodil." Storms and high wind lead her to animism and allegory. Thus one poem begins: "It sounded as if the streets were running, And then the streets stood still". In another, about a high wind, Emily beheld, "a strange mob of panting trees", and saw the fences fleeing away. A spirited image in a similar piece describes the dust scooping itself like hands and throwing away the road. The lightning resembles here a yellow beak, there a livid claw. An equally bold figure represents a bee as tossing upon a lilac sea. Finally, a distinctly modernistic poem paints a peculiarly elusive sunset as defined "By menaces of amethyst And moats of mystery."

The outstanding quality of all the foregoing images is their new brave style and hence their power to please through stimulation and surprise. But Emily is capable of rising to rarer heights not unjustly called sublime, where her image is still bold yet perfectly wedded to its lofty theme by a strange and baffling fitness. The image becomes even more moving than startling. Such is the case in her quiet and profound poem on mountains: "The mountain sat upon the plain", where the last lines boldly and magnificently describe the mountain as grandfather of the days and ancestor of the dawn. The emotional force of this imagery is indescribable.

Having no commerce whatsoever with conservative poetic diction, Emily often uses harsh, realistic figures with admirable effect. Thus in her vigorous lyric, "The soul selects her own society," this amazing woman leading a sheltered life in a small town a century ago writes of closing the valves of her attention. A vigorous poem on lovers uses an equally unsentimental diction. "We parted", she writes, "as the central flint Were parted with an adz". She is also, of course, famous for her homely imagery, all the more remarkable as being often employed in elevated poems. A celebrated instance occurs in her already quoted lines in a storm, "It sounded as if the streets were running". This piece ends with a singularly audacious figure: Nature is seen "in a beryl apron mixing fresher air". Such metaphors from housewifery help to confirm the poet's complete sincerity and to enhance the intimacy of her lines. Her imagination appears at its representative best when combining the homely with the lofty, as when in a little poem on the evening wind, "She sweeps with many-colored brooms And leaves the shreds behind", the poet concludes with a twilight scene where "brooms fade softly into stars". Such imagery is veritably Dickinsonian; no other poet achieves it. Behind it stand the many complexities and contradictions in Emily's own soul.

With her sturdy amateur psychology she vigorously probes her own imaginative processes. A highly original lyric begins: "A drunkard cannot meet a cork Without a reverie". This leads Emily to the observation that she, long intoxicated with summer, cannot encounter a fly in January without dreaming of her mid-summer happiness. The shrewd analogy virtually constitutes a metaphor. Emily never hesitates in combining, or, as the common phrase goes, in mixing even her bravest images with the utmost audacity. The well-stored mental riches of the imagination she several times likens to a mine. Of course all gold elsewhere, whether on the feathers of a bird or on coins, is ephemeral. Contrasting the casual with the permanent, she observes, "Mines have no wings."

More than once it becomes apparent that in the discovery of her images Emily has relied upon her dreams. The poem, "Wild nights! Wild nights!" is compact of Freudian figures. Such become even clearer in her long dream poem telling of her meeting with an enchanted snake in her bedroom: "In winter, in my room". How far she relied on her subconscious, however, cannot well be determined.

Finally, of outstanding importance in the power of her imagery is its terseness. Many of her finest figures depend upon a single word or the briefest possible phrase. The study of her metaphors merges with the study of her words themselves. Thus she describes the life of a mushroom as, "Shorter than a snake's delay, And fleeter than a tare". Allegorizing her own power to put much into little, she abruptly exclaims: "Bring me the sunset in a cup". The word "accent" in the line, "The accent of a coming foot", proves the most inspired moment of her thrilling poem, "Elysium is as far as to The very nearest room". Lastly, consider the force of the words "Numidian" and "roasted", in the following phrase:

> The butterfly's Numidian gown
> With spots of burnish roasted on.

Emily's terse and condensed metaphors are fairly seared upon our imagination. No phase of detail or technique has she studied more carefully or mastered more completely. All true poets are imagists, but Emily is so in a most searching sense of the word. If any one in modern times has paralleled her, it must be one among the profound French symbolists of a generation after her own. The American "Imagist" school of the present century, led by such writers as Amy Lowell, John Gould Fletcher, "H.D.", and Ezra Pound, seems superficial beside her. Her success is chiefly owing to the fact that the most brilliant pinnacles of her imagery rest upon the singularly firm foundation of her metaphysics of poetry.

6 *FORM AND PATTERN*

Though some readers fail to perceive the profound value of imagery in poetry, supposing metaphors to be mere ornaments, excrescences, and idle embellishments as a rule better omitted than included in serious verse, all immediately acknowledge the value of form. Any art work is at once perceived to be an organism whose strength and beauty alike depend largely upon shapeliness. The work must have contours fairly easily discernible, a clear beginning, middle, and end. We instinctively look for movement, development, and climax, for balance and proportion. Awkward digressions and superfluities of all sorts offend us. Construction must be at bottom economical and efficient, no matter how richly decorated the surface of the work may remain. These are clearly not requirements of any one school of art instead of another, no more classical, for example, than romantic. Although Emily Dickinson usually described poetry in terms of its emotional effect, we cannot for a moment suppose that either in her own work or in her reading she overlooked the value of formal beauty. Her brief lyrics resemble a collection of exquisite specimens of Chinese pottery from the Sung or some earlier periods, each in itself a studied work of admirable aesthetic proportions.

An analysis of the subject within bearable length must be highly selective. The following paragraphs deal with only a few brilliant and outstanding achievements illustrating the constructive principles most dear to her. To begin with, her poems at once give us the feeling that they are alive and on the move, going toward a fixed destination, and arriving at their goal. They have progress and development. A few instances of her planning in this regard throw light upon her methods. There is little or nothing esoteric in her sense of form. Unlike her genius for metaphor, it bears small relation to her metaphysics, unless we care to make ingenious deductions from her Keatsian statement that truth and beauty are essentially one. The miracle is not in the conception but in the technique, not in the theory, but in the execution. Simple formulae for progression, surprise, balance, repetition, climax, emphasis, acceleration, and retard, she merely applies more skilfully than other writers. The study of her finesse in this field should prove as rewarding as that of her more boldly inventive achievements elsewhere.

One of the simplest and at the same time effective developments of form is to be seen in her poem, "The heart asks pleasure first." Here a series of end-stopped lines proceed on the most logical march. The heart in turn asks for pleasure, excuse from pain, anodynes to deaden suffering, the gift of sleep, and permission to die. Deep feeling has seldom been so greatly enhanced by a logical construction. That the form was no accident, appears from other pieces on the same plan. Thus another octave, "Finding is the first act", carries the reader through five progressive stages of disillusionment, described as the five acts of a Euripedian tragedy. Emily's frugality is nowhere more happily evidenced than in this poem giving the germ of a five act drama in eight lines.

The reader easily recalls other examples of perspicuous formal development. Thus the little lyric, "At half-past three a single bird", describes the dawn in three acts or stanzas. The second begins, "At half-past four" . . ., the third and last, "At half-past seven . . .". Progression is meticulous. This formula is several times repeated, as in the poem, "If you were coming in the fall". The argument is that the lover's loss would be supportable if a time for reunion were possible, at either an earlier or a later date. The conclusion is that neither time nor eternity carries any assurance. The second stanza suggests reunion within a year, the third, within centuries, the fourth, in a future life. The final stanza ends with a comprehensive rejection. A similar pattern, accompanied with equal irony, gives firmness to the more elaborate and better known lyric, "I cannot live with you". Here the fourth stanza begins, "I cannot die with you", the sixth, "Nor could I rise with you", the tenth, "And were you lost", the eleventh, "And were you saved". Again, all questions are negatively answered, so that a final stanza ends the poem with despair. An even more logical structure confers firmness upon an already mentioned poem of three stanzas, "This dust and its feature", which in turn rejects the body, the mind, and the world as objects for attention of a soul already possessed of eternity.

One of the most perfectly and dramatically constructed of Emily's lyrics with deliberate deception begins, "I know that he exists". This little piece of sixteen brief lines in dipodic dimeter, commencing with the statement that the poet knows God to exist, ends with the most surprising and amazing blasphemy. The first half of the poem seems an orthodox and reasonable apology for God. Then, line by line, we awaken to the fact that the poet has thus far been deceiving us, and that her actual views of the Divine are anything but complimentary. The first line has the piety of heaven, the last the poison of hell. The lyric provides a revelation in reverse. Other of her poems are, of course, almost as skilfully built upon contrasting themes. So in "Her final summer was it", Emily poignantly compares the nervous haste of a woman who expects shortly to die with the leisurely, carefree optimism of her family suspecting no such calamity. The two concluding lines deftly summarize the whole poem, like the knot that ties the two ends of a ribbon.

Some lyrics are constructed less upon a feeling for progress or development than on a sense for balance and proportion. The planning of "Ample make this bed" has already been noted, with the first half of each of the two quatrains devoted to the bed of sleep, the second half of each to the bed of death. The two somewht longer stanzas of which the lyric, "I gained it so", is composed are most artfully contrasted. The first describes the difficulty of attaining happiness, the second the impossibility of holding it. The climax is the silence between the stanzas. One winds up the thread which the other unravels. A much more intricate balancing occurs in the lines, " 'Twas later when the summer went Than when the cricket came". This octave describes the "esoteric time" kept by the cricket, who comes earlier than the departure of summer and leaves sooner than the arrival of winter. Virtually every word throughout the octave has been balanced with another. Emily, who calls the song of the cricket a "pathetic pendulum", creates a pendulum movement in the weaving of her own words. Form and sense are exquisitely interwoven in a music and a pattern as delicate as the cricket's cry. The verses are microscopically perfect.

In poems as brief as Emily's the rhetorical patterns easily become constructive features in the major organism of the work. She has a number of poetical exercises as consciously planned as any conceits of Renaissance or baroque verse. A high degree of verbal "conceit" becomes at once recognizable in the little lyric commencing,

> If recollecting were forgetting,
>   Then I remember not;
> And if forgetting, recollecting,
>   How near I had forgot!

The poem continues in much the same vein, the theme being set by the opening lines. "Had I known that the first was the last", is a much more original and poignant lyric playing upon these opening words and their concepts. Other secondary themes are also artfully interwoven. Few poets have ever packed so much sagacious rhetoric into eight lines. Emily's fondness for rhetorical balance, of course, is often expressed in a part of a poem rather than in the whole. The final stanza of her well-known lyric with the metaphor of the gun, "My life had stood a loaded gun", illustrates this type of artistry:

> Though I than he may longer live,
> He longer must than I,
> For I have but the art to kill—
> Without the power to die.

Less pervasive patterns are also worth noticing, as certain structural uses of repetition. Some of these devices, used to enhance pathos, she presumably derived from Robert Burns. The lyric, "I should not dare to leave my friend", proves a singularly rigid organism. Among its structural elements are repetitions in the second line of each stanza. In the first stanza the word "because" is used twice, in the second, "hunted", in the third, the phrase, "so sure I'd come", in the fourth and last, the phrase, "since breaking then." Here the structure is almost too rigid for the literary lyric, though it lends itself admirably to the song. A subtler and more artful use of similar repetition occurs in the typical and very beautiful piece, "Softened by Time's consummate plush". Here the third line in each of the two stanzas reads, "That threatened childhood's citadel". Although the line is the same, the context greatly alters the meaning, much to the benefit of the poem's progress and to the reader's pleasure.

An inveterate lover of active verbs, Emily sometimes gained structure for her work by beginning each line of a poem with this most animated of the parts of speech. Her tiny and perfect little epigram, "Bind me, I still can sing", contains twenty-three words, seven of them verbs. Of the total of six lines, five begin with verbs, and notable words they are, too: "bind", "banish", "strikes", "slay", and "chanting". In "How many times these low feet staggered", six out of a total of twelve lines commence with verbs, all but one of them monosyllables. Three other of the lines begin with vigorous adverbs in an inverted position in the sentence, and still another with an important adjective. The lyric, "Taken from men this morning", is constructed on the same vigorous pattern, a trochaic rhythm adding its accent to the strong beginning of each line. The first stanza sufficiently illustrates its movement.

> Taken from men this morning,
> Carried by men to-day,
> Met by the gods with banners
> Who marshalled her away.

Emily possessed an almost inexhaustible fund of structural devices, no one of which she ever cultivated to excess or reduced to affectation or mannerism. It is this fecundity of invention that has made her inimitable. She enjoyed beginning and ending a poem with the same word or phrase. Thus the octave, "Pain has an element of blank", ends with the word "pain"; "Prayer is the little implement", ends with "prayer"; while the lyric "I'm wife; I've finished that", concludes, "I'm wife! stop there!"; and the first two words of the first and last line in, " 'Twas love, not me", are the same.

Emily is magnificent in her attack; the opening line of her poem is almost sure to be striking. Thus some of the most rewarding pages of her books are the index of first lines, which may be read with pleasure in themselves, and afford the final answers to any discussion of this problem. She also mastered an art even more difficult than that of beginning, namely, the art of ending. Sometimes her last lines are admirable summaries. Thus in her poem on books and reading, "Unto my books so good to turn", she concludes with the observation that her library enamors in prospect, and satisfies when actually read. The conclusion is a graceful summary of the whole. Her finer lyric powerfully beginning, "I had been hungry all the years", ends with equal conciseness:

> Nor was I hungry; so I found
> That hunger was a way
> Of persons outside windows,
> The entering takes away.

Mere summary is relatively tame and prosaic. With her indefatigable zest for epigram and for reticence, Emily commonly reserved the entire point of a lyric for the last few words. Time and time again the true meaning and enthusiasm of a poem are reserved for the last line or even its last syllable. So one of her poems on drowning, "Three times we parted, Breath and I", ends with the totally surprising line: "And I stood up and lived". The pith of a lyric apparently dedicated to the description of a storm, "The wind took up the northern things", is disclosed, like the kernel of a nut, only with the utterly unexpected and delightful observation: "How intimate, a tempest past, The transport of a bird!" The meaning awaits the last word. Another poem descriptive of a tempest, "There came a wind like a bugle", leaves us with the sustaining thought: "How much can come and much can go, And yet abide the world!" A pleasant epigram on the brook and the sea ends with the conclusive words of the latter, "Come now!" When ending on a strong optimistic note poems are likely to refer to the day, the noon, or the sun. So the little rhyme, "Our share of night to bear", terminates with the line, "Afterwards —day!" The impressive lyric, "If pain for peace prepares", has for its last words, "Noons blaze!" A poem on love's constancy, even beyond the grave, "The Look of Thee, what is it like?" leaves us with the vigorous line, "That thou shalt be the same". The ironical value of her lyric, "Could I but ride indefinite", where Emily wishes for herself the freedom and license of a bee, is only made clear by the closing words: "So captives deem Who tight in dungeons are". A poem full of frustration and skepticism, "Taking up the fair ideal Just to cast her down", comes abruptly to its happy ending with emphasis upon the revealing word, "smile". Finally, "Hearts, we will

forget him", an octave much like some of Heine's most
dramatic love songs, at the end totally reverses the artful
deception of the opening words. The surprising last
words, which carry the weight of the whole lyric, are:
"Haste! lest while you're lagging, I may remember him!"

Sometimes the final line provides neither the summary
nor essential meaning of the poem, but nevertheless gives
great emphasis. The exclamation, "That's all", at the end
of a stanza in the masterful lyric, "The murmur of a
bee", affords an instance of emotional emphasis achieved
by the simplest colloquialism. Metaphorical emphasis is
attained in the line, "And zero at the bone", admirably
ending Emily's poem of terror addressed to a snake, "A
narrow fellow in the grass". Her splendidly morbid lyric
on a corpse, " 'Twas warm at first like us", concludes with
the superb phrase, "And dropped like adamant". To appreciate the unique force of the word "adamant" here, it
becomes necessary, of course, to read the entire lyric.
"Porcelain" is similarly used as conclusion for the be-
guiling poem, "Death is the supple suitor". Emily never
strives for a grandiloquent last line, after the popular
fashion of Victorian verse-rhetoricians, but achieves the
desired result easily and lyrically. The conclusion flows
naturally from what precedes it. This may be seen in the
quaint little poem, "These are the signs to Nature's inn",
which ends, "The purple in the East is set And in North,
the star." Finally, in "Read, sweet, how others strove",
emphasis for the last word is achieved by using a word
in an unusual and yet a magically appropriate sense. This
lyric depicts hard struggle in life and death, which somehow terminates happily. The soul has at last, "Passed out
of record Into renown'" If Emily is a true poet through-

out the greater part of each poem, she is likely to become a super-poet in her finale.

Some of her most beautiful and assured conclusions are not crescendos. Here is, perhaps, the ultimate and classical mastery. Her magical poem, "Great streets of silence led away To neighborhoods of pause", comes to rest with the completely quiet and appropriate phrase,. "For period exhaled". Even for her light verse she discovers gentle and fitting conclusions definitely lighter than the body of the poem itself. Her fanciful rhyme on the hospitality which she once extended to the ghost of a breeze ends with the words, "And I became alone". Although Emily obviously possessed abundant passion, it should be equally clear to her readers that she acquired an extraordinary mastery of organic and expressive form, a mastery hardly to be excelled in the ancient classics themselves. On these technical matters she may be conversing pleasantly in Elysium with Sappho.

7 *HARMONY OF WORDS*

Although Emily Dickinson's poems may be as remarkable in the structure of their sense as in the structure of their sound, in the latter capacity her contributions to English poetry are more conspicuous. General principles of design, at least so far as the Western World is concerned, have apparently changed in only slight degree through many centuries. Emily introduced a certain abruptness, nervous tension, and conciseness hardly paralleled in English, but these are largely qualities of style and, broadly speaking, her compositional form reveals little fundamentally new. Though each poem introduces shades of variation hitherto unknown, such nuances are too elusive for repetition, even by the poet herself. Her form is generally without mannerism or eccentricity. In the matter of aural values, or the music of verse, these conditions become reversed. Technical devises in sound value are commonly used by her in a manner that for the nineteenth century definitely constituted innovation. Chief among her favorite discoveries of this nature is the imperfect rhyme, long known but never before practiced so extensively and intelligently. In rhythm and in euphony she is possibly less original, but hardly less inspired. Her poems cover in each respect a surprising range of achievement, their nuances in the field proving almost inexhaustible. Hence her frequent use of conventional hymn metres should not mislead a casual observer into supposing her to be relatively barren in appeal to the ear. The present inquiry examines her substantial attainments under the three general headings of her innovations in rhyme, her metres and rhythms, and her deft treatment of language sounds.

To the pedantic mind or ear, an imperfect rhyme constitutes a bad rhyme, an evidence of slovenly workmanship, and there is simply nothing more to be said. The sound and sober craftsmanship of the age of Chaucer demanded that all rhymed verse be correctly rhymed. One could write alliterative verse without rhyme, but the trained poets believed that where rhyme was used, it should be used thoroughly. Advancing centuries witnessed deviations from the conservative norm, sometimes, as in much popular verse, due to carelessness, sometimes, as in the hymns of Isaac Watts, springing from a peculiarly sensitive and delicate musical ear. But this phase of versification long remained an art superficially explored. Not until the mid-nineteenth century was time ripe for investigation of nuances in the field. As years advanced the trained ear became sensitive to new shadings in poetry, just as it explored half tones and new combinations of sound in music, and much as the infinite complexities of color were investigated by the painters. Such researches became typical especially of leading artists in diverse crafts, as Debussy with his new scale in music and Monet with his new scales in color. The half-way mark of the century began the era of half tones. Whitman's complete renunciation of rhyme was actually less in keeping with the prevailing aesthetics of the age then Emily Dickinson's explorations in new tonalisms. Her practice merely exhibited in one more phase her tireless pursuit of nuance.

Critics have already gone far in tabulating both the character of her half rhymes and the degree to which she

overlooks rhyme altogether. Since her caprices are mani-
fold, a mere description of them is not likely to con-
tribute materially to our enlightenment. It becomes fairly
obvious that her rhymes are sometimes merely assonance,
a repetition or variation of vowel or consonant. On other
occasions she repeats whole words, an equal violation of
the standard conception of true rhyme. The really interesting investigation is concerned not with the external
facts but with the inner causes of such habits. Was Emily
intelligent in her practices? What, if anything, was she
attempting to do?

In a general way it seems clear that faultless rhyme
threatened in her ear to become flat, meaningless, and
banal. She by no means wished to escape the strict rules
and obligations of her art. On the contrary, she protested
that her spirit felt freest when aided by the decorum required by poetic rules. Her whole temperament favored
discipline, restraint, and regimented conduct. Yet her
whole soul dreaded banality. Some compromise was suggested by this contradiction. Half rhyme became a natural
recourse; but how was it to be used artfully, and how
was it to express her own character?

Sympathetic scrutiny shows that the half rhyme admirably expressed her own hyper-discriminating and fundamentally skeptical nature. She repeatedly employs it in
poems voicing hesitation, doubt, resignation, or frustration. In the richly modulated music of her lyrics, full
rhyme may be compared to the musician's major mode,
half rhyme to the minor mode. The latter connotes inde-
cision, pensiveness, quiet grief, or spiritual numbness.
Although no simple formula can be given, a few illustrations at least disclose how aesthetically purposeful her

method became. It proved anything but blundering. In an eminently pensive lyric, "Of nearness to her sundered things", three out of the four rhymes are imperfect. The rhyme in the last stanza gives the key. The two words are "remained", and "mourned". In "The world feels dusty", one of her tenderest elegies, the rhyme in the first stanza only is fully consummated, while the others are imperfect: "fan-rain"; "comes-balms". Much of the heavy grief so beautifully expressed is owing to this delicately used device. One must become accustomed to this art, however, rightly to appreciate its value. In the almost incredibly lovely little octave, "Fairer through fading", depicting a sunset in a minor key, the lines perfectly follow the waning of the light. This descending tone, slipping backward, as it were, is conveyed, among many other devices, by the rhyme. The first two lines of each quatrain have a perfect rhyme, the second pair have only assonance. They are, in turn, "sun-perishing", and "dark-look". The first quatrain contains the pattern. The sun, like the rhyme, shows "half her complexion . . . Hindering, haunting, perishing". The second quatrain repeats the pattern, significantly beginning with the word "rallies". But the rally is a failure, as the evening dies out in half light and half rhyme. The whole poem constitutes an amazing instance of verse melody.

This muted rhyming becomes one of the great beauties of Emily's art. The attentive reader soon becomes accustomed to watch for it and to encounter it with an understanding pleasure. It is most effective in lyrics belonging to her graver mood. So in that moving and most representative poem, "I like a look of agony Because I know it's true", the rhyming remains muted throughout: "true-

throe; feign-strung". The device is artfully used to express frustration and doubt in the lyric, "As watchers hang
upon the east". Here Emily's thought, to put it curtly,
is that heaven makes a very charming notion—provided
it is justified in fact. Almost all the poem celebrates the
joys of the ideal state. As often, Emily reserves the sting
for the last line. A preceding line in an exuberant reference to the dawn, reads, "And lets the morning go". The
rhyme is only half-finished in the skeptical conclusion:
"Heaven to us, if true". The poem therefore ends with
an unresolved chord.

Since the muted rhyme may be described as a shadow
rhyme, it becomes especially appropriate to a poem on
shadows. So Emily's coldly aloof lines, "Like Men and
Women shadows walk Upon the hills today", contains
only partial rhyme: "today-courtesy"; "perceive-live". Dis-
appointment, tenderness, and pensiveness are often aptly
conveyed by the device. This appears more than once in
her use of the rhyme, "eyes-gaze". A poem describing the
elusive manners of the moon, "I watched the moon around
the house", employs the rhyme to this effect, as likewise
the lyric, "Sweet mountains, ye tell me no lie", where
the mountains look pensively upon the poet's failures, the
rhyme being also "eyes-gaze". Tenderness itself becomes
the chief overtone suggested by the imperfect rhyme in,
"Life is what we make it", a poem describing Christ as
a "Tender Pioneer" to those who "venture now". The
harsher and more tragic connotations of the device are
seen in such a piece as, "Too cold is this", describing a
corpse, in one line designated a "husk", and in the last
rhyme word an "Asterisk". The total absence of rhyme
where the ear is led to expect it gives the maximum of

dissonance and is often reserved therefore to express such a state of mind. The wholly cynical poem, "Drowning is not so pitiful As the attempt to rise", cheerfully rhymes "rise" with "skies", but when the dismal abyss of the ocean is considered, the ear, which expects another rhyme on the same sound, encounters the complete dissidence, "Abhorred abode". Of course on many occasions Emily employs half rhyme or omits rhymes altogether when the passage has no sinister or tragic value whatsoever, as musicians are often affirmative in a minor key. But the muted rhyme, like the minor key, does clearly possess these unhappy connotations, realized by no poet so consistently and so effectually as by Emily Dickinson.

Her versification proves considerably more varied than a public, which may too often remember her verses through anthologies, has been led to assume. It is true that she prefers familiar hymn metres, but it is also true that she uses many other forms, some of them distinctly rare. Her poems contain short lines and long, brisk dimeter and leisurely dipodic verse, a number of rare stanzaic forms, and much internal rhythmical modulation. Moreover, what proves of greater importance, all her variations are significant and dictated from within, answering the feeling and meaning of the poem. She uses rhythmical form organically and expressively.

Emily thoroughly understands the various values implied by the short line. Thus in the brilliant poem: "The soul selects its own society, Then shuts the door", the short lines alternating with the long convey a sense of tragic finality and decision. Each brief line becomes in this respect more powerful than the last, until we reach the grim finale: "Like stone". The brief line may have an ominous and portentous meaning, weighted with fear. Such is its value in the austere poem, "A shade upon the mind there passess, As when on noon . . ." In the curious narrative poem on the robbery of the lonely house at night, "I know some lonely houses off the road", the short lines have a breathless and terrifying quality:

> Day rattles, too,
> Stealth's slow . . .
> "Who's there? . . .
> Sneer— "Where?"

The short line has an austere value, with emphasis, retard, and an accent upon the intellectual, in the epigrammatic poem, "Not so the infinite relations. Below . . ." Sometimes it may have a humorous meaning, as in Emily's lyric on the rat. "The rat is the concisest tenant". The first line is much the longest of all. This shrewd piece tapers off, like the rat's tail, till the last line has only one word, "Equilibrium".

The long line likewise possesses a variety of connotations. Emily uses it especially in pieces of relaxed mood, in her lighter lyrics, and in those accenting tenderness and sentiment. She employs a surprisingly large range of long lines. Thus, "Some we see no more, tenements of wonder", is in the nursery metre so brilliantly used for literary verse by George Meredith in "Love in a Valley". Like his, Emily's lyric is idyllic. Her most affectionate address to the bluebird, coming from an overflowing heart, calls for a light and rapidly moving long line: "After all the birds have been investigated and laid aside". The relaxation of the long line is exquisitely realized in her quatrain on the cooling solace of the forest in summer-time: "These fevered days to take them to the forest".

Emily, then, finds herself at ease with many divergent verse forms. Although the customary quatrain of the Protestant hymn, derived from the popular ballad, became her norm, she mastered also the six line stanza ultimately derived from the Latin septenary and used with classical effect in many of the finest Latin hymns of the Catholic Church, as those by Saint Thomas Aquinas for the festival of Corpus Christi. Moreover, Emily employs the form intelligently, as can be seen in several lyrics composed in it and inspired with strong religious feeling. The very rhetoric of the following Thomistic lines is Latinized:

> 'Tis Kingdom—afterwards—they say,
> In perfect pauseless monarchy,
> Whose Prince is son of none—
> Himself His dateless dynasty,
> Himself Himself diversify
> In duplicate divine.

Her litany-like panegyric to the unknown God, "Bring me the sunset in a cup", appropriately has the same lusty, exuberant, and affirmative metre.

Dipodic verse, which has become so much more popular since Emily's poems were first published, occurs in many of her pieces. As a measure familiar from nursery rhymes, she happily employs it in her numerous poems conceived from the aspect of the child's imagination. It perfectly accords with her fondness for a sophisticated return to the naive. As felicitous specimens might be cited, "Now I knew I lost her", "Knows how to forget", with its references to childhood, and the wistful and naive, "Whatever it is she has tried it". Emily shows especial fondness for the equally popular dimeter, as in such a charming and perfectly wrought lyric as, "Sang from the heart, Sire".

Her most beautiful and original triumphs in rhythm naturally resist classification. No formula can describe the wistful sensitivity expressed in her lyric, "The world feels dusty When we stop to die". The delicious use of a falling rhythm, partly to be accounted for by a stanza of two longer lines followed by one shorter, in her masterpiece on autumn, "These are the days when birds come back", is a success indicating her strength but almost impossible to repeat. This lyric in five stanzas breathes as five sighs spent over the death of summer. When, on rare occasions, she radically varies her stanzaic form within a single poem, as in, "Just lost when I was saved!" she almost invariably shows uncanny sagacity. Here the variations are partly owing to the divided aim of the lyric. Two stanzas relate how near the poet came to death, yet escaped; two following stanzas contemplate her next and last approach to death's grim power. Since the mood changes, Emily changes the verse form. She uses a variant of the same device in that dramatic lyric, "Adrift! A little boat adrift!" Here the story of some sailors is that the craft which symbolizes the poet has gone down in the storm. Angels, however, report a rescue. The stanzaic movement shifts from a secular ballad form to a grave and exalted liturgical hymn of victory. An unusual type of insinuating nuance lends distinction to the poem, "Sweet safe houses—glad gay houses", as may be inferred from even the first line. How radical, or, to use a conservative expression, how rough, her verse can be, is easily seen from the final line of the poem, "It's coming—the postponeless Creature". This lyric surprisingly ends, "And carries one out of it to God." Such a harsh, uneven verse would probably have been altered under the early editorship of Mrs. Todd and Colonel Higginson. Of course Emily knew how to retard a line as well as to accelerate it. One encounters many beautifully slow and leisurely lines, such as that describing the evening glow on mountains, "Their far, slow, violet gaze". Or one may recall the spondaic line, so artfully difficult to pronounce rapidly, "Stealth's slow".

Such nuances draw us naturally from the subject of rhythm to that of the sound texture of the verse, its euphony, richness, and expressive modulations of the least sound and syllable. To dissect consonants and vowels, to tear syllables apart, and separate sound from sound, allures the hungry and ravenous critic but, like a diet of pebbles, nauseates and fatigues the sympathetic reader. Analysis of sound in poetry easily becomes too microscopic; scientific zeal discovers a notorious pitfall. The poet, like a diabolically sagacious ghost, leads his pursuer over an abyss. It will be sufficient here to leave the reader with a few expressive and well-contrasted phrases of unusual splendor and beauty on which to ponder, acknowledging the great importance of sound texture in distinguished poetry, especially lyric poetry, but realizing also the tedium of protracted analysis. The widely differing harmonies of sound in the following repay frequent rereading and reconsideration:

When Plato was a certainty,
And Sophocles a man.

And he unrolled his feathers
And rowed him softer home
Than oars divide the ocean,
Too silver for a seam,
Or butterflies, off banks of noon,
Leap, plashess, as they swim.

From some old fortress on the sun
Baronial bees march, one by one,
In murmuring platoon!

For miseries so halcyon
The happiness atone.

Such nuances Emily sustained through more than a thousand poems.

8 *LANGUAGE OF POETRY*

Emily Dickinson is one of the foremost masters of poetic English since Shakespeare, and in the severe economy of her speech comparable to Dante. Fascinating as the meaning or ideas in her poetry may be, and important as are her metaphors, verse architecture, rhythm, and euphony, it is her study of the individual word and her masterly discovery of the right word that chiefly defines her distinction. Although a word may be rich in metaphorical implications, and strictly in its rightful place in the architecture of sense and harmony of sound, it is of the word in itself that Emily apparently thought first and it is of language as built out of individual words that we ourselves chiefly think in analyzing her poetry. Emily was a worshipper of atoms, and the atoms from which her imaginative world was built were verbal. Happily, abundant proof exists of her devotion to language. The misfortune that her poems were long delayed in publication is more than cancelled by the good fortune that they now exist in copious manuscripts, some of which have already been reproduced in facsimile. These manuscripts give conclusive evidence, were any such external evidence required, of her verbal-mindedness. It became her custom to weigh words with the utmost meticulousness, sometimes writing nine or ten in the place of one to scrutinize more closely which should be preferred. Her manuscripts present some of the most amazing records of scrupulous rewriting recorded in literary history. She clearly thought even more diligently of the individual words than of any other feature of a poem. This mistress of lyrical spontaneity became also a miser of syllables, an indefatigable judge and critic of her vocabulary. Her readers do well to approach her poetry in the same spirit, viewing each poem as a medallion in the vast design of her literary creation, and each medallion as a mosaic of words like precious stones, fastidiously chosen.

Emily lived in a world of love, scorn, stars, flowers, brightness, and menacing night, where it was her one constant faith that with due labor she could always find a word for every object and every experience. If on some occasion this proved impossible, as noted in her poem, "I found a phrase to every thought I ever had, but one", the exception constituted a mere freak, curious but thoroughly unimportant. The important truth was her wholly confirmed belief in the efficacy of words. She never complains of their vagueness. Nature, she declares, did at times betray her, as it betrays all men. But she records no snake in the garden of language. Speech was something God-given, potentially errorless. What faults there were in actuality lay with the speakers. Such was her almost platonic devotion and love, not toward mankind, but toward the language of poetry.

In one of her most important aphorisms she declares that the lip would crumble could the mind conceive "the undeveloped freight of a delivered syllable." Nothing could better express her reverence for the power of words. They were to her like particles of radium, infinite power within an almost invisible substance; like the potent grains of sand envisaged by William Blake. One of her briefest poems, "A word is dead", is dedicated to the thought that the statement in its first line is an error amounting to gross atheism. Emily concludes that the word properly spoken is alive; indeed she knows nothing more tremblingly, more vibrantly alive. Had she placed more faith in the revelations of the orthodox creed, she might well have found esoteric meanings in the opening verses of the Gospel of Saint John: "In the beginning was the word". Her life became a long laboratory study of words, a laboratory of genuine experimentation, and not a mere museum. Her library, however important, was always secondary to her practice. The created word, which she sometimes called the spoken word, to her signified considerably more than the word as read. Yet more than passing notice must be taken of her researches in language. Her early love affair, some say, was with a tutor who instructed her in the mysteries of literature and vocabulary, and who left her on his premature death a devoted student of her dictionary. The dictionary was the bible of her religion, which was poetry. Her personal dictionary was Noah Webster's, the illustrious philologist who had for a time lived in the town of Amherst, laid the cornerstone of one of the buildings of Amherst College, of which her father was trustee, and left his powerful mark on the thinking of the community. The dictionary was the mine from which the gold of poetry was to be extracted, and several references to mines in her own poems show with what an awe she regarded mines. The dictionary she came to consider the one book more an essential than any other for the writing of her own poems. Yet naturally she revered her predecessors in poetry, who had so conclusively proved what words could achieve. Two books, which she probably regarded as almost equally poetical, undoubtedly in her mind surpassed all others as guiding and inspirational forces for her style. These, conservatively and almost inevitably enough, were the Bible and Shakespeare. Truly as her style is her own, it becomes evident that from these sources she won much of her sagacity in language. From the Bible she received encouragement in forthright, dignified, simple, and earnest statement; from Shakespeare she gained encouragement for the bolder flights of her imagination and fancy, for her large vocabulary, her audacious use of the parts of speech, and, occasionally, her more than Asiatic opulence. Nevertheless the most fruitful commentary on her style certainly does not lie in comments on her "influences." These are incidental. With Emily it becomes necessary to start afresh.

The starting point is undoubtedly the pointedness with which she employs the individual word. Each principal word in a major lyric constitutes for her the equivalent of a universe. Some writers never use one word where they may use ten, she never uses two where she can use one. Her rejected words would fill a volume many times larger than her actual works. It hardly becomes hyperbole to say that a single word in her poetry often contains more imaginative energy than an entire lyric by a respectable but less distinguished poet. She seeks to give the word a poetic luminence over and beyond its literal connotation as defined by the dictionary, or its prosaic meanings in familiar conversation. To use a term common in her own writing, she aims to present each word in "italic". Such is her fruitful theory of poetry, or of the poetic style, which obviously comes to much the same thing.

An example will be helpful, and clearly hundreds present themselves with equal claims. One, quite arbitrarily chosen, serves to introduce the subject. A newly published poem begins:

> He lived the life of ambush
> And went the way of dusk.

Here the vital words are obviously those at the end of the lines, namely, "ambush", and "dusk". Their meanings are not specific, as are words in simple prose, but are poetically clear, emotionally and imaginatively powerful. Neither Emily nor anyone else will use these words again with quite these shades of value. They give us the feeling of vast oceanic reservoirs of experience. And this image in itself hints at a clue to Emily's style, which is, in brief, an ideal style for lyric poetry: her words resemble oceans, while those of less successful writers resemble lakes.

Before breaking down the subject into its parts through critical analysis, two or three more illustrations of Emily's uncanny felicity should be fruitful. One of her adjectives has often been remembered as evidence of her profound understanding of the New England climate. It will be recalled that she wrote, "There is a maritime conviction In the atmosphere". Observations of a lifetime are crammed here into a single epithet. Of course when her writing is at her best, this distinguished use of words is closely sustained, so that a sentence resembles a cluster of stars. In these lines she describes a neglected burying-ground:

> Strangers strolled and spelled
> At the lone orthography
> Of the elder dead.

The analysis of such a passage is necessarily somewhat personal. These are delicate, subjective matters, difficult of approach and beyond which it is impossible to go. Nevertheless I venture to think that many readers have been left almost breathless by the calm mastery, the high felicity, of the above lines. The words themselves are, of course, not rare, though "orthography" is hardly common. The point is that no one but Emily would have been likely to use them in just this way, with just this content. Other writers would in all probability have missed both her delicate feeling and its still more exquisite expression. They would have been satisfied, as Longfellow certainly would have been, with far easier statements. Others would, presumably, never have thought of "spelled", "lone", "orthography" or "elder"; they might even have missed "stranger", and "strolled". Emily misses nothing, or, in any case, no one is inspired enough to say what it is she misses.

Frequently her customary verse rhetoric reveals in brilliant light the italic emphasis placed upon individual words. Her manner curiously resembles that of a great poet whose style cannot well have been overly familiar to her, Dante. The poem, "Who never lost, are unprepared A coronet to find", ends with the statement that angels wrote the word, "Promoted" on a soldier's forehead. This type of supernatural inscription, preternaturally condensed, closely duplicates images many times repeated in the *Purgatorio*. Similarly, in the lyric, " 'Twas like a maelstrom", graphically describing a death agony, the action of the poetic narrative terminates when "A creature gasped 'Reprieve!' " One remembers death scenes as related in the *Purgatorio*. The Dantesque practice of concluding the sketch of a character with the name, thus giving the proper name the highest possible emphasis, is repeated in Emily Dickinson's elegy on her spiritual sister, Charlotte Brontë, where the word "Brontë" is studiously reserved for the last line. Similar art gives stress and poignancy to " 'I want', it pleaded all its life", a lyric wholly based upon the sharp contrast between the pre-emptory words, "I want" in the first line and the pathetic word, "Please", in the conclusion. How Emily's spirit dwelt upon the overpowering force of single words is further hinted in her notable lyric, "I never hear the word 'escape' Without a quicker blood". The entire poem hinges on this living word, a spark kindling a considerable blaze.

The remarkable brevity of her poems in itself lends emphasis to each word. To this condition should be added her obvious dislike for the small change of language. Her style on occasions becomes almost crabbed through bold dispensing with articles, to be seen, for example, in the phrase, "As unto crowd". If she uses long or rare words, she has good reason to do so, for she utterly avoids inflated rhetoric. In her worship of directness the Bible became her tutor. In *Genesis* it is sometimes written of one who died that he merely "was not". This terse phrase impressed Emily:

> "Was not" was all the statement.
> The unpretention stuns,
> Perhaps the comprehension;
> They wore no lexicons.

Her ideal of concision leads to a statement that might well be taken to summarize her own autobiographical poetry and the relation of her verse to her life.

> Its past set down before the soul,
> And lighted with a match,
> Perusal to facilitate
> Of its condensed despatch.

The poems, and even the individual words, resemble match flames lighted to illuminate a crucial moment of the soul. Success depends almost wholly on condensation of expression. Each poem becomes a telegram from "infinity".

Often in the first or last lines of her poems there appears a word peculiarly illumined with such a supernatural brightness. "Glee! the great storm is over!" begins one of her dramatic lyrics, with evidence of her command over one of the rarer and more recalcitrant parts of speech, the exclamation. "To fight *aloud* is very brave", begins a poem contrasting bravery in battle or in the active world with spiritual courage. The meditative poem commencing, "I found the phrase to every thought", accents in its last phrases the unusual words "cochineal", and "mazarin". The brilliant, "I know that he exists", proceeds from its lukewarm and orthodox beginning to an amazingly vigorous and imaginative close, inquiring if God's jest has not "crawled" too far. Special attention is challenged by the language of the initial lines: "Softened by Time's consummate plush"; "An awful tempest mashed the air"; "The overtakelessness of death"; and "The silver reticence of death".

That the true wealth of language often depends on a frugality of syllables appears in striking passages composed wholly in monosyllables. This is Emily's monolithic style, witnessed in such expression as, "Should the glee glaze In death's stiff stare". The simplest word may prove the most potent. Thus in the harrowingly realistic little elegy, "A clock stopped—not the mantel's", the word "No" receives extreme accent, being the rhyme word at the end of a stanza and carrying on the meaning of the sentence unbroken into the stanza following. What a "No" is there! The dictionary defines no such vibrant negative. She delights in common expressions, as when, it will be remembered, she calls Elijah's chariot by no other name than a wagon. The understatement, so long a practice in Anglo-Saxon verse and further advanced by Puritan reticence and humor, also came most naturally to Emily and materially aided in the creation of her style. A good example occurs in one of the grimmest of her works, an account of drowning: "The water chased him as he fled". The lines describe the "revolting bliss" promised by some demon billow of the sea. But drowning was not really a pleasure, as harsh fact proved. The little poem ends with the menacing lines: "The object floating at his side Made no distinct reply." The particular "object" Emily in leaving undefined makes all the more terrifying. These are the devious ways of poetry.

As the last quotation indicates, the poetic word or phrase is distinguished from the non-poetic in that the former is rich in implications, a truism whose implications are themselves too seldom regarded. Poetic words are suggestive. This primary requirement of her art Emily grasps fully. "Except the heaven had come so near", begins one of her lyrics. Presumably the poem is a love poem, but denoting a love of what or whom? For what does the word "heaven" stand? The artist, like nature, preserves mysterious taciturnity.

Another instance of the same poetic strategy of hinting

rather than of stating facts literally appears in a phrase
concerning the diet of the blue jay. Of this bird it is said:

> The pillow of this daring head
> Is pungent evergreens;
> His larder—terse and militant—
> Unknown, refreshing things.

Just what the jay eats is left to the naturalist to determine,
who has opened the stomachs of dead birds; Emily is
concerned only with the spiritual or humanized meaning
of the bird and therefore of its food. Her statement
proves valueless to science but of immeasurable worth as
poetry. All the words of Apollo of necessity have a somewhat riddling and oracular tone. Such usages as the foregoing if in prose would be reprehensible, but what remains merely vague in one medium signifies power in
another. Emily cultivates the imaginative phrase, transcending logic. The literal mind can make little of such
language as, "Great streets of silence led away To neighborhoods of pause," but the poetry is all the more significant and superb.

Although most of Emily's words are sufficiently common, she employs a large vocabulary including many rare
words and some of her own manufacture. When she
writes that butterflies "Leap, plashless, as they swim", a
rare usage becomes apparent. She finds the exact use for
such an unusual word as "omnifold". A deliberate and
significant quaintness is cast upon her thought by such
terms as "farness" and "foreignhood". She avails herself
of Shakesperean license. Indeed she unobtrusively bor-
rows from Shakespeare. It was probably the great dramatist who suggested to her the frequent interchange of
parts of speech and the bold formation of vivid verbs. In

a passage rich in Shakesperean images she uses the verb "beggars", borrowed presumably from the same form in one of her favorite plays, *Antony and Cleopatra.*

Her language, then, is highly uncommon and poetic in that she employs familiar words in unfamiliar phrases. It suits her purpose to call mountains, "purple territories", to write of noon as "the parlor of the day", to address angels familiarly as "sapphire fellows", to speak of a "fleshless chant", and a "seamless company", to use "orchestra" as a verb, to speak of frost as a "blond assassin", to tell of the "gnash" of northern winds, to speak of a "pile" of wind, to use "became" in place of the less vigorous verb to be, to speak of "narrow" time, to coin the adverb "russetly", to write of a flower's "unobtrusive" face, as "punctuating" a wall, to relate the star's "Etruscan argument", to address the "staunch" dust, humorously to call hell "the Phosphorus of God", to use "again" and "until" as nouns, to write of "alabaster zest", of "sumptuous" destitution, of "sequestration" from decay, and of "phlegmatic" mountains.

Each of these words as employed by Emily Dickinson is a highly vigorous creative act, each in itself a poem. In mythology are many legends to the effect that each drop of a hero's blood comes to life. Emily's words are drops of her heart's blood. Each stands up a hero active in the triumphant wars of the spirit, armed with bow of burning gold and arrow of desire. Thus analysis of her language reduces her art to its lowest denominator, discovering it thoroughly alive and thoroughly sound. Examination can go no further, for it is a poet's ultimate claim to be a master of words ever employed in the service of the spirit of Man.